WARW
AIRF
IN THE SECOND
WORLD WAR

Graham Smith

COUNTRYSIDE BOOKS
NEWBURY, BERKSHIRE

COUNTRYSIDE BOOKS
3 Catherine Road
Newbury, Berkshire

To view our complete range of books,
please visit us at
www.countrysidebooks.co.uk

ISBN 1 85306 867 5

The cover picture shows a Spitfire Mk II over
Castle Bromwich in 1943, from an original painting
by Colin Doggett

Designed by Mon Mohan

Produced through MRM Associates Ltd., Reading
Typeset by Techniset Typesetters, Merseyside
Printed by Woolnough Bookbinding Ltd., Irthlingborough

CONTENTS

WARWICKSHIRE'S WORLD WAR II AIRFIELDS

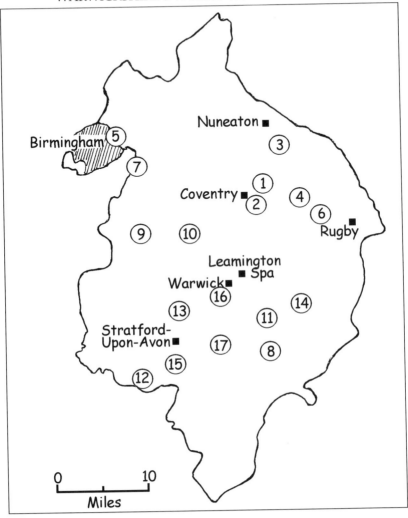

KEY TO AIRFIELDS/LANDING GROUNDS

1 Ansty
2 Baginton
3 Bramcote
4 Brinklow
5 Castle Bromwich
6 Church Lawford

7 Elmdon
8 Gaydon
9 Hockley Heath
10 Honiley
11 Leamington
12 Long Marston

13 Snittersfield
14 Southam
15 Stratford-upon-Avon
16 Warwick
17 Wellesbourne Mountford

ACKNOWLEDGEMENTS

I am greatly indebted to a number of people for assisting me during the preparation of this book, especially with the provision of illustrations. My thanks to Nina Burls and Jillian Bell of the RAF Museum, Hendon, Tim Loakes of the British Motor Industry Heritage Trust, Ruth Whalley of Birmingham International Airport and Jonathan Rock of Prodrive Live. I would especially like to thank Barry James of the Midland Air Museum for his kind and generous assistance and advice. And not forgetting Alison Hawkins for very kindly giving us a tour of the site of Stratford-upon-Avon airfield.

As usual I am most grateful for the willing assistance of the staff of Galleywood Library of Essex Libraries Services for obtaining several of the books used during my research.

Graham Smith

I
SETTING
THE SCENE

Warwickshire has a long and distinguished aviation heritage that can be traced back to the pioneer days. The county was then in the vanguard of aeroplane and aero-engine design and production. During the First World War many of the early motor-car manufacturers diverted their skilled workforces to the production of 'flying machines' and Castle Bromwich became one of the earliest military aerodromes. In the inter-war years a number of celebrated aeroplanes, both military and civil, made their first flights from Warwickshire aerodromes.

In the early 1890s a Royal Engineer Major Ross F. Moore designed and patented an 'ornithoplane or ornithopter' – such flying machines were so called because they were sustained or propelled by flapping or oscillating wings in an attempt to replicate the flight of birds; although Moore's design had been inspired by flying foxes. His machine had been constructed by John Shaw of Coventry and was driven by an electric motor built by William Mason with trailing cables linked to a power source; the wings were covered with silk or light fabric. It weighed some seven hundred pounds and cost £1,000 but never managed to get off the ground. About ten years later another Coventry man, William Weaver designed and built several ornithoplanes provided with flapping wings or rotors. From 1905 onwards he tried his various powered machines at Hampden-in-Arden Golf Course with some small success; in May 1910 it was reported that his latest machine had flown for a quarter of a mile. Even in January 1914 a Mr Shorter of the Coventry Aero Club tested his 'Cycloplane' driven by pedals and belts and achieved some short hops whilst proceeding down a slope. Such bizarre machines were not unusual in the pioneer days as men strove desperately to achieve powered flight.

There was certainly a rich vein of engineering talent and expertise in Warwickshire, especially in the field of motor transport, manifested in the number of motor-car manufacturers operating in Coventry and Birmingham – the heart of the nascent motor industry. In 1911 there were twenty-one separate car-making firms in Coventry alone, so it is hardly surprising to discover that the county should become greatly involved in early British aviation, especially in respect of aeroplane construction and the manufacture of aero-engines. From the outset there was a close affinity between early motoring and pioneer aviation, the two novel and revolutionary forms of transportation seemed to go hand-in-hand, their common link, besides speed and excitement, was, of course, the internal combustion engine. The Aero Club of Great Britain, which had been officially formed in October 1901, was really an adjunct of the Automobile Club. Furthermore many of the celebrated pioneer aviators had all been motoring devotees. Indeed Lord Northcliffe, a most vociferous and loyal supporter of both motoring and aviation, was a very generous sponsor of early British aviation and he insisted on calling flying machines 'aerial motor cars'!

It was in 1909 that aviation in Britain finally began to make some progress and there were a sufficient number of dedicated flying enthusiasts in Birmingham to set up the Midland Aero Club, which held its inaugural meeting on 3rd September, barely six weeks after Blériot had memorably crossed the English Channel in his monoplane. The Midland was one of the earliest aero clubs to be formed in the country and it would appear that several members were already constructing their own flying machines. Another club, Birmingham Aero Model Club, was founded some weeks later, with a lower subscription designed to attract 'interested artisans and working men'. Model aeroplane flying was a popular sport prior to 1914, with considerable prize money offered for the highest and longest flights.

Perhaps the most determined Midland Club member was Alfred P. Maxfield, a motor engineer from Costa Green, Birmingham. He was reputed to have been experimenting with flying machines since 1902. In early October 1909, during trials at Castle Bromwich golf course, Maxfield managed to get his latest monoplane off the ground in a series of hops; one attained the height of fifty feet. Thus Maxfield became known as 'Birmingham's First Flying Man' and joined an elite band of British aviators that had experienced the thrill and excitement of powered flight – however high or short the distance and duration. His monoplane was placed on display, along with other club models, at the

Masonic Hall, Birmingham on 13th October, an occasion that was graced by the presence of Samuel F. Cody, the first airman (albeit he was an American) to achieve powered flight in Britain.

There were other individuals and companies in Birmingham and Coventry intent on entering this new world of aeronautics. Birmingham Aeroplane Co. of Moseley Street offered to construct aeroplanes to customers' specific designs, as well as selling its own designed *Albatross* aeroplane. The Central Novelty Co., also in Birmingham, advertised a biplane (without an engine) for £50 and claimed that it would make 'a first class club glider'. But there is no evidence that any of these machines were actually built. This also was the case of the 'Man Lifting Glyders' offered for sale at £10 by Midland Aeroplane Co. Ltd of Grey Friars Lane, Coventry. Certainly W. H. Fulford of Mills-Fulford Ltd of Coventry had constructed a very small monoplane based on a French design, because it was displayed at the Stanley Cycle Show in London in November, along with a biplane built by Merlin Aeroplane Co. of Coventry, but it is highly unlikely that either machine ever flew. In November Herbert Austin briefly turned his attention from motor cars to construct a small monoplane at the specific request of the Rev. Sidney Swann of Crosby Ravensworth, Cumberland. The machine was delivered to Aintree racecourse, Liverpool on 17th November and was trialled over the next two weeks but it only managed a few hops before being heavily damaged.

The members of the Birmingham Aero Club ('Model' had been dropped from its name) tried their models at Sutton Park, Sutton Coldfield and it is reported that one member, J. H. Else-Mynard, tested his glider there in November. Over the next three years several members would trial their gliders at the park, including two built by G. Haddon Wood, who sent drawings of his gliders to the two specialist aviation journals *Flight* and *Aero*, which had first appeared in 1909, another indication of the increased interest and awareness of aviation.

By the end of 1909 the Midland Aero Club had two hundred and fifty members, and at their first annual dinner, held in December, the Lord Mayor of Birmingham expressed the opinion that 'the Midlands of all places should lead in the construction of flying machines, the district being so obviously suited to such an industry'. Two months later Major B.F.S. Baden-Powell, the celebrated military balloonist, box kite and glider experimenter, attended a club meeting and said that he looked forward to the day when he could return to Birmingham to look

9

over one of the factories building 'aerial machines for military purposes'. Little did the major, or the club members, realise how soon that day would come.

The first motor car manufacturer to turn its attention to aeroplane construction was Humber Ltd of Coventry. In September 1909 the company established an aviation division with ambitious plans to produce fifty aeroplanes of the Blériot XI type at £400 each. Early in 1910 the company took over two sheds (Nos. 4 & 5) at Brooklands, Surrey – the famous motor-car racing track that was fast becoming the centre of pioneer aviation. In January Humber took the unique decision to transport its first monoplane to Cannes in Southern France for trials because of the better weather conditions. Captain Dawes and J. V. Neale, noted pioneer airmen, also flew this machine at a meeting in Egypt. Captain T. T. Lovelace was employed as a designer and his first biplane was sent even further afield – to Allahabad, India – where some pioneering air-mail flights were made in early 1911. However, in the summer of 1912 Humber decided to abandon its aviation work and in August all its aero-engines and parts were sold by auction.

The Midland Aero Club was keen to encourage celebrated pioneer aviators to the area and demonstrate their flying skills not only for the benefit of its members but also to foster public interest in this new form of transport. In this respect perhaps the club's greatest success came during 27th June to 2nd July 1910 when the club successfully organised a large aviation meeting at Dunstall Park racecourse, Wolverhampton. This was a particularly ambitious venture considering that the first flying meetings in the country had been mounted the previous October at Doncaster and Blackpool; both had been open to international aviators and as a result were largely dominated by French airmen and aeroplanes; France was then the leading country in all aviation matters. The Wolverhampton meeting was restricted to British aviators flying British-built aeroplanes powered by British engines – the first of its kind to be held. It is a measure of the steady progress of British aviation that nineteen intrepid British airmen entered, tempted by the £4,000 prize money on offer.

The Wolverhampton meeting certainly featured most of the leading aviators of the day – the Hon. Charles Rolls, Claude Grahame-White, A. V. Roe, Cecil Grace, James Radley, Alec Ogilvie, Graham Gilmour and the Hon. Alan Boyle along with several club members and their machines. The weather over the week was not really favourable for either flying or attracting the large crowds anticipated by the Aviation

Syndicate that had been formed to run and finance the meeting. Sadly the meeting was marred by several crashes, but on the positive side it was a notable first and engendered great interest in aviation in the Midlands, especially as Humber was represented by three biplanes.

Maybe as a result of all the interest created by this meeting, the club numbered over four hundred and fifty members at the end of 1910 making it one of the largest aero clubs in the country. Coventry Aero Club also benefited from an increased membership. However, the Birmingham Aero Club was not quite so flourishing but nevertheless in April 1911 it organised an aviation exhibition at Bournville and Grahame-White, now Britain's leading airman since the tragic death of the Hon. Charles Rolls in July 1910, was persuaded to open it. By the autumn club members were regularly using Billesley Farm, King's Heath, where a workshop had been built and they had use of the club glider. In November the Midland Aero Club began negotiations to establish a landing ground at the playing fields at Castle Bromwich and by May 1912 the club was in occupation, with a club glider, a 'mechanical trainer' and at least one aeroplane shed. The aerodrome was 1,100 yards long and 400 yards wide with a flat and good surface free from trees – certainly the first recognised aerodrome in the county. A larger shed had also been provided for Ernest Willow's third airship *City of Cardiff*; he had been building airships at Cardiff since 1904 but had now transferred his operations to Handsworth, Birmingham. His fourth airship was built at Castle Bromwich and was sold (along with the shed!) to the Admiralty in July 1912 for £1,050 when it became known as H.M. Airship 2 and was used as a training and experimental ship.

Another company, Coventry Ordnance Works, entered the field of aeronautics in late 1911. It took over the works belonging to Howard Wright at Battersea along with two sheds at Brooklands. The company wanted to construct two aeroplanes specifically to compete in the War Office's military trials to be held at Larkhill on Salisbury Plain in August 1912, which if they had been successful would have led to military orders. Wright and W. O. Manning, both celebrated designers, were employed on the design and construction of the biplanes. Only one actually took part in the trials but it performed poorly and was subsequently withdrawn.

During 1911 Bentfield C. Hucks, previously Grahame-White's mechanic and now the test pilot of Blackburn Aeroplane Company, used Castle Bromwich as a stopping place whilst en *route* to the West

Bentfield C. Hucks (centre) was the first British pilot to 'loop-the loop'.

Country for an exhibition tour in Blackburn's monoplane *Mercury*. Lord Northcliffe's *Daily Mail* sponsored several airmen to make extensive tours of the country during the summer of 1912 with the object of increasing the public's awareness of 'aerial motor cars' and Hucks, along with Gustav Hamel, the new dashing 'star' of British aviation, were engaged in the Midlands. In August of the following year these two airmen competed in an air race sponsored by the *Birmingham Daily Post*, which was staged at the Tally Ho grounds, Edgbaston, the course covering Coventry, Nuneaton and Walsall. Hamel won the Trophy and £500. Hucks would return to the Tally Ho grounds in February 1914 to demonstrate 'looping-the-loop' or literally flying upside down. He was the first British airman to complete this type of aerobatic flying, which had become all the rage and no aviation meeting was complete without a display from one of the select band of 'loop-the-loopers', as they were known. In June 1914 Castle Bromwich was a mandatory stop on the *Daily Mail*'s Manchester to Hendon air race, which was won by W.L. Brock, an American airman, who was the most successful aviator in this last peacetime summer. Grahame-White in his Farman biplane entertained the crowds at Castle Bromwich.

With the outbreak of the Great War Baden-Powell's image of the Midlands factories building 'aerial machines for military purposes' was realised in no small measure. Indeed when the Society of British

Siddeley Deasy factory, Coventry, showing production of R.E.8s. (Imperial War Museum)

Aircraft Constructors (SBAC) was formed on 29th March 1916 of the forty-one original members, seven were based in Birmingham and Coventry. Austin Motor Co. at Longbridge had established an aviation department and constructed a landing field for test flying; the company would ultimately build over 2,600 military aeroplanes under licence, as well some 2,500 aero engines. In 1917 Austin had also completed several experimental prototypes of their own design, including the A.F.B.1 Austin Ball Scout, the design of which is reputed to have been suggested by Captain Albert Ball, VC, DSO, MC, perhaps the most famous fighter ace of the war. Wolseley Motors built aero-engines and some 750 aeroplanes, and Standard Motor Co. Ltd at Coventry was mainly engaged in producing Sopwith fighters. Whereas Siddeley Deasy, also based in Coventry, produced over 1,100 R.E.7s & 8s at their Parkside factory and Daimler was also engaged in producing B.E.2cs. Two Birmingham companies – Birmingham & Midland Carriage and Metropolitan Wagon & Finance – built over 150 Handley Page O/400s, the large and heavy bombers. All these companies played a major part in the rapid growth and development of the aeroplane industry, which by 1918 was producing 1,500 aeroplanes each month; nevertheless the industry was still rather disparagingly referred to as 'the trade' by senior officials of the War Office.

In August 1914 the War Office, responsible for the Royal Flying

Corps, requisitioned Castle Bromwich as a military aerodrome and in the following May No 5 (Reserve) squadron was formed there with the intention of training pilots who were needed to man a number of new squadrons formed at Castle Bromwich over the next three years; several of these became famous fighter squadrons, most notably Nos 19 and 54. The aerodrome also became an Aircraft Acceptance Park (No 14) for the receipt, flight testing and delivery of new aeroplanes. Radford aerodrome, two miles north of Coventry, was used for test flying by Daimler, also became an Aircraft Acceptance Park (No 1) and by 1918 had been supplied with nine hangars; it was returned to the city in 1919. The small Billesley aerodrome housed the Midland School of Flying.

Such a thriving centre of aeroplane production was considered a prime target for enemy airships. The first raid was experienced on the night of 31st January 1916 when two Zeppelins, L.19 and L.21, bombed the area, but with little effect and no casualities, although L.19 later crashed into the sea. The following day Neville Chamberlain, then Lord Mayor of Birmingham, complained bitterly to the Government about the lack of any advance warning! On 19th October 1917 a solitary Zeppelin, L.42, dropped some bombs on the Austin factory and two workers were injured and finally on 12th/13th April 1918 Coventry was attacked by Zeppelin L.62 – just one of a number that roamed around Lancashire, the Midlands and Norfolk. These few isolated raids merely provided the precedent for the heavy and severe bombing onslaught of the Second World War.

After the end of the war civil and private flying did not restart until 1st May 1919 with the introduction of the Air Navigation Regulations. On that day Lt. Col. W. F. Sholto-Douglas piloting a O/400 of Handley Page Transport made the first commercial flight by carrying ten passengers from Cricklewood, London to Alexandra Park, Manchester. Twelve days later Sholto-Douglas dropped newspapers over certain designated towns before landing at Castle Bromwich and returning to Cricklewood. Daimler was quick to enter the field of civil aviation. In 1919 it formed Daimler Airway, ultimately operating four aeroplanes, and was the first airline to employ a uniformed steward on board. In 1924 it was amalgamated with several other airlines to form Imperial Airways.

The Air Ministry, which had been formed in January 1918, acquired Castle Bromwich aerodrome in August and duly licensed it for civil flying and by late September the British Air Transport Co. was using its

14

One of the five Austin Whippets at Gosport, August 1924. (via R. Jones)

facilities. The aerodrome had been greatly developed and was now provided with over twenty storage sheds and nine large aeroplane sheds – a most impressive centre for post-war aviation.

Austin Motor Co., with its large workforce experienced in aeroplane production, was intent on breaking into the private and club flying market. The company's design team led by J. W. Kenworthy produced a small single-seat biplane – the A.U.1 Whippet; powered by a 45hp engine which produced a maximum speed of about 95mph, it was priced at £450. Although the aircraft was well received by the aviation press, it was perhaps too advanced for its time and suffered from the effect of the post-war recession and the plethora of ex-military machines which had flooded the market; only five Whippets were produced. The only other Austin design was the side-by-side two-seater Kestrel biplane, produced for the Air Ministry's Light Aeroplane Competition of 1920, in which it gained third prize (£1,500). However, the company felt the aviation market was then not economically viable and decided to concentrate on motor car manufacture.

The most famous aeroplane company in the county came into being in 1920, when Sir W. G. Armstrong Whitworth Aircraft Co. (AWA) was formed. In the previous year the Newcastle company had acquired Siddeley Deasy Company and both had been engaged in aeroplane manufacture during the war. John Siddeley was appointed Managing

Director of the new company. He had been instrumental, in the spring of 1919, in producing Siddeley Deasy's first original design aeroplane – the S.R.2 Siskin biplane. Although the design team would remain at Parkside until 1923, a new aerodrome at Whitley Abbey outside Coventry was acquired for the manufacture and test flying of its aeroplanes. Soon a flying school was established there under Major J. C. Griffiths, as Chief Instructor and Aerodrome Manager and in 1923 it received an Air Ministry contract to train RAF reserve pilots – one of five such flying schools owned and operated by an aircraft manu-facturer. The school remained there until 1931, when it became known as Air Service Training Ltd and was transferred to A. V. Roe's aerodrome at Hamble; three years earlier A. V. Roe & Co. Ltd had been acquired.

Considering the number of ex-Service pilots keen to continue flying and the ready availability of cheap surplus military aeroplanes, it is not surprising that many realised that there was some potential in offering the 'miracle of flight' to the public at large by providing short passenger flights, or joy-rides, as they became known. Alan Cobham, who was destined to become the most celebrated airman of the 1920s, went into partnership with Jack and Fred Holmes to form the Berkshire Aviation Co. Cobham, with the company's then solitary Avro 504K, and proceeded to set out on a 'joy-riding' tour. During 1st–5th November

Armstrong Whitworth Siskin III of No 111 squadron in 1924.

16

Moth Majors of the Midland Aero Club at Castle Bromwich. (via R. Mortimer)

1919 he was at the Polo Ground, Barby Road, Rugby before moving on to Royal Leamington Spa. In October 1920 the company offered joyrides from Billesley Aerodrome, and the next year Castle Bromwich was the venue. Indeed, Castle Bromwich had become accepted as the aerodrome for Birmingham and during 1922 and 1923 it was one of the compulsory stopping places for the King's Cup Air Race, the country's most prestigious sporting competition.

AWA had been busy developing their Siskin biplane. In 1922 a Siskin II, a two-seater trainer, was first flown in the 1922 King's Cup race and from this trainer a prototype fighter – Siskin III – was produced, which made its maiden flight from Whitley aerodrome on 7th May 1923. It was the first biplane fighter to introduce the 'Vee' interplane struts and also the first to be of all-metal construction. The Air Ministry was most impressed with its design and performance and the company received a production order; the first Siskin IIIs entering the RAF in May 1924. From then on the company did not look back. An improved Siskin IIIA was introduced in October 1925, and Siskins were built at Whitley until 1929, although most were produced under licence by other manufacturers. The Siskin proved to be an exceptional fighter and was particularly suited to aerobatics. They gave many spectacular and memorable flying exhibitions at the RAF's displays at Hendon. The company also produced the RAF's first aeroplane – Atlas I – specially designed for Army Co-operation duties. It first flew from Whitley in May 1925 and entered the Service two years later.

In an attempt to encourage and foster private flying the Air Ministry decided, in 1925, to subsidise five flying clubs in five different areas of the country – London, Lancashire, Yorkshire, the North-East and the Midlands. Each club was provided with £3,000 to help defray the initial costs and was supplied with a couple of de Havilland DH.60 Moths powered by Cirrus engines, the first really *practicable* dual-control light aircraft, which had first flown in February. Moths would dominate club and private flying in the years ahead. In September the Midland Aero Club, now operating from Castle Bromwich with a small membership, received its two Moths, which looked resplendent in their green livery (each club sported a different colour).

The year 1926 proved to be an auspicious one for Warwickshire at least as far as aviation was concerned. On 16th March Armstrong Whitworth's first biplane airliner – A.W.155 Argosy – made its initial flight from Whitley at the hands of Captain F. L. Barnard, the senior pilot of Imperial Airways. It was powered by three Armstrong Siddeley Jaguar engines and was then the largest airliner to be built in Britain. It was designed to carry twenty passengers, each of whom

A.W.155 Argosy – City of Birmingham – *in 1926.*

had a window that could be opened. It was the first airliner to provide something close to Pullman luxury air travel, carrying a steward and on-board buffet, which enabled Imperial Airways to introduce a special lunchtime 'Silver Wings' service from Croydon to Paris in May 1927. The Argosy had a range of over 500 miles, cruised at 95mph and proved far more economical to operate. It is interesting to note that the two-man crew sat in an open cockpit; the pilots (all First World War airmen) disliked cabins because they 'needed the wind on their faces better to assess the wind drift on landing approach and take-off'! Three Argosies were originally ordered by Imperial Airways, followed by four improved models in 1928. Each was named after cities – the first *City of Birmingham* (G-EBLF) and the last *City of Coventry* (G-AAEJ) – they gave admirable service to Imperial Airways for the next eight years. In January 1959 the company resuscitated the proud and famous Argosy name and bestowed it on their new and successful cargo and general transport.

On 5th October 1926 No 605 (County of Warwick) squadron was formed at Castle Bromwich with Squadron Leader J.A. Cecil Wright as its commanding officer. It was the fifth Auxiliary Air Force (AAF) squadron to be formed since the force had been authorised in October 1924. These squadrons were intended to act as a reserve for the regular RAF squadrons, with most of the officers and airmen recruited locally, and they were administered by the County Territorial Association, rather than by the RAF directly, although several regular officers were appointed to the squadron along with about seventy airmen to act as instructors. All the AAF officers were required to hold a private pilot's licence and were compelled to receive flying tuition to qualify for RAF 'wings'. All members of the squadron were expected to attend courses and a two-week summer camp. The squadron took as its crest the bear and ragged staff of Warwickshire and like the other four AAF squadrons it became a bomber unit being first equipped with DH.9As, which had become the 'workhorse' of the RAF since their introduction in 1918. They were exchanged for Westland Wapitis in 1930, then Hawker Harts, and later Hawker Hinds. Under Squadron Leader Wright No 605 became an excellent and effective unit and won the Lord Esher Trophy (a silver statuette of Perseus) on six occasions between 1927 and 1937; this highly prized trophy was awarded annually to the most efficient AAF squadron. The AAF squadrons gained a reputation for being rather select social clubs.

In July 1927 the Midland Club successfully organised the Birmingham

Aerial Pageant at Castle Bromwich, in which almost one hundred aeroplanes took part and which attracted over 100,000 spectators. The county's own squadron made a contribution to the aerial display, but perhaps the highlight of the show was the appearance of the *City of Birmingham* Argosy, in which the Lord Mayor and other local dignitaries were treated to a flight over the city. It had become increasingly obvious that the Air Ministry had no intention of releasing its hold over Castle Bromwich, although it seemed content to allow civil and club flying to continue there. In 1928 the Birmingham City Council resolved that it should consider 'the possibility of establishing a municipal aerodrome'. Initially, a site at Shirley was considered but for various reasons this was not progressed. The city council was well in tune with the mood of the time. In 1929 Sir Alan Cobham started his Municipal Aerodrome Campaign with the object of persuading cities and towns to consider establishing a municipal aerodrome. His slogans were 'Make the Skyways Britain's Highways' and 'British Towns need airports to boost British Trade'. In his large de Havilland DH.61 Giant Moth, *Youth of Britain*, Sir Alan made an exhausting tour of over one hundred towns. He visited Birmingham, Royal Leamington Spa,

Whitley Abbey aerodrome in 1928.

20

SIR ALAN COBHAM'S
GREAT AIR DISPLAY

is coming soon!

SIR ALAN COBHAM WITH SOME OF HIS PILOTS.

Sir Alan Cobham's 'National Aviation Days' were most popular during 1933–1935. (via Colin Cruddas)

Rugby and Stratford-upon-Avon, the last town council requested him to complete an aerial survey of likely sites in the area.

Nevertheless Castle Bromwich was the only aerodrome in the county available to the steadily growing number of commercial airlines. In June 1930 there were three weekly services to and from London (Croydon), Manchester (Barton) and Liverpool (Speke). Over the next five years various airlines – Great Western Railways, Midland & Scottish Air Ferries and Hillman Airways – used Castle Bromwich with increasing regularity as other inland air routes were established, more especially to south-west England and south Wales

It was during the early 1930s that flying really captured the public's imagination, its popularity seemed to know no bounds. From 1931 joy-riding returned with a vengeance: a variety of companies brought their 'air pageants', 'air displays' or 'flying circuses' to all corners of the country. These displays of 'stunt or crazy flying', aerobatics,

21

wing-walking, parachuting and, of course, passenger flights, attracted large crowds. The most popular were Sir Alan Cobham's 'National Aviation Days'. From 1932 to 1935 his display could be seen on various dates at Lawford Heath, Rugby, Cofton Hackett, Birmingham, the 'Flying Field' at Cubbington Road, Royal Leamington Spa, Whitley Abbey, Stratford-upon-Avon, Castle Bromwich and Westwood Heath, Coventry. These National Aviation Days, along with the British Hospital Air Pageants and the British Empire Air Displays, left lasting memories with all those who attended and even more so with those intrepid persons who took to the air for the first time.

From May 1934 the public were allowed to visit RAF and some civil aerodromes in celebration of what was known as Empire Air Day to be held on a Saturday in May. This was the inspiration of Air Commodore J. A. Chamier, the Secretary-General of the Aerial League of the British Empire, who was determined to make the country, and young people especially, more 'air minded'. The idea was a resounding success and over the next five years the air days became increasingly popular, with attendance figures rising sharply. On 25th May 1935 over 10,000 people attended the second Empire Air Day at Castle Bromwich. The following year (23rd May) some 6,200 visited the aerodrome, paying a shilling (children threepence) entrance fee for the privilege of seeing most of the RAF's latest aeroplanes along with a number of flying displays and also several civil aeroplanes offering short flights for five shillings. Empire Air Days gave most of the public their only opportunity to observe the work and the aeroplanes of its rapidly expanding Air Force.

Besides Castle Bromwich and Whitley Abbey, where Coventry Aeroplane Club operated alongside AWA, there were a number of small privately owned landing grounds in the county. Lord Willoughby de Broke, who had obtained his pilot's licence in July 1930, had one at his home – Woodley House, Kineton. As a squadron leader in the AAF, he would take over command of No 605 squadron in March 1936. Major J. E. Bonniken, an ex-RFC officer, also owned an aerodrome at Bishop's Tachbrook near Leamington Spa, which was the home of the Leamington, Warwick and District Flying Club. Mr J. A. Griffin had a small landing ground at Milcote Hall, Stratford-upon-Avon and David Mitchell owned one at Lawford Heath. Austin still retained their landing field at Cofton Hackett, but Billesley aerodrome had finally disappeared under housing development. All these landing grounds had been inspected and approved by the Automobile Association and

RAF Castle Bromwich on Empire Air Day – 23rd May 1936. (RAF Museum)

they were listed in its first *Register of Approved Landing Grounds* published in 1933, which contained information on the landing surfaces, obstructions, hangarage, nearest telephone and hotel. For the previous two years the A.A. had offered a weather information service for flyers, and continental touring maps for those members flying abroad, and its patrol men were frequently in attendance at air meetings and aerodromes to offer assistance – another example of how motoring and flying were closely linked.

The days of Whitley Abbey aerodrome were now numbered as Armstrong Whitworth considered that both their production facilities and the aerodrome was not really adequate or suitable for the production in quantity of large aeroplanes. However, this was not before two of the company's most famous aeroplanes made their first flights from the aerodrome. On 6th June 1932 the latest airliner, AW.15 (G–ABPI) made its maiden flight under the control of Alan C. Campbell-Orde, AWA's Chief Test Pilot. AWA had been asked by Imperial Airways to produce a nine passenger/mail airliner for its European services. The company's chief designer, John Lloyd, produced a sleek four-engined monoplane, its design perhaps owing much to the fashionable art deco of the time. It was named *Atalanta*, though in fact this name was adapted for the airline's entire fleet of eight. On 26th September 1932 *Atalanta* entered Imperial Airways' service to Brussels and Cologne, although subsequently the airliners would operate in Africa and India. The original *Atalanta* was severely damaged on 20th October 1932 when it crashed whilst taking-off from Whitley. Campbell-Orde and the Chairman of AWA, Air Marshal Sir John Higgins, escaped without injury but the co-pilot, Donald S. Green, received severe head injuries which ended his flying career.

The Atalantas were followed by AWA's largest military aircraft so far – the A.W.23 – a bomber/transport, which first flew from Whitley on 4th June 1934 and was the company's first aircraft to be provided with a retractactable undercarriage. However, it was not ordered by the Air Ministry, its competitor, the Bristol Bombay, being preferred. But when AWA's most successful military aircraft first appeared in March 1936, it outwardly showed a remarkable similiarity to A.W.23. This was the A.W.38 heavy bomber, most appropriately named the Whitley; the prototype (K4586) made its maiden flight from Whitley on 17th March 1936, flown by Campbell-Orde. The bomber had originally been designed for the Czechoslovakian government but the expected order did not materialise and the Air Ministry devised a specification B3/34 for a twin-engined bomber with a bomb load of 2,500 pounds and a range of 1,250 miles. In September 1934 two prototypes were ordered, followed almost twelve months later by a production order of eighty.

In January 1936 a new but small aerodrome opened at Ansty, about five miles to the north-east of Coventry. Its very existence owed much to the acumen of Sir John Siddeley, who had the foresight to appreciate that flying training would be an important and essential element of the proposed expansion of the RAF. Air Service Training Ltd, which had

The prototype A.W.38 Whitley (K4586) first flew from Baginton on 17th March, 1936.

been formed in 1931 as a subsidiary of the Armstrong Siddeley Development Company, had acquired about one hundred and forty acres of farmland for the new aerodrome, which was planned to house an elementary flying school to train both civilian and RAF reserve airmen. Air Service Training Ltd already had an Air Ministry contract for its other flying school at Hamble in Hampshire, which in 1935 had become known as No 3 Elementary & Reserve Flying Training School (E&RFTS). Such schools had been established with the express purpose of also training the large number of regular and reserve airmen that would be required for the RAF's expansion in the immediate years ahead. Thus, on 6th January, No 9 E&RFTS was established at Ansty, mainly staffed by civilian flying instructors, most of whom were retired RAF officers who had passed through the Central Flying School, so ensuring that the flying tuition was based on service principles and procedures.

Elsewhere, to the south-east of Coventry, another new aerodrome was also being constructed. During 1935 Coventry Corporation had acquired a substantial area of land at Baginton, about four miles south-east of the city, with the intention of establishing a municipal aerodrome. The site was close to AWA's existing works and airfield at Whitley, and the company decided to build a new production plant at Baginton, which came into use in May 1936, and it was from Baginton that AWA began the production of the Whitley Is. Like several other municipal authorities Coventry Corporation was somewhat relieved to have a large industrial tenant to defray some of the expenses of their new aerodrome. The first production Whitley I (K7183) was completed at Baginton in March 1937 and was delivered to the Aeroplane & Armament Experimental Establishment, but in the same month the first Whitley Is were delivered to No 10 squadron at Dishforth.

Two years earlier Birmingham City Council had revived the plans for a municipal airport, and not to be upstaged by neighbouring Coventry, the city council gave the final approval for the development of a municipal aerodrome on 4th February 1936. Some eight hundred acres at Elmdon, about eight miles south-east of the city, had been identified as the most suitable site and B. Sunley & Co. Ltd began almost immediately on the construction project. The airport was planned to cost £½ million and the large and impressive terminal building, designed by Holst & Co., became a feature.

The planned expansion of the RAF, which was set in motion in 1934, created a considerable number of problems for the Air Ministry and not least of these was the need to greatly improve and increase the production of aircraft. In April 1936 the Government announced the 'shadow factory' scheme, whereby it hoped to harness and apply the assembly line techniques of the large motor-car manufacturers to that of aircraft and aero-engine production. The Government would provide the new factories and equipment, and the motor car companies would be responsible for their management. The 'shadow factories' required the use of a landing ground. Once again the Midland car manufacturers became the nucleus of the pre-war scheme – shades of the Great War; Austin at Longbridge; Rover, Rootes (controlling Humbers), Standard and Daimler at Coventry. Originally they produced the Bristol Mercury radial aero-engines, but not many months after the outbreak of the war they additionally became heavily engaged in aircraft production.

Early in March 1936 Warwickshire's most illustrious airman, Flight Lieutenant Frank Whittle, who was born in Coventry, founded a small company, Power Jets Ltd, that would ultimately revolutionise military and civil flying, and gain him the title 'the father of the jet-engine'. His immense and incalculable contribution to the progress of aviation in the twentieth century fully deserves to appear under a separate chapter.

Besides being heavily involved in the Whitley project, AWA's design team had also been engaged in producing the company's latest airliner – A.W.27 Ensign. It had been ordered by Imperial Airways back in late 1934 as an all-metal four-engined airliner capable of carrying forty passengers at a cruising speed of 200mph. The long delay in developing and producing the prototype was largely due to the Air Ministry's insistence that AWA should concentrate on the production of Whitleys. The Ensign finally made its maiden flight from Hamble, not Baginton, on 24th January 1938, and the first airliner was delivered to Imperial in October and another three were in service by the end of the year.

The cost of private flying training was still quite prohibitive and largely beyond the means and aspirations of the majority of young men and women. However, in an attempt to rectify this situation the Government introduced, in July 1938, the Civil Air Guard scheme, which was intended to provide relatively cheap and subsidised flying instruction; it was advertised that 'citizens can fly for a florin [2s or 10p] a week'! The CAG scheme was also a method of creating a civilian reserve of trained pilots. An initial fee of £14 was charged, which included helmet, goggles and membership of the Royal Aero Club and then for about £10 each member could receive one year's flying instruction, by which time most had attained their 'A' licence. They were compelled to agree 'to accept service in any capacity with aviation in a state of national emergency'. The response was quite remarkable; over 35,000 applied in the first three months, of whom about 6,000 enrolled and the rest were placed on the long waiting lists at the sixty or so flying schools taking part in the scheme. By July 1939 well over two thousand had gained their pilot's licence by this method. Each had been individually classified in categories related 'to their prospective

The Terminal building at Elmdon in 1939. (via R. Mortimer)

value at a time of national emergency'! Certainly CAG pilot training took place at Castle Bromwich organised by the Midland Aero Club and at Ansty; a subsidy of £50 was paid by the Air Ministry for each successful pupil that attained their 'A' licence.

In those last peaceful months of 1939 Birmingham finally had its own airport, Elmdon, which had cost in the region of £360,000. The first aircraft landed on 20th March, a de Havilland DH.90 Dragonfly flown by Whitney Straight, the owner of Great Western and Western Airways. He announced that his airline company would use Elmdon from 17th June on its thrice daily service from Weston-super-Mare to Manchester. The airport formally opened on 1st May and Midland Aero Club was also housed there. On the same day No 44 E&RFTS was formed at the airport, operated by Airwork Ltd. Elmdon was officially opened by HRH The Duchess of Kent on 8th July but the heavy rain severely restricted the planned air display. The airport barely had time to establish itself before it was requisitioned by the Air Ministry.

Almost as if people were aware that the Empire Air Day held on Saturday, 20th May would be their last opportunity to visit RAF stations, over one million attended at the sixty-three service airfields and fifteen civil and private aerodromes open to the public. Adults were charged 1s and children 3d. More than 40,000 flocked to Ansty where during the afternoon they witnessed thirteen flying events, including a final fly-past mainly of training biplanes but also a Blenheim, Anson, Harvard and an inevitable Whitley. This proved to be the sixth, last and most successful Empire Air Day but as the crowds streamed away from these airfields, I wonder how many seriously thought that less than four months later the country would be at war.

Royal Air Force

On 1st April 1939 the Royal Air Force celebrated its coming-of-age, twenty-one years since its formation in the dark days of 1918 with the merger of the Royal Flying Corps and the Royal Naval Air Service. HM King George VI, a qualified pilot who had served as a Squadron Leader briefly during 1919/20, sent a celebratory message: 'I have known the Royal Air Force from its earliest days and am proud that its spirit remains unchanged – a spirit that has enabled it to surmount many difficulties and rise, true to its motto, to even greater heights of achievements.' This motto *Per Ardua ad Astra* dated back to the formation of the Royal Flying Corps in May 1912 and is still proudly borne by the Service today.

For the RAF to have progressed thus far in twenty-one years was no mean achievement in itself. During the 1920s the Service was compelled to strive doggedly to maintain its very independence in the face of repeated and determined attempts by the War Office and more especially the Admiralty to reclaim their flying units. Finally, when the RAF's survival as an independent service was virtually ensured, the fledgling Air Force was starved of the necessary financial resources to progress and expand, and the procurement of more advanced aeroplanes and equipment was a slow and painful procedure. This period of severe financial restraint has been memorably described as 'the years of the locust'. All this was despite the fact that during many of the inter-war years, its airmen and aircraft had been in action mainly in the Middle East and India on what has been described as a 'Colonial Policing' role.

The RAF's very survival as an independent Service can be attributed largely to one officer – Sir Hugh (later Viscount) Trenchard – who was Chief of the Air Staff (CAS) from 1919 to 1929. Indeed in January 1918 he was appointed the first CAS but resigned after just four months because he was unable to work with Lord Rothermere, the first Air Minister. To the eternal gratitude of the RAF, Winston Churchill, the newly appointed Secretary of State for War and Air, persuaded him to return as CAS in February 1919.

From the outset Trenchard had a clear vision of the way ahead, the style of Service he wished to fashion and its role in the peacetime years. Such was his foresight, conviction, utter determination and undoubted influence during this critical decade that the RAF was able ultimately to develop into an important and integral part of the Armed Services; indeed, his contribution was so immense and crucial that he became known as the 'father of the Royal Air Force', a title he is reputed to have loathed.

Trenchard strongly supported the Central Flying School, which inculcated the highest standards of flying training instruction and greatly advanced the flying skills and expertise of the squadrons. In February 1920 he founded the Officer Cadet College at Cranwell, which he intended to compare favourably with Dartmouth and

Sir Hugh Trenchard (centre) as Chief of the Air Staff – 1920. (via J. Adams)

Sandhurst, as it did, becoming known as 'the University of the Air'. The magnificent college buildings at Cranwell were not completed until the early 1930s because of severe financial restraints. A staff college for experienced serving officers was established at Andover in 1922 to prepare them for senior rank. One Service institution that is forever linked with Trenchard was his creation of the Apprentices' School at Halton to provide a regular supply of young airmen well trained in the various ground trades, a valuable legacy for the future expansion of a technical Air Force. These young airmen became known in the Service as Halton or Trenchard brats! Additionally, Trenchard established the Officers' Engineering School, which, from 1921, produced highly skilled aeronautical engineers, perhaps most notably Sir Frank Whittle. Trenchard's rationale was that pilots, after some five years of flying duties, should spend at least two years employed in a ground trade.

The introduction of the Short Service Commission scheme for young men (18 to 22 years) to be trained as pilots, with four years on the active list followed by six years on the reserve, was another of Trenchard's revolutionary initiatives. He fully realised that 'the Air Force was essentially a young man's service. Its flyers were merely birds of passage'. Trenchard was also instrumental in the introduction of the Auxiliary Air Force, despite political opposition; Winston Churchill famously commented 'Weekend flyers, Boom [Trenchard's nickname]? Never!' However it proved to be a most successful venture, and members of the AAF squadrons made an invaluable contribution to the Service during World War II. Another of Trenchard's innovations was the formation of University Air Squadrons, and no fewer than four former members of these squadrons won Victoria Crosses during the war.

In 1927 Trenchard was created the first ever Marshal of the Royal Air Force. Two years later he retired, secure in the knowledge that he had left a small but nevertheless very professional air force, which was imbued with a firm discipline, was strongly motivated and, moreover, technically trained to a high standard both in the air and on the ground. He modestly claimed, 'I have laid the foundations for a castle; if nobody builds anything bigger than a cottage on them, it will at least be a very good cottage.' Without doubt the greatly expanded RAF that faced its sternest challenge in World War II bore Trenchard's indelible imprint and by 1945 a massive and powerful 'castle' had been built! Trenchard remained an influential *éminence grise* throughout his retirement, and two of his most dedicated disciples – Sir Charles Portal and Sir Arthur Harris – were in high enough positions of power to ensure that his ideals for the Service and, more particularly, his overriding concept of an all-powerful bomber force were prosecuted to the full.

From the earliest days Trenchard had fully appreciated the need to keep the Service uppermost in the public's eye. The first RAF Tournament was held at Hendon in July 1920. Later known as pageants and then displays, they quickly became accepted as essential events in the aviation calendar, drawing high praise and attracting large crowds and ever gaining in popularity until their demise in June 1937. The displays gave the Service an ideal opportunity to demonstrate to the general public and the press, in particular, the flying skills of its airmen. With their remarkable and spectacular exhibitions of formation flying, aerobatics and mock bombing attacks, they provided a showcase to proudly display its newly acquired aircraft. During the 1930s, especially, the Service was rarely out of the

RAF Tournament at Hendon – 30th July 1920.

news: its airmen pioneered the airmail routes to the Empire, made long-distance record flights and set speed and altitude records; this was at a time when flying as a sport and aviation generally attracted much public and newspaper interest. Famously in 1931, the RAF's High Speed Flight won the prestigious international Schneider Trophy for seaplanes outright.

In the early thirties the RAF was a small and close-knit force, often described, perhaps a little unjustly, as 'the best flying club in the world'. This cosy and somewhat amateur image had been fostered to some extent by the Hendon Displays and the appearance of celebrated RAF pilots performing their 'pretty flying' at air shows throughout the country. The opening of many RAF aerodromes to the public on Empire Air Days from 1934, only strengthened this concept; their elegant and pleasing buildings created an impression of a comfortable and rather elitist club, the members of which rushed about the skies in biplanes that appeared to have little changed from those of the First World War. In those brief 'golden days of flying' airmen and airwomen were accorded celebrity status and fêted by the public as heroes or heroines for their brave and gallant long-distance flights.

In 1934 the RAF totalled 30,390 personnel, of which the elite – the pilots – were greatly in the minority – less than 2%. The aircraft they flew were all biplanes, mostly of wooden construction and really heirs of a memorable past rather than an air force for the future; in fact the

Service was jokingly referred to as the 'Hawker Air Force' because of its numerous squadrons of Hawker Hinds, Harts, Furies, Demons and Audaxes. In retrospect, 1934 may be viewed as the watershed of the Service. Over the next five years it underwent a massive and dramatic expansion in both manpower and machines. With an almost unseemly haste, the Service was modernised, with the provision of a variety of more powerful heavy bombers, far faster fighters and purpose-built trainers, virtually all of which were monoplanes. New aerodromes were built to accommodate them, and the basic command structure underwent a drastic and radical reorganisation to place it in a state of readiness to fight an air war.

The collapse of the Disarmament Conference in 1934 and a steady worsening of the political situation in Europe set in motion the first of no fewer than eight Expansion Schemes over the next four years, which were amended or abandoned with a quite bewildering regularity. The official acknowledgement to the world, in March 1935, of a powerful German Air Force – the *Reichsluftwaffe*, soon shortened to *Luftwaffe* – greatly concentrated the minds of British politicians and Service chiefs alike. And yet in July of that year, when the RAF staged 'the largest and most impressive fly-past in the world' at Duxford, in the presence of King George V and Queen Mary as part of the Royal Jubilee review of the Service, nothing could disguise the fact that the RAF gave the appearance of an outmoded air force – ponderous bombers and slow biplane fighters. Indeed, some critics claimed that 'little progress had been achieved in the last fifteen years'. One celebrated aviation journalist – Charles Grey of *The Aeroplane* – earnestly hoped that 'His Majesty may live long enough to see his Royal Air Force leading the world in every way as Queen Victoria saw her Navy ruling the sea'. This wish was not fulfilled, but it was realised for King George VI in 1945.

The task that faced Sir Edward Ellington (CAS from 1932 to 1937) and his senior commanders was formidable in the extreme, and they were then unaware of how short would be the timescale to accomplish such a wholesale modernisation programme. Indeed, the various Expansion Schemes had a completion time of ten years, a legacy of the political naiveté of the 1920s, when it was firmly believed that the country would have ten years' notice of a major European war – the infamous 'Ten Year Rule' – which bedevilled and frustrated all defence expenditure, particularly for the RAF.

The list of necessary, if not to say essential, improvements to provide a modern and well-equipped Air Force seemed to be endless – long-range bombers with powered turrets, faster fighters able to operate above 15,000 feet, variable pitch propellers, improved gun sights, better bombs, self-sealing fuel tanks, superior radio communications, the introduction of Identification of Friend or Foe (IFF), the development of ground and airborne radar, the construction of new aerodromes and the possibility of the provision of hard runways, the recruitment and training of the necessary pilots and aircrew, and so on and so forth. The Herculean task was further complicated by a sudden switch of priorities halfway through the Expansion programme, when the provision of more fighter aircraft took urgent preference over the bomber force.

In late 1935 the existing system of flying training was subjected to a radical review, and then in July 1936 the outmoded and rather cumbersome organisation known as the Air Defence of Great Britain, which had been created in 1925, was dissolved and in its place four separate and functional commands were formed – Bomber, Fighter, Coastal and Training – each with a precise and specific operational role; other commands followed later – Reserve, Maintenance, Transport, Balloon, Army Co-operation, Ferry and Transport. In June 1939 the Women's Auxiliary Air Force was created, some nineteen years after the Women's Royal Air Force had been disbanded. This then was the basic structure under which the RAF waged its bitter and costly war in Europe. There were, of course, several other Commands for units serving in the Middle East, Mediterranean, India and the Far East.

At the end of July 1936 it was announced that a Volunteer Reserve would be recruited to act as a true reserve for the regular Air Force. Unlike the AAF, it would not have its separate squadrons. Air Commodore Arthur Tedder, Director of Training at the Air Ministry, had proposed this concept of a citizen's air force to teach young men to fly in their spare time – mainly evenings and weekends. Recruitment commenced in April 1937 with the object of producing eight hundred pilots each year but it proved more successful than the Air Ministry's wildest hopes: on 1st September 1939 the RAFVR's aircrew strength was over 10,200, of which 6,640 were pilots. The RAFVR was intended to be 'a fully democratic force ... without class distinctions', and it brought about a deep and radical social change in the service. Hitherto the majority of regular pilots were of officer rank and mainly recruited from public schools and universities; now the Sergeant pilots of the RAFVR came from all classes of society and all walks of life and they

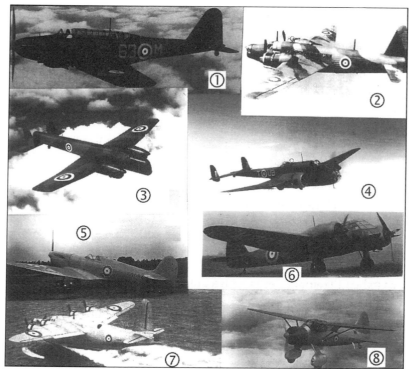

All eight of these famous WWII aircraft made their maiden flights during 1936–7. 1. Fairey Battle 10th March 1936; 2. Vickers Wellington 15th June 1936; 3. Armstrong Whitworth Whitley 17th March 1936; 4. Handley Page Hampden 21st June 1936; 5. Supermarine Spitfire 5th March 1936; 6. Bristol Blenheim I 25th June 1936; 7. Short Sunderland 16th October 1937; 8. Westland Lysander 15th June 1936.

made a most valuable contribution to the three operational Commands in the early war years. In the Battle of Britain alone over 40% of the fighter pilots involved were sergeants.

New aircraft appeared with an apparent monotonous regularity from 1936 onwards. Such well-known WWII aircraft as the Wellington, Lysander, Hampden, Blenheim, Spitfire, Whitley and Battle all made their first flights during the year – the Hurricane had arrived on the scene in late 1935. In February 1937 the RAF's latest fighter, the Gloster Gladiator, came into service and although it was a biplane, it was at least provided with an enclosed cockpit. By the end of the year it was made virtually redundant when the first monoplane fighter, the

Hurricane, entered the Service; it was also the first to exceed 300mph, followed in August 1938, by the arrival of the Spitfires. Other specifications were issued for four-engined bombers, which ultimately led to the Short Stirling and Handley Page Halifax. The RAF's long and protracted purchasing methods were accelerated by 'ordering aircraft from the drawing board'. It was really quite a revolution in so many ways. The only setback for the RAF in these Expansion years was the political decision in early 1937 that the Fleet Air Arm would be placed under the control of the Admiralty, thus finally resolving the protracted and acrimonious dispute about the control of Naval aviation. The Air Staff considered the decision as 'disastrous ... a body blow'. The FAA was formally transferred in May 1939.

Air Chief Marshal Sir Cyril Newall, the CAS from September 1937 to October 1940, is considered to have been 'the prime architect of the wartime Air Force'. Although he was born in India, he came from a Warwickshire family and in 1905 was commissioned in the Royal Warwickshire Regiment. Newall qualified as a pilot in October 1911 and joined the Royal Flying Corps in 1914, serving with distinction and personal courage; he was awarded the Albert Medal (the forerunner of the George Cross) during the First World War. Although he perhaps lacked the charisma and intellectual qualities of Trenchard or indeed his successor Sir Charles Portal, he coped with the daunting and arduous task of forging the rapidly expanding Service into a modern Air Force capable of challenging the *Luftwaffe*, which in March 1939 was considered 'the most powerful air force in the world'.

Although Newall was a dedicated 'bomber man' – a devotee of Trenchard's doctrine of the all-powerful bomber force – he accepted the initial inadequacies of Bomber Command and its early operational setbacks and losses with a calm and measured equanimity. Despite early differences of opinion with Sir Hugh Dowding, the AOC-in-C of Fighter Command, he strongly supported Dowding during his fierce struggle to preserve his precious squadrons for the defence of Britain and also allowed him a free hand to control his forces during the Battle of Britain. In October 1940 Newall was replaced as CAS by Sir Charles Portal, and he was ushered off to become Governor-General of New Zealand – an exhausted and rather forgotten man. When Newall retired in 1946 as a Marshal of the Royal Air Force, he was elevated to the peerage and took as his title Baron Newall of Clifton upon Dunsmore in the county of Warwickshire.

At the outbreak of war the RAF totalled some 175,000 personnel

Air Chief Marshal Sir Cyril Newall, Chief of the Air Staff from September, 1937 to October, 1940.

(including 1,500 airwomen) and some 1,900 operational aircraft. *The Official History of the RAF, 1939-45* claimed that 'Bomber Command was not trained or equipped to penetrate into enemy territory by day or to find its target areas, let alone its targets by night ... in 1939 it was above all an investment in the future'. Really this view could well be ascribed to the RAF in total. Fighter Command needed, and wisely used, the valuable breathing space afforded by the so-called Phoney War to strengthen its force, both in terms of the numbers of fighters and also trained pilots to fly them; this precious time enabled the Command to extend its radar coverage and also perfect interception techniques. Whereas Coastal Command, which was described in November 1940 as 'the Cinderella of the RAF', was woefully ill-equipped not only in terms of personnel but also operational aircraft: there were just nineteen squadrons to cover the whole coastline of the United Kingdom.

On 1st September 1939 the RAF was mobilised for war, and, less than an hour after Neville Chamberlain's fateful broadcast on Sunday 3rd September, its airmen went into action when a solitary Blenheim of No 139 squadron left to photograph units of the German fleet, which were thought to be leaving the Naval port of Wilhelmshaven. The following day Blenheims and Wellingtons of Bomber Command made a daylight bombing raid on German Naval ports and sadly seven of the twenty-nine aircraft failed to return, the RAF's first casualties of the air war. From that day forward, RAF units were active on patrol or operations for virtually every single day or night of the Second World War. Despite early setbacks and operational losses, especially in Bomber Command, its various Commands grew from strength to strength.

The RAF of 1940 was a vastly different force from that of just four years earlier. The memorable 'few' of Fighter Command achieved the RAF's first major and most critical victory – the Battle of Britain. Bomber Command attracted much public attention in the early war years, as it appeared to be the only armed force taking the fight to the enemy but in the process suffering heavy losses. And the airmen of Coastal Command waged a long and bitter war against the U-boats, in what was coined by Winston Churchill as the 'Battle of the Atlantic', in his opinion equally as critical as the Battle of Britain.

As the air war progressed and intensified on all fronts, existing aircraft were modified and improved, especially the classic Spitfire, and new aircraft and equipment were developed and produced, most notably the four-engined heavy bombers, the night fighters, the incomparable Mosquitos and the destructive Typhoons. New operational procedures and tactics were evolved to meet the fresh demands that were placed on its pilots and aircrews. Perhaps most crucial were the formation of fighter Wings in early 1941 to bring Fighter Command onto the offensive; the formation of Bomber Command's Pathfinder Force in August 1942; and the creation of the 2nd Tactical Air Force in June 1943.

The RAF reached a peak of manpower in July 1944 with over 1,185,000 personnel in service and some 8,400 aircraft – a mighty Air

'So much owed by so many to so few.' The Air Ministry's account of the Battle of Britain: first published 1941.

The splendid RAF Runnymede Memorial at Cooper's Hill, Surrey.

Force of quite awesome and devastating power. The cost in human terms of its long and bitter air battle was 70,253 aircrew killed or missing in action with another 22,924 wounded and over 13,100 taken as prisoners of war; furthermore, 9,671 ground crew were killed and 4,490 made prisoners. Bomber Command suffered grievously with over 47,000 killed or missing in action. Many of these airmen are buried in the various British war cemeteries on the continent and other corners of the world. Those airmen, over 20,450, that flew from this country and have no known graves are commemorated in the splendid Runnymede Memorial at Cooper's Hill, Surrey.

The junior Service had paid a very high price for its share in the ultimate victory but it had clearly demonstrated that by the skills, determination, courage and bravery of its airmen the RAF had truly 'come of age' as a superb fighting service. Twenty-nine Victoria Crosses were awarded to its airmen. Many of its commanders and airmen etched their names permanently in the annals of aviation history – Hugh Dowding, Arthur Harris, Donald Bennett, Guy Gibson, Douglas Bader, John Cunningham, Leonard Cheshire – to name but a handful. Without a shadow of doubt the Royal Air Force had fully justified the faith and confidence placed upon it by HM

King George VI in his message to the Service on 4th September 1939: '... you will have to shoulder far greater responsibilities than those which your Service had to shoulder in the last war ... I can assure all ranks of the Air Force of my supreme confidence in their skill and courage, and their ability to meet whatever calls may be made on them.'

Flying and Operational Training

Most of Warwickshire's wartime airfields were engaged in flying training of some description, from elementary through to operational, but predominant was bomber crew operational training. Many famous training aircraft of the Second World War were evident in the skies above the county – Tutors, Tiger Moths, Masters, Oxfords, Ansons and Harvards, with Whitleys and Wellingtons equipping the several Operational Training Units (OTUs). Therefore it is appropriate to examine in some detail the growth and development of flying and operational training within the Service.

Those intrepid military officers who volunteered to serve in the country's first flying service – the Air Battalion of the Royal Engineers – from April 1911 were required to learn to fly by first arranging their own private flying tuition and secure a Royal Aero Club certificate before being accepted into the air battalion. They did, however, receive a compensatory payment of £75, an amount that barely covered their expenditure.

The first military flying school came into being in December 1911 at Eastchurch, Kent, where the Admiralty established a Naval Flying School. In May 1912 the Royal Flying Corps (RFC) was formed, and one month later the Central Flying School (CFS) was established at Upavon on Salisbury Plain, equipped with just seven aeroplanes and with the objective of producing one hundred and eighty pilots each year for both the Military and Naval Wings of the Corps, although the Admiralty still preferred to use its existing elementary flying school at Eastchurch. At this time applicants still had to be in possession of their Royal Aero Club's certificates before acceptance into the CFS. One of the earliest entrants was Major Hugh Trenchard, who had gained his pilot's certificate at the Sopwith School, Brooklands in August; two months later he was appointed as an instructor and effectively became the school's adjutant.

By August 1914 there were only 881 certified pilots in the whole of the country and over 55% of these were military officers. Less than four years later there were over 6,500. The almost insatiable demand for pilots to man the new RFC squadrons and replace the mounting losses of pilots over France and in training accidents resulted in the development of a vast training organisation. Soon pilots were being trained at the rate of over one thousand a month, although their courses amounted to less than twenty flying hours; indeed, some pilots went into action in France with only twelve hours' flying experience, often with fatal consequences. By 1918 there were over seventy training depots throughout the country and a number of schools of aeronautics as well as fighting schools. There were also some twenty specialist or 'finishing' training centres. One laboured under the title of the School of Navigation and Bomb Dropping at Stonehenge!

One of the most famous early graduates of the CFS was Robert Smith-Barry, a superb pilot who had served in France. In 1916, as the colonel in charge of Gosport, he had his training aeroplanes fitted with full dual control, with the pupil occupying the pilot's seat, and he developed a system of flying instruction which was adopted by the CFS as the standard RAF practice and still prevails today. The school gained a high reputation for the quality of its training and became dedicated to the training of flying instructors; by repute the school had 'turned the art of flying into a science'.

In the immediate post-war years the RAF was reduced to a fraction of its size and therefore the provision of flying training posed no real problems. Aspiring pilots went to one of the Service Flying Training Schools (SFTS), where in approximately six months they completed some one hundred and fifty flying hours before joining a 'front-line' squadron to continue their training up to an operational standard. Their initial training had been completed in Avro 504s – the 'Immortal 504' – which dated back to 1912; it had become one of the classic training aircraft of all time. The 504s survived until 1933, then being replaced by Avro Tutors and more especially by the equally famous and ubiquitous de Havilland Tiger Moths. For the more advanced stages of their instruction the pilots flew Bristol F2Bs and DH.9As – both of which had served during the First World War. Later, other 'front-line' aeroplanes, once they had been superseded, would be adapted to act as advanced flying trainers. The officer cadets entering

The 'Immortal 504' – Avro 504K of No. 1 Flying Training School over Netheravon. (RAF Museum)

the RAF College at Cranwell received their flying training at the college but were relatively few in number (including Frank Whittle), so it is no small wonder that they were considered 'the elite' of the Service.

Although it was universally accepted that the RAF produced highly trained pilots, there were some deficiencies in the flying training programme. Navigation barely merited a mention, although map-reading did; 'air navigation' in RAF circles largely became the art of following railway lines, known as 'Bradshawing' from the famous railway timetables. Gunnery and bombing practice were minor elements in the programme. Observers were not trained to a sufficiently high standard and wireless operators were given too much of the theory of radio rather than practical operation and maintenance. Furthermore, instrument flying was in its infancy; it was the CFS that introduced blind flying or 'cloud flying' – as it was shown in the syllabus – into the flying training schools and front-line squadrons during the early 1930s.

These rather unsatisfactory elements of flying training and the proposed Expansion plans for the Service caused the Air Ministry to initiate a radical reappraisal of flying training. It was now considered to be an urgent priority, especially as it was estimated that 10,000 pilots

Formation of pre-war training aircraft – many flew from Warwickshire airfields in the Second World War. (RAF Museum)

would be required in the first year of any future war along with other aircrew categories. In 1933 there were just five SFTSs (including Cranwell) and this number increased in the next three years. Furthermore the prospect of faster and more advanced aircraft planned to enter the service in the foreseeable future gave an added dimension to the flying training programme.

In 1934 Air Commodore Arthur Tedder, Director of Training at the Air Ministry, was given the task of reorganising flying training. He was asked to make full use of all the available resources in the country and he proposed to utilise the many existing civilian flying schools to train regular and reserve airmen for initial flying instruction; these schools were placed under contract to the Air Ministry and by the end of 1935 eight were involved in the Air Ministry scheme. From these schools the student pilots progressed to an SFTS, where in the fullness of time they would qualify for their Flying Badge – the highly prized and coveted RAF Wings. The number of SFTSs was increased to ten in order to cater for the expected influx of students.

A serious disaster in December 1936, which resulted in three deaths and two injuries, highlighted the inherent weaknesses in the existing system of 'operational' training, certainly in the case of bomber squadrons. Six out of seven Handley Page Heyfords of No 102

Students set off to their training aircraft – Ansons and Harvards.

squadron flying from Aldergrove, Northern Ireland to Finningley, Yorkshire crashed in the Pennines. Although there was a combination of circumstances that brought about this tragedy, the lack of extended training and insufficient air experience of the bomber crews, especially in navigation and radio communication skills, certainly played a part.

With the reorganisation of the RAF in 1936, Training Command was established, with its headquarters at Market Drayton controlling all

Service training under four Groups. In February 1937 Reserve Command was formed, which became responsible for the E&RFTSs. The introduction of the Volunteer Reserve in April saw another seven E&RFTSs open, and another seven would commence instructing Reserve airmen during 1938; by the outbreak of war forty-five were in operation. Instructors from the CFS monitored the performance of these E&RFTSs with regular inspections, and the school was also given the responsibility of producing pilot's notes, describing in detail the layout of controls of each type of service aircraft as well as its flying characteristics. Hitherto there had been precious little printed information on new aircraft.

New training aircraft began to emerge. In May 1937 the RAF received its first monoplane advanced two-seater trainer – Miles Magister – fondly known as the 'Maggie'. It had been developed from the company's successful Hawk series of civilian aircraft. The Magister, with its low-wing layout, proved to be particularly suited for fighter pilot training. It was followed in November by Airspeed Oxfords, the Service's first twin-engined advanced trainer with dual control as standard. Oxfords were destined to train other aircrew categories besides pilots. Also Avro Ansons were being used for initial navigation training in addition to their intended role as coastal reconnaissance aircraft.

The sheer pressure of training the large number of pilots passing

Miles Magister I – fondly known as the 'Maggie'.

46

*North American Harvards of EATS at Cranbourne, Rhodesia – September 1941.
(Imperial War Museum)*

through the E&RFTSs created a number of problems. There was a dearth of experienced flying training instructors, although many instructors previously serving on the reserve had been recalled to assist and even WWI pilots (notably Cecil Lewis of RFC and *Sagittarius Rising* fame) were encouraged to return as instructors. There was also an acute shortage of training aircraft: every available machine was being used. In 1938 the Air Ministry was forced to look to the United States for a suitable two-seat advanced training aircraft, finally settling on the North American BC-1 trainer, designated the Harvard I, and the first of the initial order of two hundred arrived in December 1938. It was not until 31st March 1939 that the first British-built advanced trainer – Miles M.9A Master – made its maiden flight, but only seven had entered the Service by the outbreak of the war.

Although Tedder had continually stressed that 'the object of training must be to produce pilots capable of going straight from the training organisation to operational work in squadrons', the reality was far from this ideal; Bomber Command particularly was suffering in this respect. However, there was some improvement as far as other aircrew categories were concerned. The observer flying badge had been re-introduced in October 1937 and their first specialist schools had opened. Navigation was still a thorny problem, although the School of Air Navigation at Manston along with two civilian schools (one at Ansty) was manfully striving to improve matters. The broad concept of dedicated bomber crews was not yet realised. It was not until December 1939 that air gunners were made full-time crew members, given the rank of sergeant and awarded their half-wing 'AG'; previously they had joined crews on a part-time basis flying with any pilot.

Perhaps the most serious defect in the training programme, at least in respect of Bomber and Coastal Commands, was the inadequate experience of long-distance and night flying. During 1938 less than 10% of Bomber Command's flying hours had been conducted at night, Station Commanders were reluctant to order night exercises because of the wide difference in skills between senior and junior pilots and some Commanders even claimed that they had kept night flying to a minimum in deference to the local civilian communities! A more sobering fact to consider was that were no fewer than 487 forced landings at night in two years due mainly to faulty navigation. The AOC-in-C of Bomber Command, Sir Edgar Ludlow-Hewitt, maintained that 40% of his crews were unable to find a target in a friendly city in broad daylight, let alone at night! One of the reasons given for the large number of 'Nickels' (the dropping of propaganda leaflets) operations by Bomber Command in the early months of the war was that they gave crews valuable experience of long-distance flying and navigation over enemy territory.

With commendable foresight the Air Staff, fully supported by Ludlow-Hewitt, decided in January 1939 to allocate fifteen of Bomber Command's precious squadrons to undertake the necessary conversion and advanced training – a wise and judicious investment for the future; they became known as Group Pool Squadrons. On 5th September they were taken over by No 6 (Training) Group to form seven Group Pools. The intake was eleven pilots for each six week course, with heavy bomber pilots flying fifty-five hours including twenty-two at night. The idea was to convert individual aircrew members onto an operational bomber and then weld them together as a crew. Yet in the autumn of 1939 Air Vice-Marshal Arthur Harris, then AOC of No 5 Group, Bomber Command, considered that 'there is not an adequate organisation for training crews up to the standard or in the numbers required for a modern war'.

Fighter Command appeared to have far fewer operational training problems, although when its pilots gained their first experience of air combat against the *Luftwaffe* over France in May 1940 they found that the operational tactics practised at their two Group Pools were outdated and unsuited to modern air combat. Fighter pilots were compelled to learn new attack and defence procedures from trial and error and bitter experience. Few of the new pilots entering the squadrons had more than a dozen or so flying hours on Hurricanes, and no Spitfires became available for operational training until September 1940. On the other hand, their colleagues in Bomber Command were receiving their operational training in front-line bombers – Blenheims, Whitleys and, mostly, Wellingtons.

Despite the fact that the whole period of flying training had been shortened because of a desperate need for pilots and aircrews, the flow of trained personnel was still not sufficient to cope with the normal demands of the rapidly expanding Service, let alone to replace those lost during the first six months of 1940. This was far more pronounced in Fighter Command, which had lost many experienced pilots in the Battle of France during May. The biggest problem during the Battle of Britain was not the supply of replacement aircraft but rather that of trained pilots to fly them. A welcome and valuable addition to the RAF was the number of already qualified pilots from the Commonwealth and European countries. About 20% fought in the Battle of Britain and throughout the war almost 46% of all aircrews came from the Commonwealth and Europe, making the wartime RAF a truly cosmopolitan Service.

In an attempt to keep pace with the ever increasing training requirements, in late 1939 discussions took place with the Dominion governments to establish a scheme whereby flying training could be undertaken in their own countries. The agreement was signed in December, and in May 1940 the Empire (later British Commonwealth) Air Training Scheme (EATS) commenced, which has been described as 'one of the most brilliant pieces of imaginative organisation ever conceived'. Certainly it proved a saviour for Training Command, as the severe winter of 1939/40 had caused serious delays in all forms of flying training. The vagaries of the British weather greatly impinged on flying and operational training throughout the war.

The first EATS school opened at Belvedere near Salisbury in Southern Rhodesia on 24th May 1940, followed shortly by flying training schools being transferred to Canada; throughout the war more airmen received their flying tuition in Canada than in any other Commonwealth country. It was not quite the novel expedient it at first appeared, because even in the First World War pilots had been trained in flying schools in Canada and during the interwar years No 4 SFTS was based at Abu Sueir in Egypt, where it had been found that the better weather conditions and clearer skies enabled the courses to be completed on time. A wide variety of flying training schools were later established in Canada, Australia, New Zealand, South Africa and India, and by the end of 1942 there were over one hundred and twenty providing initial to advanced flying tuition, as well as specialised instruction for other aircrew categories. Flying training was also conducted at six American private flying schools under contract to the United States Army Air Force, known as the Arnold Scheme after General H. H. 'Hap' Arnold of the USAAF; ultimately fourteen thousand RAF airmen received much of their flying training in the United States. The EATS proved to be a great boon for Flying Training Command. Over one hundred and sixty-eight thousand pilots and other aircrew categories passed through the scheme, almost 50% of them pilots. The pilots would then return to the United Kingdom to undertake refresher and acclimatisation courses at (P) Advanced Training Units; there were similar courses for observers.

Senior commanders of Bomber Command expressed a growing concern about the standard of crews passing out from the Group Pool Squadrons; it was decided that operational training for pilots and aircrews would be placed on a more formal, efficient and hopefully more effective basis. On 8th April 1940 the existing Group Pools were reorganised into OTUs; the first eleven bomber OTUs were placed under the control of No 6 (Training) Group. By January 1941 there were nineteen OTUs in operation within the three operational commands. It had been recognised that whatever the drawbacks of this system, these units seemed to be the most effective means of producing highly trained pilots and crews for operational squadrons. Each command was responsible for the standard of operational training its airmen received. Over the next few years the number of OTUs would increase markedly.

Training Command, as such, was officially disbanded in May 1940 and was replaced by two separate commands – Flying Training and Technical Training. Air Marshal Sir Arthur Longmore, who had been in charge of Training Command since July 1939, moved to Egypt as Commander of the RAF Middle East. He was replaced by Air Marshal L. A. Pattison, who controlled six Groups – Nos 21, 23, 25, 50, 51 and 54. Each was specialised in character and responsible for a particular aspect of flying training: for instance, No 21 was solely engaged in the training of pilots and No 25 in armament and gunnery training. There were now over eighty FTSs and in excess of three thousand aircraft engaged in flying and operational training, ranging from Tiger Moths right up to Wellingtons; it was said that no fewer than sixty-five types of aircraft were engaged in training. Most of them (other than those in OTUs) bore yellow colourings on the underside of their wings and fuselage. This colour was universally used as the International Flag Code for Quarantine – in other words, a warning to other aircrews to give these training aircraft a wide berth.

During 1941/2 the three operational commands grew with remarkable pace, resulting in the seemingly insatiable demand for pilots and aircrew, not only to man the new squadrons but also to replace aircrew killed or missing in action as well as those airmen fortunate to have completed their operational tours. Despite enemy night activity over training airfields and adverse flying weather, Flying Training Command still managed to produce over seventeen thousand aircrew of all categories. Bomber Command, in particular, experienced heavy losses during these years and their nineteen OTUs were finding it difficult to produce enough trained crews. The command's training situation was eased somewhat when it was decreed in March 1942 that heavy bomber crews would only include one pilot rather than two and a new aircrew designation of navigator was introduced; previously the second pilot had been responsible for navigation.

The seventeen OTUs in Bomber Command were based mainly at airfields in those counties that might loosely be defined as 'middle' England. The introduction of four-engined bombers – Stirlings, Halifaxes and Lancasters – had resulted in another stage in the operational training programme – Heavy Conversion Flights (later Units). As more Lancasters entered the Service, an additional twelve or so flying hours had to be completed by crews at a Lancaster Finishing School. Therefore it was not surprising that Air Chief Marshal Sir Arthur Harris later maintained that 'the education of a bomber crew was the most expensive in the world; it cost some £10,000 for each man, enough to send ten men to Oxford or Cambridge for three years'.

Since 1942 the responsibility for flying training had resided with Air Marshal Sir Philip Babington, and at the end of 1943 – the wartime peak for flying training – almost twenty-four thousand pilots and aircrew of all categories had qualified. The manpower and resources devoted to flying/operational training were immense. There were over one hundred and fifty flying schools in the United Kingdom besides another one hundred and eighty in Commonwealth countries. In Bomber Command alone twenty-three OTUs and ten HCUs operated in three Groups – Nos 91 to 93. Furthermore, over one third of its

The highly prized and coveted RAF Wings.

operational aircraft were engaged in training and 55% of its annual flying hours were devoted to the training of crews.

In addition to all these training schools and operational and conversion units, there were myriad other specialised schools and units along with flying training courses – Central Navigation, Air Armament, Beam Approach Flights, Pathfinder Flights, Glider Pilots, Flying Instructors, Air Gunners, Observers, Fighter Leaders, Ground Support, Torpedo Training, *et al*. Furthermore, the majority of aircrew personnel on completion of their operational tours became involved in some form of training instruction either at these specialised schools or more often at the operational and conversion level.

By January 1945 Flying Training Command had grown to seven Groups with another seven devoted to training of some description in the four operational Commands. The Service's commitment to flying and operational training during the war was a massive undertaking conducted on a grand scale. Without doubt it produced the most highly trained pilots and aircrew of the Second World War. There were no fewer than 193,000 serving aircrew of all categories at the end of the war, and it should be remembered that all of the RAF aircrew personnel were volunteers. At no period of the war did the Service have to resort to conscription for flying duties; in fact there were far more volunteers than were required. Many Warwickshire airfields made essential contributions to this remarkable and impressive flying and operational training enterprise, which certainly deserves far more acclamation and praise than it has subsequently received.

Airfields

The term *airfield* was of very recent coinage, at least in the context of this account. The earliest airfields were simply known as 'landing grounds' and were little more than large, open and level spaces with few natural or man-made encumbrances, some perhaps supplied with a couple of 'sheds' for the storage of the fragile flying machines. This name was perpetuated during the Second World War with a variety of 'Satellite ... Relief ... Advanced ... Emergency Landing Grounds'. It was Claude Grahame-White who really introduced the name *aerodrome* into common parlance with the establishment of London Aerodrome at Hendon in March 1911. The name was taken from the Greek word *dromos* and can be literally translated as an 'aerial racecourse'.

From the earliest days of flying, *field* was used in the United States of America to describe an aircraft landing ground, and it was thus that *airfield* came into common usage in Britain, mainly to describe a military aerodrome. However, I think that *aerodrome* has a more romantic resonance, redolent of the 'golden days of flying', and it is gratifying to know that some seventy years later the old name has been preserved in the number of aerodromes dotted about the country.

At the outbreak of the Second World War there were two hundred and twenty aerodromes in the United Kingdom, of which one hundred and sixteen were military. At the end of 1942 it was judged that seven hundred and forty airfields would ultimately be required for the RAF and the USAAF; this estimation proved to be over generous because in 1945 there were over six hundred airfields occupying some 360,000 acres in all. Nevertheless, to build over four hundred airfields in just a few years was a truly remarkable achievement, brought about by an airfield construction programme that was carried out on a massive and monumental scale, probably the largest and most ambitious building project ever completed. It is not really surprising that Great Britain was likened to a 'massive and unsinkable aircraft carrier anchored off the coast of Europe'!

Each wartime airfield cost in the region of £1 million, although if they were provided with tarmac instead of concrete runways, there was a saving of perhaps £200,000. In five years over £600 million (equating to perhaps £15/16 billion in today's values) was expended on the construction of new airfields and improvements to existing ones. Some of the statistics in this immense programme almost beggar belief – 160

Work on concrete runways. (John Laing plc)

million square yards of concrete were laid down, over 60,000 men (a third of the total manpower of the building industry) were involved in their construction besides another 70,000 providing the myriad of support services required. Ernest Bevin, Minister of Labour and National Service, had the overall responsibility of directing the country's building labour for this airfield programme. Despite opposition from Winston Churchill, he delayed the conscription of building workers as well as postponing urgent repair work on bomb-damaged houses until the peak of airfield construction had passed. 1942 was the height of airfield construction, when one hundred and twenty were completed, equating to one new airfield opening on average every three days.

With the proposed expansion of the RAF from 1934, the Air Ministry established the Aerodromes Board in May of that year; it was given the task of selecting suitable aerodrome sites for the burgeoning Service. The Board was headed by two retired RAF officers and because the potential enemy had been identified as Germany, the eastern counties were scoured for potential sites for operational squadrons. The Board reported directly to the Air Ministry's Works Directorate General, which was responsible for the maintenance, repair and construction of RAF aerodromes. The Directorate was familiarly known as 'Works and Bricks' and perhaps more unkindly as 'Wonders and Blunders'.

In pre-war years the Board had the relative luxury of being more selective in their choice of sites. The main criteria were relatively flat and well-drained land, preferably clear from natural and man-made obstructions, and free from the incidence of hill fog; for this reason five to six hundred feet above sea level was taken as the maximum altitude. The sites were invariably chosen well away from large areas of population for safety reasons, and the board also tended to work to a constraint of five to six miles between aerodromes.

Most of these 'Expansion' aerodromes, as they became known, took about four years to complete from the initial legal negotiations to obtain the land to the arrival of the first airmen. This prolonged and lengthy procedure appeared to be inordinately leisurely compared with the building of wartime airfields, when twelve months or less was the normal time scale. However, the Board had to operate under an antiquated legal procedure to obtain the land – the Defence Act of 1842 – and the new aerodromes were built to rigorous and exacting engineering and construction standards; after all, they were intended to be permanent, and many of these splendid airfields have survived to this day.

They were specially designed to blend into the local landscape as far as was possible. All the buildings were of brick and tile construction, the roadways, normally arranged to a set pattern, were laid in tarmacadam or concrete, and trees were planted to soften the aspect. Great care had been taken to make all of the buildings aesthetically pleasing: imposing and well-proportioned structures on neo-Georgian lines with impressive fronts and high-porched entrances. This was due to the main architect, Sir Edward Lutyens, who had been commissioned by the directorate to impose his distinctive style and design on many pre-war RAF aerodromes. It could be said that by producing such elegant, commodious and comfortable buildings, the Air Ministry had achieved a splendid 'corporate image' for the junior Service; they were famously described as 'a cross between an elegant country club and large hotel'.

After the trauma of the Munich crisis of 1938 there was a strong urgency imposed on the Aerodromes Board to seek out likely sites for new airfields to house the proposed new squadrons. Therefore it could ill-afford to be as selective as hitherto and was constrained to compromise on airfield locations, with the result that many fell far short of the existing pre-war criteria. By 1940 the Board had located some 4,000 possible sites, although for a variety of reasons only about 10% were ultimately developed into airfields. Of course the Air Ministry had already requisitioned the existing civil and private aerodromes, but many were considered unsuitable for military use or further development.

The Aerodromes Board initiated their formidable task by a laborious scrutiny of one inch Ordnance Survey maps, followed by an aerial assessment of the locality before a careful and accurate survey was made on foot, field by field, which included a detailed investigation into the nature of the sub-soil. At this time the majority of RAF aerodromes had only grass runways; so the quality of drainage was an important factor. Once a location was deemed to be suitable, the Air Ministry's Lands Branch entered the arena and commenced the legal requisition of the necessary land (on average about 600 acres). The regulations under the Emergency Powers (Defence) Act of 1939 virtually ensured almost instant acquisition by the Air Ministry, and, although there was an appeals procedure, precious few appeals were upheld. Usually the most vehement opposition came from the War Agricultural Committee, who were perhaps under greater pressure to ensure that all available agricultural land was under cultivation. Many large private estates, which had hitherto being considered sacrosanct, found that the families' objections carried little weight in such extenuating circumstances, although there was, I believe, a plan to build a mile-long taxi runway from Baginton to Stoneleigh that was abandoned after considerable pressure from influential local residents. To my knowledge Copston Magna, a couple of miles east of Bramcote, was the only proposed and approved site (for a medium bomber station) in the county that was not further developed.

Once the proposed site had been requisitioned and its status agreed, the Directorate General of Works took over. It was responsible for the allocation of building contracts to one of the large civil engineering companies – such household names as Wimpey, McAlpine, Taylor Woodrow, French, Costain and John Laing – or maybe to smaller local building contractors. John Laing & Son Ltd of Mill Hill in north-west London seemed to be the most active company in Warwickshire. It had gained the contract to construct Bramcote followed by Gaydon, Honiley, Long Marston and Wellesbourne Mountford.

The intense urgency created by the demands of war compelled the Directorate to look for far speedier and more economic methods of construction. It produced hundreds of standard working drawings for airfield layouts, essential services, runways, hard-standings, buildings, bomb stores, pillboxes, etc. As a result the majority of wartime airfields were built to a fairly uniform pattern and standard, with perhaps

Some of the heavy equipment used in the construction of airfields. (John Laing plc)

minor alterations and adjustments because of local conditions and topographical features.

The earliest indications to the local communities that the peace of their rural life would be shattered in the short term was the invasion of coaches and buses carrying the hordes of building workers as they moved into a tented camp alongside the site. They would be followed by the whole paraphernalia of their trade – massive earth-moving equipment, heavy tractors and lorries, cement mixers, portable cranes etc. Soon roads in the vicinity were either closed or clogged with traffic and some remained closed for the rest of the war. For months on end the whole area resembled a battlefield: land was flattened, trees and hedges uprooted, ditches and hollows filled in, trenches dug for the vital services, and seemingly in no time at all the site and surrounding area either became a sea of mud or disappeared under thick clouds of choking dust depending on the season of the year. Such was the urgency that the construction work continued day and night with little let-up in the disturbance, and many local inhabitants who lived through the ordeal would later recall it as their worst experience of the war. These wartime airfields left a lasting and indelible mark on the local landscape: the sheer bulk of the large hangars, the high and gaunt water towers, the myriad buildings and huts and ultimately the constant presence of noisy low-flying aircraft day and night certainly ensured that the countryside would never be the same again, nor indeed would the peace and tranquillity of the 'leafy Warwickshire lanes'!

The first real construction work was the provision of a concrete perimeter road around the whole of the airfield site, normally fifty feet wide; it provided access to the aircraft dispersal points or hardstandings. Early in 1939 the Air Ministry had decreed that all aircraft should be dispersed around the airfield perimeter as a precaution against aerial attack. The hard-standings were of two types – 'frying pan' or 'loops'; the latter became standard on bomber airfields and OTUs. The next stage was the laying of the runways, mostly in concrete, but some were finished in graded tarmacadam. It is interesting to note that virtually all pre-war aerodromes were grassed. However, in 1937 with the advent of heavier aircraft, the Air Ministry was forced to consider 'hard' runways. Hitherto their main objections had been on the question of cost, but it was also thought that they would be difficult to camouflage and that they did not possess the 'natural braking powers of grass'. In December 1937 a Whitley was used for taxiing trials at the grass airfield at Odiham; at 22,000 pounds laden weight it was the heaviest aircraft in service and for the trials its weight was increased to 40,000 pounds. Another trial was undertaken at Stradishall in March 1938 and the Air Ministry concluded that 'properly prepared grass surfaces were quite satisfactory up to 40,000 pounds'. But in May 1939 a number of fighter airfields were provided with hard runways and it was decided that all future bomber airfields should be constructed with hard runways.

According to local folklore, the bomb debris from Coventry and Birmingham was used as hardcore for the concrete runways laid down at some of the county's wartime airfields, as was the procedure with several wartime airfields built around London. The prescribed lengths of the three runways changed during 1940/1 and ultimately a standard specification was introduced, which became known as a Class A standard bomber station. The main runway measured two thousand yards (maximum) by fifty yards wide, with two secondary runways each not more than fourteen hundred yards long. They were placed as near as 60° to each other as possible and were invariably laid down in the shape of a letter 'A'. This wartime concrete, which was initially 6 inches in depth and later increased to 8 inches, appears to have survived the rigours of time in spite of the pace at which it was laid, often in unfavourable weather conditions. Several strips of runways, perimeter roads and hard-standings can still be discovered along the

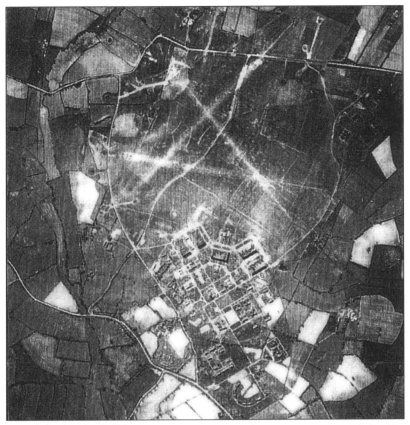

Bramcote airfield in 1944; the three runways in the shape of a letter 'A'. (RAF Museum)

edges of fields, and in many instances this surviving concrete is the site's sole link to its wartime past. The tarmac runways were laid on a subgrade mixture of tar, stone and bricks, with a top layer of graded tar to a thickness of $2\frac{1}{2}$ inches, and a coat of asphalt for waterproofing.

Most Warwickshire airfields were provided with either concrete or tarmac runways, although there was one notable exception – Bramcote. In its early days it had three steel matting runways and the airfield was too advanced in its construction when the Air Ministry made its decision on hard runways. These Sommerfeld metal track runways were constructed of 13 gauge 3 inch mesh wire netting secured by metal pickets and strengthened with flat steel bars. Originating from the First World War, it had been developed by an Austrian engineer, Kurt Sommerfeld. The track was cheap, easy and quick to lay, and provided a reasonably secure and dry landing surface, especially during the winter months. It was used to good effect on fighter airfields and in North Africa, where it gained its nickname 'tin lino'! Relief and Satellite Landing Grounds were not accorded the luxury of hard runways: they were merely grassed landing areas.

The most distinctive and prominent landmarks on any airfield were the large hangars, although on the majority of the Air Ministry's detailed airfield plans, they are listed as 'Aircraft Sheds'. All six of the most prevalent types of wartime hangars could be seen at the county's airfields – T2, Bellman, B1, J, C and Blister. Up until mid-1942 the hangars were all painted in camouflage colours but from then onwards they were finished in black bitumen.

It was the 'T' type hangars that were usually provided for wartime airfields. 'T' stood for transportable and they had been developed and

A 'J' type 'Gaydon' hangar still in use at Gaydon. (British Motor Industry Heritage Trust)

built by Tees-Side Bridge & Engineering Works. They were of galvanised corrugated iron construction and were specially designed to be simple and quick to erect. They came in various sizes but the T2s were the most usual and were two hundred and forty feet long and about half as wide, with a door clearance of twenty-nine feet. Another popular hangar was the type B1, also constructed of steel, but it was even larger, with a high gabled end, and they were used mainly for the major servicing of aircraft. Some airfields were also provided with a single J type hangar, which was produced by William Arrol & Co. Ltd and constructed mainly of metal, with curved roofs of steel plates.

Until the appearance of the T types, the most common hangar was the Bellman. It dated from 1937 and was named after its designer, N. S. Bellman, an Air Ministry engineer. Built of steel, it was developed by Head & Wrightson Co. Ltd; it became the RAF's first really transportable hangar and was simple to erect. The hangar was one hundred and seventy-five feet long with a span of almost eighty-eight feet and a maximum clearance of twenty-six feet. By 1940 over four hundred had been produced but they were then somewhat outmoded with the introduction of larger operational aircraft and were largely superseded by the T1 and T2s. The smaller Blister hangars first appeared in late 1939 and perhaps were more common at fighter and flying training airfields. They were of a far simpler construction and comprised arched wooden or welded steel ribs covered by curved corrugated iron sheets, and were normally forty-five feet long. Produced by C. Miskens & Sons Ltd, they were economical, simple and quick to erect and because they did not require either foundations or flooring, they could be erected on uneven land. Over three thousand were built in several different designs – Double, Over and Extra Over.

Prior to 1939, air traffic control in the RAF was fairly basic and minimal; each pilot was required to log his flight with the duty control officer. But with the advent of the war and the vast increase of air traffic this all changed and one of the most vital buildings on every airfield was the watch office, or control tower, as it became more familiarly known – yet another aviation term originating in the United States. This building housed the air traffic control personnel and meteorological office. It was the nerve centre of the airfield during operational and training flying. By late 1941 the building had become fairly standardised and constructed to an accepted pattern – Type 12779/41, a functional and rather basic two-storied brick building rendered with concrete, with six windows on its front elevation. The building was

Wartime control towers were built to a standard design.

provided with a railed balcony as well as railings along its flat roof and it was from here that the number of the runway in current use was displayed. Some control towers were also provided with an exterior iron stairway and several had crew and operations rooms added later.

Such was their importance that the impressive RAF memorial at Runnymede is dominated by a symbolic control tower. One airwoman who spent many long hours in control towers remembered them as 'built like a functional Puritan square, jutting up blindly, covered with brown and green undulations of camouflage, impotent against its unnatural shape'. Many have survived throughout the country and they appear rather gaunt and forlorn buildings beset by the ravages of time. Some have been preserved and now house either aviation museums or commercial offices, and several have been converted into private houses.

The airfield's unique identification code was displayed on the ground close to the control tower; this comprised two large white letters about ten feet wide. These letters dated back to pre-war days, when it was the accepted practice to display the aerodrome's name in large white letters as an aid to navigation. The letters were required to be large enough to be read from an altitude of two thousand feet. For security reasons these names were removed at the outbreak of war and a two letter code was introduced. For example, Church Lawford was represented by CL and Gaydon by GD, but Baginton was allocated NG, Long Marston JS, and Stratford-upon-Avon NF. The reason for these less recognisable codes was the multiplicity of existing airfields starting with B, L or S. At night a mobile beacon unit, known as a 'pundit', was sited some distance from the airfield and was moved regularly. The beacon flashed the airfield's code in a red Morse signal, hence the identification code was more normally known as the Pundit Code.

In marked contrast to the permanent stations, life on these wartime airfields could be quite spartan and less than congenial. Most of the buildings and huts were of prefabricated construction, some of timber and plasterboard and others of precast concrete slabs. John Laing's had a factory at Elstree, Hertfordshire producing their 'Laing huts', many of which adorned Warwickshire airfields. They were fashioned out of timber and plasterboard with felt sheeted pitched roofs. The lasting image of these wartime airfields was the omnipresent Nissen huts. They were invariably used on the accommodation sites for the living, messing and sleeping quarters for both airmen and airwomen, as well as on the airfield for a variety of technical purposes. These curved corrugated iron-sheeted huts in various spans of sixteen, eighteen and twenty-four feet had originated in the First World War, when Colonel Peter Nissen, a Canadian by birth, had set up a factory in this country to manufacture them. They were bitterly cold in the winter with ill-fitting draughty windows and a solitary coke stove for heating and then in the summer they were unbearably hot. Nevertheless they are still fondly remembered by many wartime airmen. Perhaps the long passage of time has somewhat clouded their memories? However, many wartime airmen have recalled that despite being uncomfortable, they considered these huts as their homes, the place they yearned to return to safely whilst on their bombing operations.

The number of sites at wartime airfields varied but the main ones were the Administration/Operations block, Instructional and Technical site, communal site, sewage disposal farm, bomb stores, radio/transmission site and a number of separate living and messing quarters for officers, airmen and airwomen, usually well away from the airfield proper. There was a multiplicity of buildings – administration blocks, technical workshops, photographic sections, motor vehicle repair huts, equipment and parachute stores, squadron and flight offices, briefing and crews' rooms, fire and rescue rooms, armoury, guard room,

The ruined remains of the odd hut still stand amongst the ploughed fields.

mortuary, and so forth. Also it should be noted that other buildings were added during the progress of the war as and when needed. Although over a half a century has passed since these buildings were crowded with airmen and airwomen, the ruined remains of the odd hut still stand amongst the ploughed fields but now they have become well camouflaged by nature. Flying training airfields, especially those devoted to operational training, required various types of specialised instructional buildings, which will be described in greater detail later.

These wartime airfields became virtually closed communities, self-sufficient and catering for the needs of maybe two and a half thousand personnel. They were provided with an intricate system of radio, telephone and teleprinter services. For the welfare of the regular staff and the large multitude of training airmen there was normally a dental surgery, sick quarters, hairdresser, grocery store, NAAFI or YMCA, gymnasium/concert hall, and church and/or chapel, besides a variety of air raid shelters. Sporting facilities were also provided with a football field for the airmen, and the officers' site normally housed a squash court (always *de rigueur* at pre-war stations!) along with at least one tennis court. Although most of these airfields were constructed to a similar design, each airfield seemed to acquire its own separate and

A pillbox that has survived on the site of Stratford-upon-Avon airfield.

unique identity. As Richard Hough, an RAF fighter pilot and later famous author, recalled, 'I know of nothing more distinctive and memorable than a wartime airfield. To the outside world they may have looked the same. To anyone who was going to live there for a while – and maybe die there – each stamped its nature indelibly on your mind'.

As the construction of the wartime airfield neared completion, the question of a system of defence was determined; the contractor liaised with the local military commander as to the siting of pillboxes and other defences. By the summer of 1941, after the immediate threat of invasion had disappeared, a scale of airfield defence had been agreed depending on its strategic importance and its distance from the coast. In the case of Warwickshire airfields they were considered Class Three, which meant a single ring of pillboxes providing all-round fire protection, but of course there was an abundance of barbed wire and piquet posts. In the autumn of 1940 a new RAF trade of 'ground gunner' had been formed and by the end of the year almost forty thousand were engaged on airfield defence. The RAF Regiment was formed on 1st February 1942, which largely took over the defence of airfields from Army personnel. This, of course, necessitated the building of extra living and messing accommodation, usually on a separate site, and kennels for the guard dogs.

The airfield's defence was controlled and co-ordinated from the Battle Headquarters, a specially-built strongpoint, normally underground with thick reinforced concrete walls, and earth banks were added if it projected too far above the ground. It was dominated by a six foot square observation post about three feet above the ground with viewing slits affording all-round observation. A standard type evolved, known as 11008/41. Largely because of their stout construction and the fact that they were quite unobtrusive and sited well away from the main airfield site, several have survived, perhaps most notably at Wellesbourne Mountford, which now houses a wartime museum.

RAF airfields fell into certain categories. The main ones were considered parent stations, a self-accounting service station in any of the RAF Commands. The Station Commander was normally a Group Captain but at some smaller stations he could be a Wing Commander. The main station may or may not administer one or even two satellite airfields, a relief landing ground and/or an emergency landing ground. There was no set standard size of an RAF station. Many grew during the war as the operational and training demands increased.

All but three of the twelve major Warwickshire wartime airfields have survived the passage of time. Of course Elmdon quickly returned to civil aviation, as did Baginton, but somewhat later. Wellesbourne

An old battle headquarters building (Type 11008/41).

Mountford is still alive with private and club flying along with Long Marston, and Snitterfield is the home of a flourishing gliding club. Ansty, Gaydon, and Honiley are in the hands of various motoring companies, with Gaydon and Honiley being used for the trials and testing of motor vehicles. Bramcote is now an Army barracks. Castle Bromwich has long since disappeared for housing development; Stratford-upon-Avon has returned to agriculture; and Church Lawford is used for industrial purposes. It may be of interest to note that the Royal Air Force Museum at Hendon holds a comprehensive stock of airfield site plans (mostly relating to wartime airfields). These can either be examined at the museum or photocopies may be obtained by post for the requisite fee.

The following account of the various Warwickshire airfields is essentially related to their activities during the Second World War, as the title of the book confirms. But I am aware that several of these airfields had a longer and perhaps more interesting existence in the post-war years. Therefore I have *briefly* outlined their subsequent growth and development where I considered it relevant to bring the account up-to-date.

2
ANSTY

From midnight on 31st August 1939 all civil flying over eastern England, Scotland and other specific areas was banned under the Air Navigation (Restriction in Time of War) Order, and most of the one hundred and five civil and private aerodromes were virtually closed to flying. Any flight of whatever distance required a special permit. In due course these airfields, of whatever size, were requisitioned by the Air Ministry for military use and in this respect Ansty was no exception. The aerodrome, owned and operated by Air Services Training Ltd, was situated almost 1½ miles south of Ansty village and had been operating for over 3½ years.

For some strange and unaccountable reason Ansty does not appear in several of the published works on Second World War airfields. It has

Ansty Airfield in 1936. (via B. Hardy)

either been conveniently forgotten or totally disregarded. Nevertheless this relatively small airfield operated as an RAF elementary flying training station from January 1940 until March 1944 as well as being used for the assembly, test flying and delivery of Airspeed Oxfords and de Havilland Mosquitos produced by Standard Motor Company. Also Armstrong Siddeley remained in residence, undertaking turbojet experimental and development work. In fact for most of the war Ansty was a hive of activity and industry, with flying training almost forced to take a back seat.

In 1936 the original aerodrome site covered about one hundred and forty acres but since then another fifty acres had been purchased and even by July 1940 Ansty was still less than two hundred acres in area, probably about a third of the size of an average wartime airfield. The maximum grassed landing and take-off run was no more than one thousand yards due north-south and was only really adequate for training aircraft. However, it was well appointed, with the provision of a large hangar, workshops, living quarters and a fine administration block.

From January 1936 No 9 E&RFTS had been training civilian and service airmen to a Licence 'A' standard. For this task the school had been supplied with a fairly rare training aircraft – the Avro A631 Cadet. This aircraft had first appeared in 1932 and was designed for the private and club market. It owed much of its design to yet another successful Avro training aircraft – the Tutor. An improved version Avro 643 Cadet II appeared two years later, which was powered by an Armstrong Siddeley 150hp Genet Major IA engine giving the Cadet II a cruising speed of 100mph. Thirty-four were ordered by the Royal Australian Air Force but Air Service Training Ltd was the largest civilian user of Cadets at its school at Hamble, which was why Cadets equipped the new flying school at Ansty. Although never as commercially successful as the Tutor, the Cadet proved to be an excellent aircraft for basic flying instruction, blind flying and aerobatics.

No 4 Civil Air Navigation School had formed at Ansty in September 1938 to provide a high standard of navigational training for both civil and service airmen. It would be fair to say that at this time air navigation was rather a neglected science. In fact considering the poor standard of RAF navigation generally, Air Chief Marshal Sir Edgar Ludlow-Hewitt, the AOC-in-C of Bomber Command deliberated for a considerable time before sending selected airmen on one of these

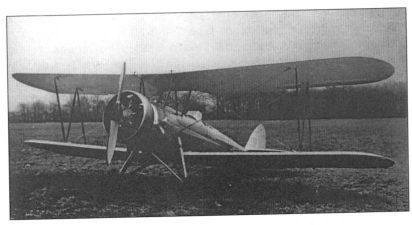

Avro A631 Cadet. (RAF Museum)

courses. The school used Avro Anson 1s, along with Blackburn Bothas and a few Saro Clouds. As will be noted later, the Anson, despite its original purpose to operate as a reconnaissance bomber with Coastal Command, became the standard RAF aircraft for basic navigational training. Not so the A.29 Cloud, which was a rather clumsy twin-engined amphibian and not really suitable for training purposes. It had been produced by Supermarine back in 1932 and its Siddeley Serval engines were rather less than reliable. The few surviving Clouds were sent to Air Service's other Navigation School – No 11 – at Hamble. The Botha had originally been designed as a torpedo bomber and first appeared in December 1938. However, it proved to be woefully underpowered, unsuitable for operational duties and quickly relegated to training units.

It was not until 1st January 1940 that Ansty was *formally* taken over by the RAF and was placed under the control of Flying Training Command. No 9 School dropped 'Reserve' from its title and, as No 9 EFTS, it became a full service flying training school under Flight Lieutenant (later Wing Commander) R. P. P. Pope, DFC, AFC. On 25th June five bombs fell on and near the airfield and it was thought they had been jettisoned by an enemy bomber unable to find its designated target. Certainly on this day there were several recorded instances of small numbers of enemy bombers – three or four in number – making what were officially described as 'reconnaissance raids' over a wide area. Whatever the reason for the bombing, it was the first occasion that any bombs had fallen in the county. In the following month the Navigation School, now known as No 4 Air Observers Navigation School, moved to a new airfield at Watchfield, Oxfordshire, where it would be joined by No 11 School from Hamble. Thus for the immediate future, at least, Ansty was solely devoted to elementary or ab initio flying training.

Like virtually all the other EFTSs Ansty became the home of scores upon scores of Tiger Moths, which along with Tutors, were then the standard elementary flying trainers used by the RAF. The de Havilland D.H.82 Tiger Moth was a modified version of its successful Gipsy Moth and became the most famous and successful training aircraft of all time. The majority of pilots who served in the Second World War experienced their first taste of flying and received their initial flying instruction in this excellent little aircraft; universally admired for their easy handling and forgiving traits they were familiarly known as 'Tiggies'. The aircraft had first flown on October 1931 and in February 1932 a number of Tiger Moths were delivered to No 3 Flying Training School at Grantham and the Central Flying School; its long and legendary service life had begun.

The company developed an improved version – D.H.82A – with a 130hp Gipsy Major engine and a plywood rear fuselage in place of the original fabric-coated one; it was also fitted with a hood for instrument flying instruction. The engine had been inverted to provide an improved forward view and the wings swept back to allow easier exit from the front instructor's cockpit when wearing a parachute. The Moth II had a maximum speed of 109mph at 1,000 feet but it more normally cruised at about 93mph. Despite its rather fragile appearance, it nevertheless was a very sturdy and reliable aircraft well able to survive the rough treatment it received at the hands of raw and inexperienced student pilots. However, Moths did demand a high standard of precise control on the part of the pupil pilot. Over 4,660 were produced for the RAF, the majority by Morris Motors at Cowley and they equipped no fewer than eighty-three flying schools in the United Kingdom and abroad under the Empire Air Training Scheme. With the threat of enemy invasion during the summer of 1940, bomb racks able to carry eight 20 pound bombs were fitted to training Tiger Moths, although none was ever used operationally. They were, however, frequently used for communications flights. They were such a delight to fly and with their open cockpits they brought back the days of 'real flying with the wind on one's face ...' that many Station

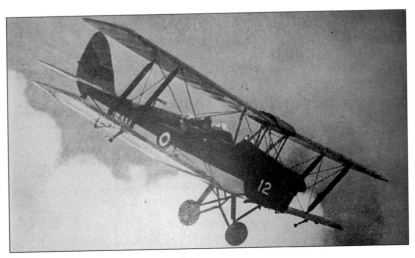

A de Havilland D.H.82A Tiger Moth.

Commanders at operational stations tried to obtain at least one Tiger Moth as their own personal aircraft. Tiger Moths survived as elementary flying trainers well into the post-war years, remaining in service with Reserve Flying Schools and University Air squadrons until February 1955.

Initially the elementary flying course lasted about three months and was planned to give the student pilots maybe sixty flying hours of dual and solo flying. But in the summer of 1940, largely due to pilot losses in France and in the Battle of Britain, along with the formation of new bomber and fighter squadrons, the duration of the course was shortened in an attempt to increase the number of pilots passing through to the advanced stage of flying instruction. This imposed considerable pressure on the flying instructors, the ground crews tasked with the maintenance of the Tiger Moths and also the sheer availability of flying time at the airfield. By mid-1941 the length of the course had settled down to about ten weeks and was planned to provide at least fifty flying hours, that is, depending on the weather, which was always a major factor in the maintenance of tight flying schedules in all types of flying training.

Before the trainee pilots arrived at the EFTSs they had already passed through a fairly lengthy and rigorous selection process – the initial Aircrew Selection board followed by a searching Medical Board – to ensure that they were both mentally suitable and medically fit for flying duties. Many wartime (and peacetime) pilots reckoned that it was quite an achievement to get this far. The trainees were then sent for an eight week course at one of the Initial Training Wings, where they were taught to march, salute and conduct themselves in 'an airmanlike manner'; an introduction into the rigours and disciplines of service life. They were now Leading Aircraftsmen (LACs) and known officially as 'pilots under training' or 'UT' for short, which was marked with a modest pay rise. Shortly after arrival at the EFTS, they were divided into two sections; one section received flying instruction in the morning and attended lectures in the afternoon and vice-versa.

Each student pilot was issued with a Sidcot coat (a one-piece flying suit), a pair of overalls, a flying helmet and a pair of goggles – at least now they looked like pilots but as yet they were far from the finished article. Their next indoctrination was into the intricacies of the parachute harness, which was adjusted to fit each individual. They were given instruction on how to pack and use the parachute, as well as being constantly reminded that the 'chute' was their precious lifeline; it was further emphasised that parachutes were very expensive items of equipment (about £70) and should be treated with the utmost care.

Perhaps the proudest and most memorable moment of the course came when the Chief Flying Instructor, after a successful dual landing, told the student pilot 'Off you go, one circuit and a landing' – the student's first solo flight. If this was accomplished to the satisfaction of the instructor, it was now a matter of improving and refining his newly acquired flying skills both by day and night until he was adjudged sufficiently competent to proceed to the more exacting regime of flying at an Advanced Flying School and hopefully finally qualify for his wings.

Besides receiving flying instruction up to a good solo standard, the students were given a thorough grounding in the theories of flight, navigation, armaments, radio communications, airframe and engine construction, along with photography. Their copy of the RAF *Flying Training Manual* was to prove their constant reference book. They also attended lectures on service organisation and law as well as more general subjects such as mathematics. Throughout the course there were written examinations and their progress, both in the air and on the ground, was closely monitored by their instructors. Their aptitude and temperament for either single-engined or multi-engined aircraft

The student pilot climbs into the rear cockpit of a Tiger Moth – the great moment has arrived.

was carefully assessed and this evaluation would ultimately determine the Service Flying Training School they would proceed to and the advanced training aircraft they would encounter there, providing, of course, that they had successfully completed the course. Since the Battle of Britain and all the attendant official propaganda surrounding 'The Few' most trainees had a burning ambition to be fighter pilots but the plain fact of the matter was that there was a far greater demand for multi-engined pilots for Bomber and Coastal Commands, which since 1938 required two pilots for each aircraft.

Soon the student pilots and their Tiger Moths would have to share the airfield with aircraft that had been built by Standard Motor Company at Canley and Fletchamstead. In December 1939 the Ministry of Aircraft Production had invited Standard Motor to build aircraft along with the company's pre-war commitment for the production of Mercury and Pegasus aero-engines. It was planned that the sub-assemblies would be built at the various factories and transported to Ansty by road, where they would be assembled and test flown before being delivered to the RAF by pilots of the Air Transport Auxiliary (many of them young women pilots). For this purpose assembly and flight test facilities were erected at Ansty along with a concrete runway and a perimeter track.

Standard Motor's first aircraft contract was for the production of three hundred Airspeed AS.10 Oxfords, familiarly known as the 'Oxbox' to RAF airmen. The aircraft was the result of an Air Ministry specification, T23/36, for a twin-engined trainer. Airspeed (1934) Ltd of Portsmouth specially developed the Oxford from its moderately successful small passenger airliner, the Envoy, which had first flown in April 1934. The Envoy had gained a high reputation for its reliability, and perhaps this was an aspect that influenced the Air Ministry to order one hundred and thirty-six 'direct from the drawing board' (a rare occurrence) before the Oxford's maiden flight on 19th June 1937. The Oxford was of wooden construction with stressed-skin wings and tailplanes, which not only facilitated the production of sub-assemblies but was less expensive to build. The aircraft made its public debut at the end of June 1937 at the RAF annual display at Hendon, and Oxfords entered the Service five months later, with six being delivered to the Central Flying School. The Oxford was well advanced for its time with a retractable undercarriage and a well-equipped cockpit to give the trainee pilots a sound introduction to the multiplicity of instruments they would encounter on larger twin- and four-engined operational aircraft; it was the RAF's first twin-engined monoplane for advanced flying training.

At the outbreak of the war the RAF had three hundred and sixty

The last of 750 Airspeed Oxfords was delivered from Ansty in July 1943.

Oxfords in service but the outstanding success of the aircraft brought about more orders than Airspeed's two factories in Portsmouth and Christchurch could cope with; thus Oxford production was sub-contracted to de Havilland's at Hatfield, Percival at Luton and Standard Motor. At the end of the war the number of Oxfords in service had grown to over four thousand one hundred, the second most numerous RAF aircraft after Spitfires. When production of Oxfords finally ceased in July 1945 over eight thousand five hundred had been produced, and of these the seven hundred and fifty built by Standard Motor can be identified by the V, DF, LB and MP range of serial numbers. The last Oxford was delivered from Ansty in July 1943.

One of the perennial problems faced by all flying training schools was to cram as many flying hours into the day as was humanly possible. The innumerable and seemingly endless round of practice take-offs, landings and airfield circuits required to be completed by the trainee pilots, both with their instructors and later solo, placed a considerable strain on the available facilities at the parent airfield. Therefore the Schools were always seeking alternative landing grounds to ease this burden. The small grassed airfield that No 9 EFTS used from mid-1940 was at Southam Fields to the east of the village along the A425 road. Southam had been laid out with two landing runs of 800 and 600 yards and was later provided with a number of Laing prefabricated buildings as well as some Nissen and wooden huts for the use of about seventy or so personnel who manned the Relief Landing Ground. There were also some maintenance facilities, with the erection of four standard Blister hangars. Southam closed for flying in 1944.

It was in July 1943 that the first Mosquito was completed at Ansty by Standard Motor. Without doubt the de Havilland D.H.98 Mosquito was the most remarkable, versatile and successful aircraft of the Second World War. It had started life in October 1938 as a private venture for a high-speed unarmed wooden bomber. At that time the Air Ministry was engaged in developing a medium and heavy all-metal bomber force and were more than a little sceptical about a wooden unarmed bomber however fast it might be. Nevertheless quite undaunted de Havilland decided to continue with the project on their own. However, one member of the Air Council, Air Marshal Sir William R. Freeman, who was responsible for Development & Production, had faith in the project and after the first mock-up Mosquito had been produced, Freeman ordered fifty 'high-speed wooden reconnaissance bombers'

ɛr 1,000 Mosquito FBVIs were test flown and delivered from Ansty. This FBVI
₁ed with No 487 (RNZAF) squadron – February, 1944.

₁er Specification B1/40 dated 1st March. His decision to back the
squito so wholeheartedly, resulted in the aircraft becoming known
Service circles as 'Freeman's Folly' during its early stages of
₁ elopment.

he prototype 'Wooden Wonder' had first flown at Hatfield on
25th November 1940, and official trials began in February 1941. The
performance was so outstanding that thenceforth the Mosquito
never looked back. Out of the original fifty, ten were developed for
photographic reconnaissance, thirty as day and night fighters and ten
as bombers, and already a prototype training version had been
developed. The most prolific Mosquito Mark was the FBVI, which first
appeared with No 418 squadron in May 1943. In total 2,718 FBVIs were
built, 40% of them by Standard Motor from 1942, and ultimately they
equipped fifty-four RAF squadrons. The Mark had been developed
from the F.IIs, which had first flown on 15th May 1941, and was
powered by twin Merlin 21, 23 or 25 engines giving a maximum speed
of 378mph; its armament comprised four 20mm Hispano cannons in
the nose and four .303' Browning machine guns. The total bomb load
of the Series 2 was 2,000 lbs and the wings were fitted with points for
either bomb racks or long-range fuel tanks; from 1944 they were
adapted to carry eight rocket projectiles with 60 lb warheads. Up until
15th August 1945 (VJ Day) Standard Motor had produced nine
hundred and sixteen Mosquito FBVIs and ultimately a most creditable
total of one thousand and sixty-six passed through Ansty. Some of
these might have found their way to No 605 (County of Warwick)
squadron, which had been re-equipped with FBVIs in July 1943.
Mosquitos remained in production until November 1950, by which

time over seven thousand seven hundred and eighty had been built and, according to Sir Geoffrey de Havilland, in forty-three different versions.

Those last two years of war must have been exhilarating times at Ansty, to witness these splendid and exciting Mosquito FBVIs taking-off on their test flights, many in the hands of Squadron Leader P. V. Williams, who was Standard's Chief Test Pilot, and previously the Chief Flying Instructor for Air Service Training Ltd. Certainly they provided quite a dramatic change from the rather sedate Oxfords and the leisurely Tiger Moth biplanes. From March 1944 these Mosquitos had the airfield for their sole use as No 9 EFTS closed down owing to congestion at the airfield and also because the RAF had more than enough pilots coming through the EATS and other larger EFTSs in the United Kingdom. Therefore the control of Ansty passed from Flying Training Command to the Ministry of Aircraft Production.

It was another seven years (1951) before RAF trainee pilots returned again to Ansty when No 2 Basic Flying Training School, operated once again by Air Service Training Ltd, opened in the wake of the Korean War. The school was mainly intended to give flying instruction to National Service pilots. Tiger Moths had virtually disappeared from the regular RAF but they had been replaced by yet another training aircraft from the de Havilland stable – the Chipmunk – which along with Percival Prentices was now used for basic flying training. The school had a fairly brief existence: it closed in March 1953 along with all the other similar civilian-operated schools. The school's closure brought about the demise of flying at Ansty after some eighteen years as a flying training airfield.

Ansty had been considerably developed in the immediate post-war years. By early February 1950 the airfield site covered almost two hundred and eighty-five acres and was greatly involved in the development and testing of turboprop aero engines by Armstrong Siddeley Motors; the company's first jet engine, the ASX, had been built in 1942 and tested there. Armstrong Siddeley now trialled and tested such engines as the Python, Mamba, Double Mamba and Sapphire at Ansty. Like many other wartime airfields, Ansty was also used on occasions for motor-cycle racing; the runway and perimeter road made an excellent circuit track. But, because of the resumption of flying training in 1951, competition racing ceased unlike at other wartime airfields such as Silverstone, Snetterton Heath, and Boreham.

A large new Engineering and Development Centre was opened at

Ansty in 1957 and over the next decade it was the centre for the development of rail and marine diesels, industrial gas turbines, as well as rockets. In March 1966 Rolls-Royce merged with Bristol Siddeley Engines Ltd and in the following March the company announced the formation of a new division to be known as the Rolls-Royce Industrial and Marine Gas Turbine Division based at Ansty. Although Rolls-Royce was forced into receivership in 1971, the company became state-owned and Ansty continued to produce gas turbines for marine propulsion, along with gas and oil generation.

At the time of writing Ansty is still very involved in marine and industrial gas turbines. The airfield site, now exceeding three hundred and ten acres, can be found by leaving the M6 motorway at Exit 2, and then taking the B4065 through Ansty before turning right on to the B4029. Take another right under the motorway bridge and the site can be found about half a mile on the right-hand side.

3
BAGINTON

Baginton is now perhaps best known as West Midlands International Airport, which is claimed to be 'the best located airport in Britain', but in 1939 Baginton's chief claim to fame was that it was the site of Sir W. G. Armstrong Whitworth Aircraft Company's large factory producing the company's famous Whitley heavy bombers. AWA was also urgently engaged in modifying its Ensign airliners. Thus the airfield was intrinsically linked to Armstrong Whitworth Aircraft and would remain so for another twenty-six years.

In January 1939 Imperial Airways had withdrawn the original five Ensigns from service and returned them to AWA for a number of quite drastic modifications. The airline's pilots had been unhappy with certain aspects of the aircraft's flying controls and its 880hp Tiger IX engines were considered to be underpowered for the aircraft's weight, especially on take-off, and they had also proved somewhat unreliable. The Ensign had turned out to be 20% heavier than the original estimate

A.W.27 Ensigns operated with BOAC during WWII – G-ADSR Ensign in its wartime livery.

The first production Whitley V – 4th August 1939.

and AWA was obliged to pay Imperial Airways £42,500 as compensation for lost passenger revenue. By October remedial work on the twelve Ensigns had been duly completed and they had been returned to Imperial Airways, now refitted with Armstrong Siddeley 920hp Tiger VIII or IXc engines along with new constant-speed propellers. The two additional Ensigns, ordered back in late 1936, were not delivered until 1941 but were powered by American Wright Cyclone engines. All fourteen Ensigns operated with British Overseas Airways Corporation (BOAC) during the Second World War. Four were lost in 1940 (three to enemy action); a fifth – *Enterprise* – was abandoned in French West Africa in February 1942. The other nine, each bearing BOAC's famous 'Speedbird' insignia, survived the war. They had been used to transport military personnel, VIPs, ammunition and supplies mainly to Gibraltar and north and central Africa, but by 1947 all had been scrapped.

The company's major priority during 1939 and beyond was the production of Whitleys. At the outbreak of war No 4 Group of Bomber Command had six Whitley squadrons. It was especially engaged in the two new Marks – IV and V. The decision had been taken to increase the aircraft's power and as there was no in-house engine capable of developing 1,000hp or above, the company opted for Rolls-Royce Merlin X engines, which were rated at 1,075hp on take-off and more above 5,000 feet, thus increasing the aircraft's maximum speed to 230mph. The operational range was extended to 1,500 miles and Whitleys could now carry 7,000 pounds of bombs although none larger than a thousand pounder. A new Nash & Thompson FN4A four-gun powered turret was installed in the tail, and the bomb aimer's position in the nose was improved by the provision of a plexiglass 'chin' extension. The first production IV flew in April, followed in early August by the V. The fuselage had been slightly lengthened to provide the rear gunner with an improved field of fire, the fuel capacity had been increased and de-icing boots installed along the leading edges of the wings. In August the two-hundredth Whitley rolled off the assembly line at Baginton, and the company had already received an order for over three hundred Mark Vs; the first were delivered to No 77 squadron in September.

The Whitley gave the appearance of a cumbersome and inelegant aircraft with its distinctive 'nose-down' flying attitude and was often referred to as 'the Flying Barn Door'. Nevertheless, the aircraft gave sterling service to the RAF, despite its relative slow cruising speed and low operational ceiling. In its early days, the lack of cockpit heating made it somewhat uncomfortable for its five-man crew, but it was spacious and very sturdy, with good overall reliability. The aircraft claimed several notable firsts – the first to drop leaflets over Germany on 3rd/4th September 1939, first to bomb mainland German targets on 10th/11th May 1940, and then Italian targets on 11th/12th June. They also operated in Bomber Command's first bombing operation over Berlin on 25th/26th August 1940 and dropped the first British airborne troops to go into action on 10th February 1941.

From 1st September all civil flying was placed under the strict control of the National Air Communications, the government organisation established to co-ordinate all civil aviation activities in the event of war. Virtually all of the commercial airliners, large or small, had been transferred to Whitchurch near Bristol. However, many of Imperial Airways' Ensigns and Frobishers were diverted to Baginton, from where they would be directed to various RAF airfields to ferry the airmen and equipment of the ten Fairey squadrons of the Advanced Air Striking Force to their new bases in France. In fact an Ensign flown by Captain H. H. Perry, the oldest captain of the airline, made the first trip to France. With considerable skill he landed the airliner in a large field near Reims, which ultimately became the headquarters of the AASF during its stay in France.

There was no doubt that the Air Ministry would find some use for Baginton, despite the fact that it was only a grassed airfield with three landing runs of 1,730, 1,350 and 1,060 yards. Nevertheless, few people anticipated that during the early war years Baginton would house a number of fighter squadrons. Within days of the outbreak of war Baginton was duly requisitioned and the erection of four large hangars at the west end of the airfield was started. Early in September the first of several RAF units was formed there – No 1 Camouflage Unit. Its express purpose was to check from the air the effectiveness of the camouflaging of airfields, aircraft and armaments factories and anti-aircraft gun batteries – perhaps not the most glamorous of roles but nevertheless a quite demanding task both for the pilots and observers, especially considering the number of barrage balloons sited around Birmingham and Coventry. In fact, No 916 (Balloon) squadron established its headquarters at Baginton and was responsible for half of the fifty-six balloon sites in and around Coventry.

The Camouflage Unit was equipped with various aircraft – de Havilland Dominies, Lysander, Oxford and Blenheim – but its most unusual aircraft were the handful of Stimson SR-9 Reliants. This American-built high-wing cabin monoplane had been very popular in the United States, where it had been used largely as a mail carrier to remote townships not blessed with an airfield. The unit's Reliants were British registered civil aircraft that had been impressed into the service. Another impressed aircraft was a de Havilland DH.85 Leopard Moth, also a high-wing cabin monoplane, which dated back to April 1933. These aircraft, along with the Reliants, were just a few of the 1,017 civil registered aircraft pressed into service with the RAF during the war. The unit remained at Baginton until 12th November 1940, when it left for RAF Hendon.

During early 1940 it was proposed that AWA should be given a contract to build three hundred Avro Manchesters, the latest twin-engined bomber. Then there was a change of plan when it was thought that perhaps the company should be contracted to build Handley Page Halifaxes, the new four-engined bomber that made its maiden flight in October 1939. However, when the bustling Lord Beaverbrook was appointed the first Minister of Aircraft Production in May 1940, he decided that priority should be given to the production of established and well-tried aircraft, one of which was the Whitley; this resulted in an order for over eleven hundred Whitleys. The company's old factory at Whitley Abbey built the fuselages, Coventry Ordnance Works at South Street produced panelling and various parts, and the production of wings and final assembly took place at Baginton, whence the aircraft were test flown and delivered to the RAF.

In June 1940 Winston Churchill ordered that the War Office should establish a strong corps of airborne troops, with training to commence in the summer; it was therefore necessary to find a suitable aircraft for parachute training and the Whitley then offered the best option. Accordingly, AWA adapted six Mark IIs by making two exits, one through a circular hatch fitted with split doors, and the other fitted in the fuselage floor. These Whitleys were capable of carrying ten paratroops plus stores and supplies. In July they were operating at the Central Landing School at Manchester's Ringway airfield, where the first paratroops were trained. In August two Mark Vs, similarly adapted, were sent to Stapleford Tawney, a small grassed airfield in Essex where a highly secret unit, No 419 Flight, was in residence. This flight had recently been formed as the operational air-arm of the Special Operations Executive (SOE). The Whitleys were used to drop agents, supplies, radios and arms to resistance fighters in enemy occupied countries. Two successful drops were made in late August, the start of these clandestine operations, which continued virtually until the end of the war, famously by the two Special Duties squadrons, Nos 138 and 161.

As the Battle of Britain raged during the summer of 1940, the Air Ministry was concerned about the vulnerability of the Midlands and Merseyside to enemy air attack should the *Luftwaffe* turn to bombing operations. At that time the squadrons of No 12 Group theoretically provided the air defence cover for the Midlands but these squadrons had become increasingly engaged in the battle. Therefore, it was decided to form a sixth Fighter Command Group with responsibility for the defence of this vital and heavily industrialised area. On 8th August No 9 Group was established, with its headquarters at Barton Hall, Preston, Lancashire, but it was almost five weeks before an Air Officer Commanding was appointed – Air Vice-Marshal W. A. McClaughry – or indeed before the new Group was allocated any squadrons.

It was perhaps surprising that Baginton was earmarked as a Sector Station for the Midlands, virtually all the other Sector Stations were already established fighter airfields. But in reality the Air Ministry had very little choice. Nearby Bramcote, which had opened in June, was allocated to Bomber Command and the other RAF station in the vicinity – Castle Bromwich – was heavily engaged in Spitfire production. With Fighter Command being stretched almost to breaking point during September, there were certainly no established fighter squadrons to spare for the new Group. The Group's first allocated squadron was No 308, which had formed at the Polish Air Force depot at Squires Gate, Blackpool on 5th September and naturally was composed mainly of Polish airmen. The new squadron moved briefly to Speke, Liverpool, and on the 25th it arrived at Baginton. Within a week or so its first operational aircraft began to arrive – Hurricane Is.

Polish fighter pilots with 'Poland' shoulder flashes and PAF cap badges. (RAF Museum)

Polish airmen had first been assimilated into the RAF in January 1940, but after the fall of France some six thousand Polish airmen had managed to escape to England and were eager to continue the battle; most of them were fighter pilots. The initial Polish Air Force (PAF) squadrons in the RAF had been formed in July and by early August General Wladyslaw Sikorski, the Commander of the Polish Armed Forces in Britain, had finally obtained an agreement with the British Government that the PAF was recognised as a sovereign force in its own right and its airmen swore allegiance to the Polish government. However, it would remain subject to the RAF in all organisational, training, operational and discipline matters; its airmen wore RAF uniforms but with Polish buttons, Polish eagle cap badges and 'Poland' shoulder flash. The Polish Air Force ensign was allowed to fly beneath the RAF ensign on stations where Polish squadrons served. Approval was given for the formation of four bomber and four fighter squadrons along with an army support squadron, but it was acknowledged that there would be room for expansion. Already the first two Polish fighter squadrons – Nos 302 (Poznán) and 303 (Kościuszko) – were fully engaged in the Battle of Britain; one hundred and forty-one Polish airmen flew in the battle and twenty-nine were killed. These pilots gained effusive praise from Dowding: 'Had it not been for the magnificent material contributed by the Polish squadrons and their unsurpassed gallantry, I hesitate to say that the outcome of the battle would have been the same.'

The majority of the pilots of No 308 (Kraków) squadron were drawn from No 2 Kraków Air Regiment, hence its title. It was the fifth Polish fighter squadron to be formed and was commanded jointly by Squadron Leader J. A. Davies and a Polish commander, with the assistance of two RAF flight lieutenants. The squadrons were allowed to display their Polish identity on their aircraft and No 308 adopted 121 Eskadra's Winged Arrow Badge. The squadron used the Baginton Oak at the west end of the main grassed runway as its headquarters and officers' mess, and soon the pilots took to wearing coloured scarves, in order to denote their squadron: white for No 308, light brown for No 302, scarlet for No 303, and so on. The courage and bravery of the Polish fighter pilots became almost legendary, especially after their exploits in the Battle of Britain. They possessed a fierce determination and an almost obsessive hatred of Germans. This fervent aggression gained them the nickname of 'mad Poles'. However, their lack of discipline and scant indifference to all kinds of authority created continual problems wherever they served, and, of course this was not helped by the language barrier. As one RAF officer recalled, 'They were a complete law unto themselves. Nobody could control them not even their own officers'.

The main task for Squadron Leader Davies was to meld his inexperienced but highly motivated pilots into a cohesive fighting unit and bring them up to operational readiness in the minimum of time. This was not made easier by the fact that the squadron had become part of the Command's embryonic night fighter force. Although the Hurricane was an admirable fighter in many ways, it was not really suited to night operations. It was difficult and dangerous to land in the dark even in the hands of an experienced pilot. Also, the glow from the aircraft's exhausts not only impaired the pilot's night vision but also acted as an early warning to enemy aircraft. Matters were not improved when Squadron Leader Davies was tragically killed in a training accident, which not only delayed the training programme but also caused a loss of confidence by the pilots. Squadron Leader Morris took over command of the squadron in October.

The heavy and concentrated night bombing offensive by the

Luftwaffe from September 1940 had found Fighter Command at a severe disadvantage with the lack of a specialist night fighter. Blenheim Ifs had been modified for this role, mainly because they were the only fighters then capable of carrying the first heavy and cumbersome AI (Airborne Interception) radar sets. Boulton Paul Defiants had been quickly adapted to carry AI, but it was the arrival of the first Bristol Beaufighters in the autumn and the formation of the first night fighter OTU in December that offered some promise for an improvement in the night fighter force. The problem the Command faced can be illustrated by the infamous bombing of Coventry on 14th/15th November 1940; a total of 121 fighter sorties were flown that night – 40% of them by AI fighters – but only twelve sightings were made and just one of the estimated 450 enemy bombers was destroyed by anti-aircraft fire.

Although the squadron was not declared operational until 1st December, seven days earlier two of its pilots sighted and intercepted a Junkers 88 bomber and they succeeded in bringing it down over Stoneleigh. Night fighting was a lonely, demanding and exhausting task; long hours spent patrolling the night skies vainly searching for the merest shadow or silhouette. This was repeated night after night before returning to Baginton and a difficult landing, and all to no avail. It was all most frustrating and demanded infinite patience – a type of air warfare which was hardly suited to the temperament of Polish pilots, who were ever eager to get into battle and destroy as many German aircraft as possible.

By January 1941 No 9 Group had five night fighter squadrons all equipped with Hurricanes, known as 'cat's eyes' squadrons because they solely relied on the excellence of their pilots' night vision. The Air Ministry had finally and reluctantly agreed that once a Polish squadron was fully operational, the command could be passed over to a Polish officer. Thus in February Squadron Leader Orzechowski took over command of No 308.

As if to illustrate the cosmopolitan nature of the RAF, the Polish airmen were joined at Baginton by members of the Royal Canadian Air Force. The Canadian airmen moved in on 19th February to form a new squadron – No 403 'Wolf' – the third RCAF squadron to serve in the RAF. It was proposed to serve in the Army Co-operation Command, which had been formed in the previous November with Air Marshal Sir Arthur S. Barratt as its AOC. Hitherto most Army Co-operation (AC) squadrons had been equipped with Lysanders but they were now

Curtiss Tomahawks equipped No 403 (RCAF) squadron. (RAF Museum)

reaching the end of their operational life and were being replaced by an American aircraft – the Curtiss Tomahawk. The aircraft had been introduced into the US Army Air Corps in late 1939 and was known as a P.40; 'P' stood for 'Pursuit aircraft', as all fighters were called in the States. Originally the RAF had intended Tomahawks to operate as escort fighters and had ordered one hundred and forty as well as taking those produced for the now non-existent French Air Force. However, the aircraft's overall performance was less than impressive; its rate of climb and poor manoeuvrability made it unsuitable for escort duties, and they were relegated to a training role until drafted into Army support duties. Thirteen AC squadrons were ultimately equipped with Tomahawks.

As the Tomahawks began to arrive at Baginton, the squadron's unique identification code, KH, and the aircraft's individual letter were quickly applied to the fuselage, either side of the RAF roundel. Each RAF squadron had its individual code, No 308's was ZF. Soon the harsh rasp of the aircraft's Allinson V engines became a familiar sound around the airfield. However, it was now decided to move No 403 into Fighter Command and soon the Canadian pilots were converting to Spitfire Is. By the end of May the squadron was at operational readiness and it left for Ternhill, Shropshire.

Because of the better night facilities and firm runways at Bramcote, the Polish pilots increasingly used this airfield for their night patrols. But it was during a day patrol that the squadron notched up its second victory; on 28th March, another Junkers 88 was shot down over Coventry. The squadron had already received its first Supermarine Spitfire Is. Their arrival was greeted with great enthusiasm by the Polish pilots; not only were they thrilled to fly this legendary fighter but their arrival heralded the fact that soon the squadron would be moving on to the day offensive. In May the squadron was re-equipped with Mark IIAs, the first production variant, built at nearby Castle Bromwich, and at the end of the month the Polish airmen left for Chilbolton, Hampshire. Later at Northolt, No 308, along with Nos 303 and 306 squadrons, formed the First Polish Fighter Wing. During 1941 No 308 became the most successful Polish fighter squadron, with fifty-two confirmed victories and another ten probables.

The squadron was immediately replaced by the county's 'own' squadron No 605, making a welcome return to Warwickshire after an absence of almost two years. During that time it had served at a number of fighter stations but most successfully at Northolt during the later months of the Battle of Britain. Sadly, on 1st November, the squadron had lost in action its celebrated Commander, Squadron Leader Archie A. McKellar, DSO, DFC & Bar; at the time of his death he was credited with twenty victories. No 605 was now commanded by Squadron Leader Gerry R. Edge, DFC, one of the senior members of the original AAF squadron. Since November its pilots had been flying Hurricane IIAs. Hawker Aircraft had been developing the Hurricane from early 1940 in order to exploit the potential of this remarkable fighter. Two new sets of wings were designed, one having twelve .303 inch Browning machine guns, and the other four 20mm Hispano cannons. Each wing could also carry two 250 or 500 pound bombs. These changes had necessitated a strengthened fuselage, and the new variants were known as IIA, B and C. The first IIAs appeared in August 1940, powered by Merlin XX engines but still retaining the original eight Browning machine guns.

Another squadron, No 457, was formed at Baginton on 16th June and this time predominantly with pilots of the Royal Australian Air Force, but the ground crews were RAF. It was equipped with Spitfire Is and commanded by another Battle of Britain pilot – Squadron Leader Peter M. Brothers, DFC. The squadron was deemed operational in July but on 7th August the Australian airmen moved to Jurby on the Isle of Man after a brief stay at Honiley. A week later another new, or rather re-formed, squadron was established at Baginton – No 135 – under the command of Squadron Leader Frank R. Carey, DFC & Bar, DFM. He was one of the Command's most experienced pilots and a credit to the RAF's pre-war training regime. Carey had entered the Service in 1927 as an apprentice and became a Sergeant pilot in 1935 with No 43 squadron. He then served in France during May 1940, followed by the Battle of Britain, and survived the war, retiring as a Group Captain with twenty-four victories, including seven Japanese aircraft. No 135 squadron was allocated 605's Hurricane IIAs as and when they were replaced by Mark IIBs. Both squadrons moved off to Honiley on 4th September, largely as a temporary staging-post prior to overseas service. The days of Baginton as a Sector Station were fast coming to a close. During August both squadrons used Bramcote and a new airfield at Ramsey (Honiley), especially for 605's night patrols. In early September the Sector Headquarters moved to Honiley and a new role was found for Baginton, that of an overseas kitting-out centre.

The speedy and sleek Hurricanes and Spitfires that operated from

Whitleys in production at Baginton. (via M. Harris)

Baginton made the Whitleys that regularly emerged from AWA's factory seem even more clumsy and ponderous. Production had reached ten a week and in the following year it would peak at twelve a week. Buoyed by Coastal Command's successful use of Whitley Vs in its bitter battle against U-boats, AWA was preparing a Mark V (P4949) to accommodate the ASV (Air-to-Surface Vessel) Mk.II radar set. Extra cabin space was needed for the additional two crew members, and the fuel capacity was increased to extend the aircraft's operational range and endurance. This adapted Whitley was designated a Mark VII and was fitted with an array of aerials along the top of the fuselage as well as another beneath the nose. No 502 squadron at Chivenor, Devon received the first Mark VIIs and on 30th November it was credited with destroying *U-206* in the Bay of Biscay, then thought to be the first victory by use of ASV. However, in 1992, an Admiralty reappraisal of wartime U-boat sinkings discovered from German naval records that this was not so: *U-206* had in fact been sunk by a mine. The Whitley crew had attacked *U-71* without causing any serious damage. Nevertheless, Whitley VIIs gave valuable service to Coastal Command until replaced in 1943.

On 26th September 1941 the Prime Minister, Winston Churchill, visited Baginton to inspect the production of Whitleys. He must surely have been most interested in some experimental work that was on hand at Baginton, which was close to his heart. Trials were being conducted at both Baginton and Honiley using Mark Vs to tow Hotspur gliders, then used for training airborne troops – yet another operational role for the indomitable Whitley.

For several months the airfield was relatively quiet and peaceful after the departure of the Hurricanes to Honiley. However, on Christmas Eve, Hurricane IIBs of No 79 squadron arrived from Fairwood Common near Swansea. This brought yet another famous Battle of Britain pilot to Baginton – Squadron Leader Arthur V. Clowes, DFC, DFM. As a sergeant pilot with No 1 squadron, Clowes had been in action in France from the outbreak of war and by the end of the Battle he had nine victories to his name. His squadron remained at Baginton until 4th March 1942 when it started to prepare for its move overseas to India. All too briefly Baginton played host to the best known and certainly the most prolific Spitfire mark – the V. They arrived on 26th March 1942 from Eglinton, Northern Ireland as No 134 squadron, under Squadron Leader K. T. Tofts, DFC, making what can only be described as a fleeting visit. Uniquely during August to November

Hurricane IIBs of No 79 squadron operated from Baginton from December 1941 to March 1942. (via J. Adams)

1941 the squadron had served at Vaenga, Russia and was then flying Hurricane IIBs. It was now equipped with Spitfire VBs, which were armed with two 20mm Hispano cannons and four .303 inch Browning machine guns, and their Merlin 45 engines gave them a top speed of some 370mph. On 10th April the squadron left Baginton on the first stage of its journey to Helwan, Egypt.

The year 1942 brought some remarkable changes for AWA. In the previous year the company had been awarded contracts to produce nine hundred and ten Avro 683 Lancaster Mark Is along with three hundred Mark IIs, the new variant which had flown for the first time on 26th November 1941. Undoubtedly, the Lancaster was one of the truly great aircraft of the Second World War; indeed, Sir Arthur Harris considered it 'the finest bomber in the world' and maintained in December 1945 that it was 'the greatest single factor in winning the Second World War'. The Lancaster owed its existence to the unsuccessful twin-engined Manchester. The four-engined prototype, really a Manchester III (BT308) but already named Lancaster, made its maiden flight on 9th January 1941. There was a little concern about the continued availability of its original Rolls-Royce Merlin engines, so, to ensure continuity of production of this outstanding bomber, it was decided that the Mark IIs would be equipped with four Bristol Hercules VI or XVI engines. Further details of this outstanding bomber will appear under Castle Bromwich and Elmdon.

Although it was planned that the company would change

production to Lancaster Is and IIs, nevertheless the Ministry of Aircraft Production maintained that it should continue to build Whitleys, despite the fact that they had been withdrawn from Bomber Command's front-line squadrons in May; the last Whitley bombing operation was made on 29th/30th April to Ostend. Whitleys had made a total of 9,858 sorties for the loss of 317 aircraft (3.22%), but another 558 operational sorties were made by OTUs. By now the stalwart and steadfast Whitley had acquired a more kindly and favourable name – 'The Grand Old Lady of Bomber Command'! Perhaps the most famous Whitley pilot was Flight Lieutenant (later Group Captain) Leonard Cheshire of No 102 squadron.

The production of Lancaster IIs commenced at Whitley in August and the first production aircraft (DS601) left Sywell in October and first saw service with No 61 squadron. The American aero-engine company Packard had begun to produce Rolls-Royce Merlin 28 and 38 engines under licence, so the ministry's concern about the dearth of Merlin engines proved to be groundless. All of the three hundred Mark IIs were produced by AWA before turning to Mark Is and IIIs, the latter powered by the Packard Merlin engines. Warwickshire could almost be described as 'Lancaster country', with Vickers-Armstrong at Castle Bromwich, and Austin Motors at Longbridge and

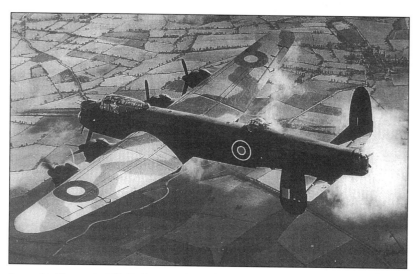

Lancaster II on a test flight from Baginton – August 1943.

Marston Green engaged in their production. Over 1,950 were built in the county or about 28% of the total number of Lancasters produced in this country.

Early in 1942 BOAC had requested that AWA convert fifteen Whitley Vs into straight transport aircraft. The gun turrets were removed and auxiliary fuel tanks were fitted into the bomb bays, which increased the operational range to 2,500 miles. They were duly registered as civil aircraft and from April to August 1942 were used on BOAC's route to West Africa. They also transported stores and supplies to both Gibraltar and Malta, although on these trips they were found to be less suitable, and in 1943 twelve were returned to the RAF.

The last fighter squadron to use Baginton during the Second World War was No 32. It arrived from Honiley on 19th October with Hurricane IIBs under the command of Squadron Leader J. T. Shaw, DFC. The squadron stayed until 25th November before moving out on its way to serve in Operation Torch – the Allied Invasion of North Africa – where its pilots would be engaged in shipping escort duties from Philippeville, Algeria.

On 12th July 1943 the final Whitley – a Mark V (LA951) – rolled out of the AWA factory at Baginton, making a grand total of 1,814. LA951 had been adapted as a glider tug but was not in fact delivered to the RAF; it was retained by the company until scrapped in 1949. AWA now had factories at Leicester, Nuneaton, Northampton, Sywell and Bitteswell. The last was an airfield in Leicestershire where the company had built a large hangar system and the airfield was also used for the test flying of production Lancasters. By the following year AWA had a workforce of some 12,000 and had made a massive contribution to the quite remarkable growth and development of the British aircraft industry during the Second World War.

In October 1944 AWA converted a Douglas C.54B Skymaster (EW999) into a VIP transport for the personal use of the Prime Minister. The Skymaster had been presented to Winston Churchill by President Roosevelt earlier in the year. The conversion included a rather splendid conference room, panelled in walnut, with a large walnut table seating eight persons. Charles Turner-Hughes flew the Skymaster to Northolt on 3rd November where it was later inspected by the Prime Minister. However, the aircraft was returned to the USA after the election of the Labour Government in the first post-war election.

During 1945 AWA was engaged in preparing Lancasters for service with the 'Tiger Force' in the Far East. They were known as Lancaster I(F.E.)s. The upper surfaces were coloured white and the undersides black, also additional fuel tanks were installed along the top of the fuselage to the aft of the cabin. It was also producing Avro 694 Lincolns, which were virtually scaled-up versions of the Lancaster. In fact, the original Lincoln I and II were first designated Lancaster IV and V respectively – another improved design for the Far East with a better performance, heavier armament and very long operational range. The Lincolns had been fully re-armed with .50 inch machine guns, provided with a greater bomb load and had a range of some 3,000 miles. They remained as the RAF's front-line bomber in the immediate post-war years until replaced by Boeing Washingtons (B-29s) and English Electric Canberras.

When the Second World War ended, contracts for both Lancasters and Lincolns were drastically reduced, and aircraft production work ceased at Whitley and the other dispersed factories, with the exception of Bitteswell. The final Lancaster left AWA on 2nd February 1946, making a total of 1,329 built by the company. The airfield returned to civilian flying in 1946, and two years later AWA built a new control tower to replace the old RAF watch office. In an attempt to re-enter the world of civil aviation, AWA began in late 1947 the design and development of a new airliner – A.W.55 Apollo. The first prototype was

Gloster Meteor NF11 – Meteor night fighters were produced at Baginton from 1950 to 1954. (RAF Museum)

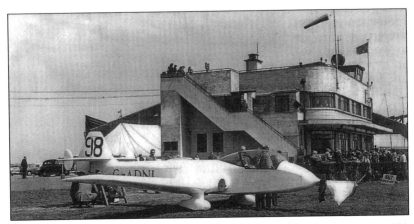

Miles Sparrowjet at Baginton during the King's Cup Air Race, June 1954. (via J. Adams)

completed in March 1949 and made its maiden flight on 10th April. The Apollo was a handsome four-engined turbo-prop airliner, able to carry twenty-four passengers at a cruising speed of 300mph. But problems with its Mamba engines and other shortcomings meant that the airliner lost out to its close competitor, the Vickers Viscount. In June 1952 it was decided to abandon further development of the aircraft; only two were built.

Nevertheless, military aircraft production continued at Baginton until late 1949, when over three hundred and eighty Lincolns had been completed. These were followed by 1,072 Gloster Meteors, more especially the night fighter versions, NF11 to NF14, which AWA had been asked to develop. The NF11 first flew on 31st May 1950 and over five hundred and forty night fighters of all marks were produced until May 1954. Hawker Seahawks and finally Gloster Javelins were built by AWA, but the Javelin production came to an end in 1958. Some 4,030 aircraft designed by other companies had been built by AWA. The last aircraft to bear the famous Armstrong Whitworth name was the Argosy cargo and general transport – A.W.650 and 660 (military version). The Argosy first flew on 8th January 1959, it was also the last aircraft designed by the company's 'veteran' chief designer, John Lloyd. The Apollo was not quite as commercially successful as the company would have liked; just sixteen were sold to civil operators, although fifty-six were ordered by the RAF. In 1961, as a result of the merger with Gloster Aircraft Company, AWA became Whitworth Gloster Aircraft Ltd; sadly, four years later aircraft production ceased at Baginton.

The airfield underwent major development from 1952, including the building of a passenger terminal along with a 5,300 feet hard runway, which was well used by both civil and private aircraft. Jersey Airlines operated services from there from 1952, followed by British United and other smaller airlines. Baginton also hosted a number of air shows and pageants, as well as being used as a staging post for the King's Cup Air Races. In 1998 the Atlantique Group secured the lease of the airfield from the city council and at the time of writing administers and operates West Midlands International Airport.

One of the major attractions now at Baginton is the superb Midland Air Museum, which houses a unique collection of aircraft and exhibits. The museum's centrepiece is 'The Sir Frank Whittle Jet Heritage Centre', dedicated to the life and work of the inventor of the jet engine. The museum is open all the year round and certainly well deserves a visit.

4

BRAMCOTE

Early in 1939 John Laing & Son Ltd started construction work on an airfield site to the south of the B4114 road at Bramcote, about four miles south-east of Nuneaton. Those airmen who would ultimately serve or train at this airfield could consider themselves rather fortunate, because Bramcote was one of the last 'Expansion' stations to be approved prior to 1939. It was built to high specifications and standards, with attractive brick buildings, spacious accommodation blocks and messes, tarmacadamed roads, and good working conditions with the provision of five 'C' hangars and ample social and sports amenities. In this respect Bramcote was in very sharp contrast to the other wartime airfields in the county, and sixty-four years later it still remains a Ministry of Defence property, a fine testimony to the contractor's workmanship.

Within a week of the outbreak of the war, when construction work at the airfield was far from complete, No 215 squadron's Wellingtons flew

Wellington IC of No 215 squadron: the first of countless Wellingtons that operated from Bramcote.

in from Honington, Suffolk. Their arrival was in accord with the Air Ministry's 'Scatter Plans', which decreed that some bomber squadrons should be dispersed away from their operational bases in the advent of war; a purely precautionary and temporary measure in case the *Luftwaffe* directed a pre-emptive strike against certain airfields, which were mainly sited in East Anglia. These aircraft proved to be the first of countless Wellingtons that operated from Bramcote during the next six years. On 24th September the squadron moved to Bassingbourn, Cambridgeshire, where, in April 1940, it was disbanded to form the nucleus of No 11 Operational Training Unit (OTU).

Considerable pressure was placed on Laing to complete the airfield as speedily as possible but the severe weather conditions during the winter of 1939/40 seriously delayed the construction work and the airfield was not formally opened until 4th June 1940. It had been allocated to Bomber Command and had been belatedly provided with three steel matting runways, one at 1,600 yards and two at 1,400 yards, although they would be extended later. Bramcote had also been provided with a 'decoy' site at Wibtoft, about 4½ miles due east, just off Watling Street. At this time the Command was in dire need of airfields to house the additional OTUs that had been formed mostly from Group Pool squadrons. Bramcote was placed in No 6 (Training) Group, based at Abingdon, Oxfordshire and was earmarked for one of the recently formed OTUs.

It was a rather special OTU – No 18 – that arrived at Bramcote in early November. It had been formed at Hucknall, Nottinghamshire on 15th June and was the eleventh such unit to be established. No 18 was intended to train Polish Air Force aircrews, and comprised mainly those airmen already serving in the existing Polish Flying Training Unit at Hucknall. The original agreement with the British Government was that the PAF would comprise four bomber squadrons equipped with Wellingtons, but sadly there were insufficient Wellingtons available to form new squadrons, and therefore they were temporarily provided with out-dated Fairey Battle light bombers. This decision caused much dismay and disappointment to both the Polish government in exile and its eager and enthusiastic airmen. However, one senior RAF officer remarked at the time, 'the Pole was an individualist and an aircraft like the Wellington, with a crew of five, was not really suited to their temperament'! The fine record of Polish squadrons in Bomber Command proved otherwise.

The first Polish bomber squadron was formed at Bramcote on

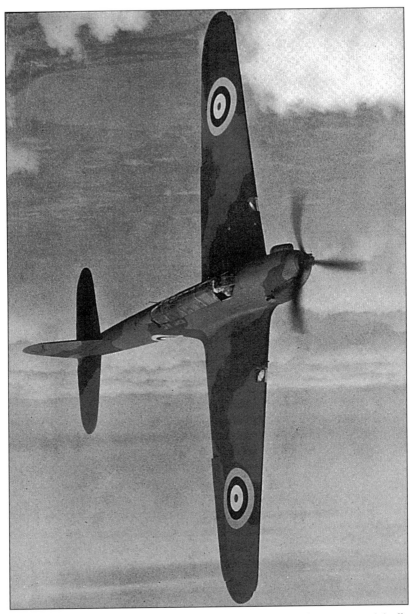

An early production Fairey Battle: the Polish bomber squadrons were originally equipped with Battles.

1st July – No 300 (Mazovian) – with Lieutenant-Colonel Wactan Makowski and Wing Commander K. P. Lewis in joint command. By RAF standards Makowski, aged forty-three, was perhaps rather old to command an operational squadron. He had first served in the PAF in 1920 and then had gained wide experience in civil aviation, latterly as the general manager of the Polish airline LOT. The second squadron was formed twenty-one days later – No 301 (Pomeranian) – under Lieutenant-Colonel Roman Rudkowski and Squadron Leader C. G. Skinner; both were experienced airmen and by repute were tough and resilient characters. Each squadron comprised some thirty aircrew and one hundred and eighty ground crew, with British adjutants as well as a number of RAF technical advisers. They were placed in the newly re-formed No 1 Group of Bomber Command under Air Commodore J. J. Breen, with its headquarters at Hucknall. The Group then comprised the Battle squadrons that had served in France with the Allied Expeditionary Striking Force, but by February 1941 its eight squadrons (half Polish) were equipped with Wellingtons.

The Fairey Battle was a single-engined light bomber, which dated from March 1936 when it was a significant advance over the Hawker Hart it was designed to replace. The Battle was a rather sleek and well-designed monoplane of a light alloy and stressed skin construction. It cruised at slightly over 200mph, carried a 1,400 pound bomb load and had a range of 1,200 miles. However, it was lightly armed with a single .303 inch Browning gun forward in the right wing and a Vickers gun aft. They entered the service in May 1937 but two years later had become virtually obsolete owing to their under-powered engines and poor armament. Nevertheless, by the outbreak of the war, there were more than 1,000 Battles equipping seventeen squadrons with the AASF; many had been built by Austin Motors at Longbridge. During May 1940, especially, their inadequacies were cruelly exposed. In just five days, from 10th to 14th, sixty Battles (55%) were lost in action in France, gaining the macabre name 'flying coffins'. With their mediocre performance and evil reputation, one can well understand the Polish airmen's discontent and mistrust as they became familiar with their new aircraft. In fact, by the autumn, Battles were withdrawn from front-line squadrons and were relegated to target-towing duties or converted to dual-control trainers.

With the creation of the Polish bomber squadrons, Bramcote became a mecca for VIPs, especially as it was such a pristine station. Such visits provided propaganda material to show the 'many brave Polish airmen who had escaped the tyranny of Nazism'. On 3rd August Air Chief Marshal Sir Charles Portal, Chief of Bomber Command, came to officially welcome the Polish squadrons into his command. He was said to have been highly impressed with the way the crews flew their Battles: they experimented with them 'as dive bombers and flew them almost like fighters'; in fact it was claimed that the majority of Polish airmen were really 'all frustrated fighter pilots'. Seventeen days later HM King George VI visited Bramcote and met many Polish airmen. When one of the Polish commanders was asked by the king what had been the most difficult problems to adjust to since their arrival in Britain, he quickly replied, 'King's Regulations, Your Majesty.' Another example of how they considered the majority of the RAF's procedures and rules so irksome.

A third squadron was formed on 22nd August – No 304 (Silesian) – under Wing Commander J. Bialy, followed a week later by No 305 (Ziemia Wielkopolska), commanded by Wing Commander J. Jankowski. Both squadrons were mainly formed from Polish airmen who had briefly served in the French Air Force. Thus, Bramcote has been described as 'the cradle of the Polish bomber force' and holds a special place in the history of the PAF during WWII. These four Polish squadrons would be in the forefront of the Command's bombing offensive over the next two years. In fact No 300 squadron carried out more bombing raids, flew more sorties and suffered more losses (seventy-seven aircraft) than any other allied bomber squadron. The squadron also flew the last Wellington bombing sorties on 3rd/4th March 1944. In total 929 Polish airmen were killed or missing in action whilst serving in Bomber Command.

By the end of August Nos 300 and 301 squadrons had moved out to Swinderby, Lincolnshire and took their Battles into action for the first time on the night of 14th September, when they bombed invasion barges massed in Boulogne harbour. The other two squadrons remained at Bramcote until early December before moving to Syerston near Newark, Nottinghamshire. The Polish airmen met King George VI and Queen Elizabeth once again, when royal visits were made to Swinderby and Syerston on 27th January 1941.

With the departure of the squadrons Bramcote became predominantly devoted to the operational training of Polish crews. The Unit was now virtually manned by Polish airmen, except in respect of the various instructors. It was said that there were ten Polish airmen to each RAF man – one commented that Bramcote was like 'being posted overseas'. Certainly it could be considered as 'little Poland' sited in leafy Warwickshire. The Unit was stood down briefly as the Battles finally disappeared from operational squadrons and were replaced by one of the outstanding bombers of the Second World War – the Vickers Wellington. No 18 was the fifth OTU to be equipped with this quite remarkable aircraft.

The Wellington, beloved by crews and the public alike, had been designed by Barnes Wallis, of later 'bouncing bomb' fame. It was in response to an Air Ministry specification (B.9/32) of October 1932 for a twin-engined medium bomber, which also gave rise to the Handley Page Hampden and Harrow bombers. The Wellington's unique geodetic lattice construction proved capable of sustaining a considerable amount of battle damage and still survive; its crews had an unbounded faith that their aircraft would bring them home safely despite being severely damaged. Originally called the Crecy in honour of the famous victory of 1346, its name was changed to Wellington after the Iron Duke. However, the aircraft later acquired the nickname 'Wimpy' after J. Wellington Wimpy Esquire, a favourite character from the popular Popeye newspaper strip cartoon. The British public's fondness for the aircraft was ensured in 1941 with the very successful propaganda film, *Target for Tonight*, which featured Wellingtons, especially 'F for Freddie', and 'starred' operational RAF aircrew, perhaps most famously Squadron Leader (later Group Captain) Charles Pickard, DSO, DFC.

The prototype Wellington (K4090) first flew on 15th June 1936, production started in December 1937 and the first Wellingtons entered the Service in October 1938 with No 99 squadron. Flying Officer (later Group Captain) A. Montagu-Smith of No 99 later commented '[They] brought a whole new era of military flying for the pilots of Bomber Command … it was something entirely new.' Powered by two Bristol Pegasus XVIII engines, which gave a top speed of about 235mph at 15,500 feet, it could carry a 4,500 pound bomb load. In April 1941 it was the first bomber to drop the 4,000 pound bomb. There were Frazer-Nash nose and tail turrets with twin .303 inch Browning guns as well as two single Brownings in beam positions. Wellingtons suffered Bomber Command's first heavy losses, and in the early war years they formed the backbone of Bomber Command. Over 47,400 operational sorties were flown (third behind Lancasters and Halifaxes) and 1,386 (2.9%) Wellingtons were lost in action. Just like the Whitley, the Wellington proved to be a most adaptable aircraft and was used in many

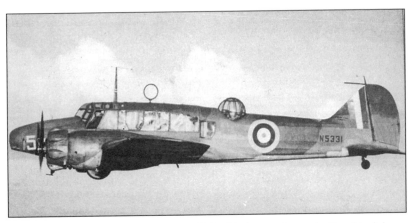

Avro 652A Anson: all OTUs were supplied with Ansons for navigational training.

operational roles, notably with Coastal Command. Some 11,460 were built in a variety of marks, the largest total of any British bomber. Its use as an aircrew training aircraft extended right through to 1953, although production ceased in October 1945. The majority of heavy bomber crews received their operational training on Wellingtons, so the aircraft held a very special place in the hearts of 'The Bomber Men'.

The other aircraft that was invariably used at OTUs was the Avro Anson, another fondly-loved wartime aircraft known as the 'Faithful Annie', which was used for navigational and radio training. Ultimately, the Unit would be equipped with nine Ansons, and indeed its first training loss from Bramcote was an Anson. On 19th December 1940 Sub-Lieutenant (A) C. R. Coxon, RN, whilst engaged on a wireless procedure exercise, made an emergency landing at Staverton, Gloucestershire and ran into soft ground; the crew escaped without injury, but the Anson was so badly damaged that it was written-off.

OTUs normally comprised four large flights usually commanded by a Flight Lieutenant although later Squadron Leaders were sometimes placed in charge, especially those devoted to all aspects of operational or applied flying training. The other flights covered initial or conversion training, navigation, radio communications, aerial arma-ment and fighter affiliation. This system invoked a certain amount of criticism because trainees had to change their instructors about midway through their course, but it proved to work, producing a high standard of aircrews. Certain changes and modifications were introduced later, largely dictated by experience and different priorities. In the early days an OTU was not considered to be a full Unit until it was provided with a satellite airfield. Until then, it counted as a ¾ OTU and its complement of training Wellingtons was set accordingly.

The intake of crews was normally on a fortnightly basis, with anything from eleven to sixteen crews joining, depending on the size of the Unit. The course was planned to last ten weeks, though this time period varied, depending on the time of year. Up until mid-1942 each intake had a greater number of pilots because of the necessity of a second pilot in heavy bombers. The rest of the intake would consist almost equally of air observers, radio operators/gunners, bomb aimers and air gunners. The OTU was the first occasion these aircrew categories had come together for training; previously they had trained at the various specialist units or schools. The pilots had spent the longest time on training, from initial through to advanced instruction, and those trained abroad under the Empire Air Training Scheme received refresher training before arriving at an OTU; this process could take about twelve months or maybe longer.

Prior to any flying training, all trainees undertook two weeks of lectures and ground training. The other essential feature of these early weeks in the OTU was the neccessity of the individual categories to form up into a crew. All wartime memories of bomber airmen express considerable surprise that they had not been officially nominated into a crew but rather were given a free choice. The trainees were all herded into a large hangar and told 'to sort themselves out into crews' and were usually given about seven days to do just that. As one pilot later remarked, 'I didn't know any of them. I needed four of these men to fly with, live with and go to war with.' What attracted individuals to crew up ranged from nationality, physical appearance, smoking or drinking habits to sociability. This system appeared to be most haphazard and disorganised but quite amazingly it worked very well. Strong and binding wartime friendships were made at this stage of training, and those crews fortunate enough to survive an operational tour remained friends for years ahead. From now on the training would be concentrated on the five chosen airmen working together as a team, which was so essential for the effective operation of their aircraft and their ultimate survival. The pilot was designated the captain or 'skipper' of the crew, regardless of rank, and he would be responsible for his crew members arriving on time at lectures, roll calls, parades, exercises, etc. Of course in the early days all the trainees at No 18 OTU

Hurricane IIC (of No 87 squadron) in matt black night finish. Several Hurricane squadrons used Bramcote for night patrols.

were Polish airmen and perhaps they crewed up on a regional or town basis, but subsequently RAF airmen were also trained at the Unit as there became a shortage of Polish aircrews; indeed, No 301 (Pomeranian) squadron was disbanded in April 1943 for this very reason.

There must have been a touch of envy amongst the Polish airmen when, on 28th November 1940, No 151's Hurricane Is arrived from Digby, Lincolnshire. The squadron had been involved in the Battle of Britain, operating from Martlesham Heath and Stapleford Tawney, and had been posted to No 12 Group for a rest and regrouping. The squadron was now transferred to night fighting, and its pilots became engaged in night training exercises and endless night take-offs and landings. They also began converting to Boulton Paul Defiant Is, the stop-gap night fighter, but the squadron operated both fighters in the months ahead. One of its pilots, Pilot Officer Richard P. Stevens, DFC, was destined to become the most successful Hurricane night fighter pilot of the war. During 1941 he was credited with fourteen enemy aircraft, with another six probables. Sadly, he was killed in action in December after he had been awarded a Bar to his DFC and DSO. On 22nd December the squadron moved away to Wittering, Cambridgeshire, where some of its crews were already on detachment. Over the next twelve months or so the Polish airmen became accustomed to the matt-black Hurricanes of several squadrons using the airfield for night patrols.

All forms of flying training were hazardous but operational training posed the greatest risks, and unfortunately OTUs suffered far higher accident rates than any other flying training. In some units this was as high as 20% over a period of six months. Some factors to account for this were youthful and inexperienced crews flying 'aged' aircraft that were passed down from front-line squadrons and were therefore more prone to mechanical failure, especially the engines and radio equipment. Also trainee crews were often required to fly in unfavourable weather conditions, and the many and various night flying exercises presented considerable problems for the inexperienced crews. After all, according to an old RAF adage, 'only owls and fools fly by night'! However, the majority of OTU accidents were a result of human error of some description. It should be borne in mind that the young trainee pilots were coping with large and heavy aircraft – thirteen tons fully loaded – after only recently mastering Oxfords, which by comparison were a mere three tons.

Since the first OTUs had been formed in April 1940 two hundred aircraft had been lost in accidents or written-off in eight months, with over two hundred and ten airmen killed. The Unit had lost one airman, LAC E.V. Rozmiarek, the first Polish airman to be killed during operational training. Tragically, his Battle crashed onto a house at Hucknall on 23rd September, killing a family of four. On the night of the Coventry raid of 14th/15th November 1940, a couple of Polish airmen saw a parachute descending upon the airfield and, thinking that it was an airborne landing, they fired at the parachute and the aerial mine exploded killing three airmen.

During 1941 No 18 lost sixteen aircraft (about 4% of total OTU losses). Not all were due to flying accidents, but nevertheless thirty-six airmen were killed, twenty-four of them Polish. Then Polish airmen were buried in Nuneaton (Oaston Road) cemetery, whereas RAF airmen were buried in cemeteries selected by their next-of-kin. A tragic accident occurred on 4th February when a Wellington IC on a night navigation exercise flew into a barrage balloon cable near Middlewich,

Wellington IC in No 301 squadron's markings: it was destroyed on the ground at Bramcote on 4th February 1942 whilst with 'C' Flight.

Cheshire. The instructor pilot, Flying Officer D. Warburton, and the nine crewmen (six Polish) were killed. This was the highest death toll in a single OTU accident so far.

On the night of 13th March a stray *Luftwaffe* bomber dropped at least eight bombs on the airfield, and one of the hangars was slightly damaged but no casualties were suffered. However, two Wellingtons were destroyed along with a Miles Magister. These low-wing two-seater elementary trainers were provided to OTUs as 'dog's-body' aircraft to carry out general communication duties, act as enemy fighters on affiliation exercises, and to be used sometimes by desk-bound officers to increase their flying hours.

It was a grim fact that barrage balloons brought down more friendly than enemy aircraft, and in April (29th) one of the Unit's Ansons collided with a balloon cable over Coventry and all five crew members were killed. During the summer the Unit experienced almost five months free from accidents, a quite remarkable run of good fortune considering the accident rate at other OTUs; perhaps this can be seen as a measure of just how weather conditions contributed to accidents.

The Unit was allocated Bitteswell near Lutterworth, Leicestershire as a satellite airfield in late June, relieving the pressure of arranging all the necessary flying exercises from Bramcote. Bitteswell had been constructed during 1940/1 and even in June it was far from finished. In fact, it was not until early August that the first night flying exercises were mounted from there. The Unit's D Flight, equipped with six Wellingtons, moved into Bitteswell. Even when the airfield was finally completed, it was not a particularly comfortable or congenial place, further emphasising the vastly different living and working conditions prevailing at pre-war and wartime airfields.

Sadly, 1942 proved to be far worse for fatal accidents – fifty-six airmen killed – although this included those lost in action. Perhaps the most remarkable story concerns Sergeant J. Fusniak, PAF, an air gunner. He was a member of a six-man Polish crew that was engaged on a night cross-country exercise on 30th/31st January. Their Wellington IC was flying in severe weather conditions – snow and heavy icing – and in an attempt to reduce height the aircraft crashed into Buckden Pike in North Yorkshire. Fusniak and the radio operator were the only survivors, and despite a broken leg Fusniak struggled through the snow to reach the village of Cray to raise the alarm, but not in time to save the life of the radio operator. Nevertheless, Fusniak was awarded the British Empire Medal. Almost seven months later (21st/ 22nd July), Fusniak was again the sole survivor of No 301 Squadron's Wellington IV struck by flak en route to Duisburg. He was blown out of his turret and landed safely by parachute. Although injured and suffering from shock, Fusniak almost managed to escape but he was captured by the Germans and spent the rest of the war as a prisoner-of-war. In 1972 he returned to Buckden Pike and placed a stone cairn surmounted by a cross in remembrance of his old crew.

A tragic accident in 1942 relates to a five-man Polish crew that left Bramcote on the night of 17th May for a cross-country exercise. It was

The end product of all OTUs: bomber crew preparing for take-off. Oil painting by Dame Laura Knight, RA. (Imperial War Museum)

scheduled as the crew's final training flight prior to posting to an operational squadron. Their Wellington IC was seen to burst into flames and crash near Hexham, Northumberland. The five airmen were buried at the Polish Forces Cemetery, Newark, Nottinghamshire, where there is now a PAF memorial.

In April 1942 the OTU had attained full strength with fifty-four Wellingtons, eighteen Ansons, and a couple of Lysanders to act as fighters for affiliation exercises. From May the Unit came under the control of No 91 Group at Abingdon, Oxfordshire, commanded by Group Captain Hugh S. P. Walmsley, but in September No 18 was re-allocated to the newly formed No 93 Group under Group Captain C. E. Maitland, originally at Lichfield, Staffordshire, but later moving to Egginton Hall, Derby. It was now a rather smaller Unit than in April because the Polish Flight had moved on to No 6 (C) OTU at Thornaby, Durham, which trained Coastal Command crews. The reason for this move was that No 403 (Polish) squadron ceased as a bomber squadron on its transfer to Coastal Command in May; nevertheless, the squadron operated Wellingtons throughout the war.

Many trainee crews passing through OTUs during the summer of 1942 found themselves engaged on bombing operations a little sooner than they had anticipated. In April the relatively new AOC-in-C of Bomber Command, Air Marshal Arthur Harris, conceived the idea of launching a 1,000 bomber raid against a major German city. To achieve this 'magical' figure he needed the assistance of Coastal Command, and at the late stage of preparation the Admiralty baulked against such a proposal: it would do nothing to weaken the unremitting battle against the U-boat menace. Harris was far short of his 1,000 bombers and the Command was forced to provide every available aircraft and crew. The decision was taken to reinforce the regular bomber squadrons by using training aircraft and trainee crews then approaching the end of their courses, although every effort was made to provide these crews with at least an experienced pilot.

The first 1,000 bomber raid took place on 30th/31st May with Cologne, the third largest city in Germany, as the target. This massive force of bombers, the largest ever assembled, was planned to attack in successive waves and there was a concern about collisions but the Command estimated that only two aircraft would be lost to collisions, but, as one trainee airman quipped, 'Ah yes, but which two?' A total of 1,047 bombers were despatched, 602 of them Wellingtons, of which 299 came from OTUs. Bramcote supplied eighteen crews. It was estimated that the maximum loss would be 10% – well over double the 'tolerable' loss rate of 4%. However, the overall loss was forty-one, of which, quite surprisingly, 3.3% were training aircraft, which was less than the 3.9% suffered by regular squadrons. Moreover, it was revealed that those aircraft flown by trainee pilots suffered lower losses than those with experienced pilots! All the Unit's crews survived the ordeal or 'Flap', as these operations were called by trainee crews.

The operation – 'the Greatest Air Raid in History' – was considered a huge success: a high proportion of the crews managed to bomb the city, considerable damage was inflicted, and it provided a fine propaganda coup for Bomber Command and a sorely needed morale boost to the country. The fine performance of the trainee crews ensured that they would be used on similar raids in the near future. The next night, 1st/2nd June, Essen was the target but only 956 bombers were available. A Wellington IC from Bramcote was one of the thirty-one aircraft lost (3.2%); it was flown by Flight Lieutenant W. L. Tweddie with two Polish and two RAF airmen, and one of these, Warrant Officer J. A. Nott, was the last of three brothers to be killed in action with the RAF.

But worse was to follow. On 25th/26th June the 'Thousand Force' was reassembled for a raid on Bremen; with 1,067 aircraft dispatched, it was larger than the Cologne raid, mainly because Churchill had ordered the Admiralty to participate. The force comprised every RAF bomber of WWII – Wellingtons, Halifaxes, Lancasters, Stirlings, Blenheims, Whitleys, Hampdens, Bostons, Manchesters and even four Mosquitos. Forty-eight aircraft were lost, exactly 5%, and the OTUs suffered harshly this night. Thirty failed to return, three from No 18 – ten Polish airmen killed and five prisoners-of-war. A further five bomber operations included OTU crews, the last to Essen of 16th/17th September. No 18 survived these operations without incurring any further casualties – a quite remarkable record. However, another five Polish airmen were killed in action on 15th October when engaged in a night exercise over France. The Court of Inquiry into the loss reported: 'It is presumed the crew decided to drop their 'live' bomb in German occupied territory'!

At the end of October eight Airspeed Oxfords took up residence for the duration of the war. They equipped No 1513 Beam Approach Training (BAT) Flight, which had been previously based at Honington, Suffolk. These Flights instructed crews in the complexities of the Beam Approach System. By 1941 most RAF airfields operated the Standard Beam Approach, which was based on short distance radio beams transmitted from a ground station along the runway approach path, maybe up to thirty miles from the airfield. A receiver in the aircraft indicated to the crew any deviations from the centre line, both visually and aurally. The left-hand beam transmitted Morse dots and the other beam dashes; when the beams locked, a steady note was heard and it was by this tone the aircraft was navigated safely down. The SBA proved to be a most valuable aid to night landings and landings in unfavourable weather. Originally such Flights had been known as Blind Approach Training Flights, from the first Blind Approach School, formed at Watchfield in October 1940. Strangely the system was of German origin; it had been developed by Lorenz A. G. and Telefunken. The British rights to the system had been acquired by Standard Telephones and Cables in 1936. By 1945 there were more than forty BAT Flights and originally they had been controlled by Bomber Command but from 1943 Flying Training Command assumed responsibility for them.

Early in February 1943 the Unit's personnel moved back from Bitteswell and the Flight's Wellingtons were allocated to No 21 OTU at Moreton-in-the-Marsh, Gloucestershire. Bitteswell was closed to flying in order that its facilities could be upgraded. Nevertheless, Bramcote was allocated another satellite airfield – Nuneaton – although known locally as Lindley. It had been built during 1941/2 and was sited about 4½ miles NNE of Nuneaton between Higham on the Hill and Fenny Drayton just across the boundary in Leicestershire. It was provided with three concrete runways of standard lengths (one at 2,000 yards and the other two at 1,400 yards) and was not approved for flying until early August, by which time No 18 OTU was no longer at Bramcote. On 27th February it had moved to Finningley, Yorkshire. After almost three years the PAF ensign was ceremoniously lowered for the last time. Over 14,300 Polish airmen and airwomen served in the PAF during the Second World War and 2,408 were killed. In November 1948 Air Chief Marshal Lord Teddar unveiled the Polish Air Memorial at Western Avenue on the edge of Northolt airfield. It lists the 1,241 airmen killed in action and is inscribed in English and Polish 'I have fought a good fight. I have finished my course. I have kept the faith.' The memorial, which was subscribed by the British public and the Polish armed forces, is a mecca for veteran Polish airmen and women and their families.

Such a prime airfield as Bramcote, along with Nuneaton, was soon occupied by another training unit, when, on 5th April, No 105(T) OTU formed at Bramcote. It was controlled by No 44 Group of Transport Command, which had formed only on 25th March, under Air Chief Marshal Sir Frederick Bowhill. The Command comprised three Groups with No 44 responsible for the training of ex-bomber crews for the far less dangerous task of flying transport aircraft. Very little changed at

The Polish Air Memorial at Western Avenue on the edge of Northolt airfield.

Bramcote. It was a relatively smooth transition, largely because the new OTU was equipped with the omnipresent Wellingtons. The course did reflect the different kind of operations they would fly, with the inclusion of far more night navigation exercises and over longer distances. The trainee crews also became involved in flying the ferry service to and from Nutt's Corner, County Antrim, in Northern Ireland. The Unit's first known accident occurred on 4th December 1943, when a Wellington IC crashed in flames at Tilstock, Shropshire, but the crew managed to parachute to safety.

In November 1944 Bitteswell returned to the fold and became the Unit's second satellite, housing B and C Flights. In June 1945 Bramcote and its satellites were transferred to No 4 Group of Transport Command and almost immediately began to receive Douglas C-47s (Skytrains), far better known as Dakotas – perhaps the most famous transport aircraft of all time. The C-47 was the military version of the successful DC-3 airliner and quickly became the workhorse of the USAAF, fondly dubbed the 'Gooney Bird'! It was able to transport two tons of freight or twenty-eight fully equipped troops and carried a crew

Douglas C-47 Dakotas operated from Bramcote with No 105(T) OTU. (RAF Museum)

of three with side-by-side dual controls but it was unarmed. The first
Dakotas arrived in this country in February 1943, when a number went
to BOAC. In March No 24 was the first RAF squadron to operate
Dakotas from Gibraltar. Over 1,900 Dakotas served in the RAF and the
aircraft was equally successful operating in the post-war years with
many commercial airlines (including BOAC) and countless freight
companies worldwide. In excess of 20,000 of all versions were
produced, making it the most successful aircraft ever.

Bramcote also housed Transport Command's Air Crew Examining
Board. On August 10th 1945 the Unit was redesignated No 1381
(Transport) Conversion Unit, although the new Unit was not destined
to spend long at the airfield because on 19th November it moved to
Desborough, Northamptonshire. There was now an empty feeling
around Bramcote, with just the BAT Oxfords in residence. They left in
May 1946 but were swiftly replaced by more Oxfords of No 1510 BAT
Flight, which departed in November.

Most wartime airfields were now placed on a Care and Maintenance
basis, whilst the Air Ministry considered their ultimate fate. Flying had
ceased at both Bitteswell and Nuneaton. In September 1947 Nuneaton
was taken over by the Motor Industry Research Association and fifty-
seven years later is still used by MIRA. Bramcote, on the other hand,
was ceded to the Royal Navy in December 1946 for the use of
squadrons of Naval Aviation, as the Fleet Air Arm had recently been
renamed. The airfield was renamed HMS *Gamecock*, following the long-
established naval practice of naming its shore establishments after
birds.

Supermarine Seafires of Naval Aviation flew from Bramcote in the post-war years. (FAA Museum)

Considering the rather ponderous Second World War aircraft that had used Bramcote, the immediate post-war years saw the appearance of naval fighters, especially Supermarine Seafires – latterly mainly those of No 1833 (RNVR) squadron. They were the naval version of the Spitfire. The first successful trials of aircraft carrier landings of Spitfire Vs had been made in early 1942. As a result, many were converted for carrier operations by the provision of 'sting ray' arrestor hooks beneath the fuselage and some had catapult spools. Later versions had the famous so-called praying mantis manually folding wings, which afforded easier handling and stowage on carriers. Over five hundred and ninety Spitfires were converted to Seafires, with another eighteen hundred specially produced as Seafires. They served the FAA with great distinction during the Second World War and indeed one Seafire squadron (No 800) operated in the Korean War during 1950. In the following year Seafires were withdrawn from operational service but remained with RNVR squadrons and training units. When the RNVR squadrons were disbanded in 1957, flying ceased at Bramcote. The airfield was retained by the Ministry of Defence and handed over to the Army and known as Gamecock Barracks. At the time of writing, it is the home of the 30th Signals Regiment and also the county training centre of the Warwickshire & West Midlands Army Cadet Force.

5
CASTLE BROMWICH

Certainly few RAF stations during the Second World War could lay claim to such a long and rich aviation history as Castle Bromwich; as 'a flying ground' it even pre-dated the formation of the Royal Flying Corps. During the 1920/30s it was the centre of aviation activity in the county – private, club, commercial and military – and thousands of local people had visited the airfield during the Empire Air Days. They felt, with some justification, that it was 'their' airfield, after all it was the home of their own squadron – No 605 (County of Warwick).

In 1937 the Air Ministry decided to spend almost £¼ million on improvements to the station, which included a large 'C' type hangar, impressive headquarters buildings, accommodation blocks for all personnel, tennis and squash racquets courts but, alas, no hard runways! There were already two aircraft sheds at the airfield, each noted on the official plan as 'Old Midland Type', whatever that meant. All this new development work took place in the north-west corner of the airfield and the size of the investment, considering the amount that was then being expended on the construction of new stations, perhaps implied that the Air Ministry had plans for its future use either as an operational base or perhaps a major training station, actually neither of these materialised.

It can be said that Castle Bromwich's wartime future was really sealed in 1937 when plans were drawn up for a huge 'shadow factory' to be built near Birmingham. The site, covering three hundred and forty-five acres between Fort Dunlop and Castle Bromwich, was acquired from Birmingham Corporation by the Nuffield Organisation and construction work, financed by the Government, commenced in July 1938. The original intention of this new shadow factory was to manufacture Wellington bombers but this decision was speedily revoked in favour of the production of Supermarine Spitfires. The large flight shed situated on the eastern boundary of the airfield, complete with Spitfire turntable, was crowded with Spitfires in various stages of production throughout the Second World War.

The first Air Ministry contract for this truly legendary fighter was placed with Vickers (Aviation) Ltd (Supermarine had been acquired by Vickers in November 1928) in June 1936 and totalled three hundred and ten; this was just three months after the prototype Spitfire (K5054) made its maiden flight from Supermarine's works at Woolston near Southampton on 5th March 1936. The initial order was followed by another two hundred in 1937 and a further one thousand in April 1938. In October of that year Supermarine became a division of Vickers-Armstrong Ltd. It was quite clear that production figures of such magnitude were far beyond the resources of Supermarine's relatively small plant at Woolston, hence the reason why the large Castle Bromwich factory was designated for the manufacture of Spitfires. Indeed, it proved to be the largest factory of its kind in the country. By the outbreak of war orders for Spitfires totalled over two thousand.

In that uneasy interlude between the Munich crisis and the outbreak of war No 605 (County of Warwick) squadron changed from a light bomber unit to a fighter squadron, as did the majority of AAF squadrons. Thus in April 1939 the squadron began to re-equip with Gloster Gladiator Is and IIs – the RAF's last biplane fighter – which had entered the RAF in January 1937, by which time it was effectively obsolete with the emergence of the new monoplane fighters. During 1939 most of the Gladiator squadrons were being re-equipped with Hurricanes. In August 1939 No 605 left, as usual, for its summer camp at Tangmere, Sussex, and whilst there the pilots began to receive their first Hurricanes. The squadron returned briefly to Castle Bromwich but by the 27th of the month it was ordered back to Tangmere, thus leaving the airfield that had been its permanent home for the previous thirteen years.

At the outbreak of war No 14 E&RFTS, which had been managed by Air Work Ltd at Castle Bromwich since July 1937, amalgamated with No 20 E&RFTS (then at Gravesend, Kent) and No 44 at Elmdon, to form No 14 Elementary Flying Training School; within a week the new EFTS moved away to Elmdon. The official reason given for the transfer was that 'the barrage balloons defending Castle Bromwich factory posed a serious risk and hazard for the student pilots', although it might be said that Elmdon was perhaps only marginally safer in this respect.

In late September Blenheim IVs of No 90 squadron made a fleeting visit to Castle Bromwich. The squadron had recently moved from its pre-war base at West Raynham, Norfolk to Upwood, Huntingdonshire, where it had been removed from operational duties to become a Group training squadron; in April 1940 it would form the nucleus of No 17 OTU. I am not aware of the reason for its sudden appearance at Castle Bromwich. Perhaps it was part of Bomber Command's 'Scatter Plans'?

Castle Bromwich was now placed under the control of No 22 (Army Co-operation) Group of Fighter Command, and towards the end of April 1940 No 7 Anti-Aircraft Co-operation Unit (AACU) arrived from Ringway, Manchester, to establish its headquarters and set up maintenance and servicing facilities. Such Units had been formed in order to assist in the training of anti-aircraft gun and searchlight crews, assess their effectiveness and report back to the Anti-Aircraft Command, which was under the control of the redoubtable General Sir Frederick Pile. The Unit worked particularly closely with the Wolverhampton Searchlight School, providing 'live' targets for its trainee crews. Like all similar AACUs, No 7 had a number of Flights detached at other airfields, notably Abingdon. Orginally the Unit had been supplied with a motley assortment of civil aircraft impressed by the Air Ministry, including a few de Havilland D.H.90 Dragonflies, General Aircraft Monospars and Spartan Cruisers, but slowly these were replaced by 'proper' if somewhat redundant RAF aircraft such as Fairey Battles and Westland Lysanders.

The Lysander was a two-seater monoplane with a most distinctive high-wing configuration, which dated from June 1936, when it had been specifically designed for Army support duties. Unfortunately its operational inadequacies – low speed and inadequate firepower – had been severely exposed in France during May 1940, when losses of over 20% were suffered. By late 1940 they were being withdrawn from UK-based squadrons and thus new operating roles had to be found for them. The Lysander's STOL (short take-off and landing) ability meant it could operate from small airfields and landing grounds, and so there was a wide variety of suitable alternative tasks – target-towing, air-sea rescue and fighter affiliation, for instance. Of course, the black painted Lysanders of Nos 138 and 161 (Special Duties) squadrons gained

Westland Lysander: No 7 AACU and No 116 squadron operated Lysanders from the airfield.

lasting Second World War fame by delivering and picking-up agents of the Special Operations Executive by night in enemy-occupied Europe. Over 1,650 Lysanders ('Lizzies') were produced.

At the end of 1940 Castle Bromwich was allocated to the newly formed Army Co-operation Command and was one of the relatively few airfields in the country placed under its direct control. In the spring of 1941 a detachment of Lysanders of various marks of No 116 squadron arrived at the airfield. The squadron had been formed at Hendon on 15th February largely as the result of the advent of radar. This had brought a new task for the RAF in addition to the various radio calibration and other duties undertaken by the AACUs and their myriad flights. This squadron's main duty was the calibration of predictors and AA radar used by gun and searchlight batteries. It had taken as its motto 'Precision in Defence', which in the circumstances proved rather apt.

However, Castle Bromwich will be forever linked with the production of Spitfires during the Second World War; some 11,560 were built and assembled there and in its ancillary factories. Although the grand total appears to vary from 11,555 to 11,939, the exact figure has not been specifically established. With certainty, over half of some 20,400 Spitfires produced until February 1948 emanated from Castle Bromwich, a remarkable contribution to the manufacture of this legendary aircraft. The Spitfire was the most famous RAF fighter of all time. In the dark days of 1940 it was a symbol of defiance and hope, and some sixty-four years later the sight and sound of a Spitfire at air displays up and down the country can still thrill crowds of spectators, both young and old alike.

The Spitfire was the only Allied aircraft to remain in continuous development, production and active service throughout the Second World War (the last Hurricane was produced in September 1944). From its entry into the RAF in July 1938 until production ceased in October 1947, some twenty-two versions along with numerous variants were produced. The aircraft's power more than doubled, its maximum speed increased by a third, its rate of climb doubled and its fire power increased by a factor of five. No other Allied aircraft was so highly developed and improved in such a short space of time. Spitfires were used for high and low-level reconnaissance, as high-altitude interceptors and heavy bomber escorts, for photographic reconnaissance and meteorological duties and as tactical fighter-bombers. They also operated with the FAA, USAAF, Commonwealth Air Forces and another nineteen overseas air forces. The Spitfires operated in the RAF for nineteen years. The last operational sorties were made in Malaya on 1st April 1954, and the final meteorological flights were flown in June 1957.

Production of Spitfires by Morris Motors Ltd at Castle Bromwich started in 1939 but there was obviously a certain amount of friction between the management at Castle Bromwich (Oliver Boden was the General Manager until replaced by his Deputy, Herbert Clarke in March 1940) and the Supermarine Division of Vickers-Armstrong Ltd at Woolston. It was claimed that Supermarine were forever requesting parts from Castle Bromwich, which delayed the factory's production, and it was not until January 1940 that the first Spitfire fuselage, to be used as a pattern, was received from Woolston. Also, the wing sections caused problems before satisfactory assembly techniques were established. Lord Nuffield was a perfectionist, well used to the mass production of motor cars, but the various and constant modifications of the aircraft frustrated him greatly.

Nevertheless, within days of Lord Beaverbrook's being appointed the Minister of Aircraft Production in May 1940, he was deeply concerned to discover that not a single Spitfire had yet emerged from the Castle Bromwich factory. At this time Spitfires were in short supply and Sir Hugh Dowding was jealously conserving his Spitfire squadrons. Quite obviously the abrasive and ruthless Beaverbrook and Lord Nuffield (Sir William Morris) had a heated discussion about the reasons for the long delay. It was said that Lord Nuffield attempted to call Beaverbrook's bluff by saying: 'Perhaps you would like me to give up the control of the Spitfire factory?' Whereupon Beaverbrook quickly accepted the 'offer'! He handed control of the Castle Bromwich factory to Vickers. Lord Nuffield realised that he had been out-manoeuvred and he desperately tried to persuade Winston Churchill to reverse this decision, but Churchill adamantly refused to intervene.

Vickers proceeded to move a number of management staff and skilled workers from Woolston to Castle Bromwich to get production moving, and Stanley Woodley of the Supermarine division was appointed manager of the factory. Castle Bromwich had been earmarked to produce Spitfire IIs, which had first flown in the summer of 1939. In June ten Spitfire IIs were completed at Castle Bromwich, the first being delivered to the RAF on the 27th of the month and entering No 611 squadron in August. In June five hundred additional Spitfire IIs were ordered and Castle Bromwich could be said to be really up and running, with twenty-three built in July, thirty-seven in August and fifty-six in September; this was despite bombing raids in August.

The Spitfire II was essentially a Mark I but powered by a 1175hp Rolls-Royce Merlin XII engine with certain modifications and improvements to the airframe and extra armour-plating provided for the pilot and fuel tanks. It was produced in three variants – 'A' with the

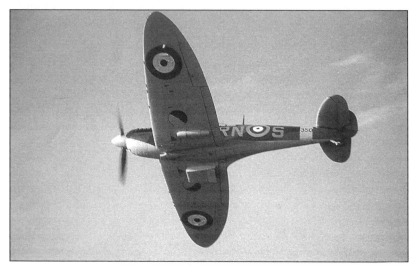

Spitfire II of No 72 squadron: all 921 Spitfire IIs were built at Castle Bromwich.

normal eight .303 inch Browning machine guns; 'B' with two 20mm Hispano cannons and four Brownings; and those used on air-sea rescue duties were designated 'C'. All of the nine hundred and twenty-one Spitfire IIs were built at Castle Bromwich.

The large factory at Castle Bromwich was obviously a prime target for the *Luftwaffe* and, in order to maintain production targets, it was clear that a number of dispersed sites should be found. Ultimately they included, for instance, a carpet warehouse in Kidderminster, an old prison in Worcester, Dudley Zoo, a silk works in Leicestershire, and, importantly, at Desford, an RAF airfield about six miles south-west of Leicester, where component parts were delivered from Castle Bromwich and within a week completed Spitfires appeared. Castle Bromwich's team of sixteen test pilots trialled the Spitfires at Desford. Such a dispersal of Spitfire production was not unusual as Supermarine would spread its production facilities far and wide to numerous factories in Wiltshire, Hampshire and Berkshire; also Westland Aircraft Ltd at Yeovil, Somerset, and Cunliffe-Owen Aircraft Ltd at Eastleigh, Hampshire were engaged in this mammoth wartime Spitfire production programme.

One thousand Spitfire IIIs were ordered in late October; it was the first serious attempt to improve the design and a Mark III first flew in March 1940. Largely because of a shortage of Merlin XX engines, the Mark III never went into production, and the order was ultimately completed as Mark Vs. By February 1941 the five-hundredth Spitfire had been completed at Castle Bromwich, and five months later the thousandth fighter left the works. At the end of 1941 almost one thousand three hundred Spitfires had been produced. The factory was now mainly producing Mark Vs in three versions – A to C. They were powered by Rolls-Royce Merlin 45 engines, which gave a maximum speed of 378mph. The 'A' and 'B' had a similar armament to the Mark II, but the Mark 'C' had been built with a so-called 'universal wing', which could accommodate four 20mm cannons and also carry a 500 pound bomb or two 250 pound bombs. The Mark V was the most prolific individual mark with some 6,470 being produced and they first entered the RAF in February 1941 with No 92 squadron. Spitfire Vs would equip one hundred and seventeen RAF squadrons at home and abroad. By the end of the year almost every day-fighter squadron had re-equipped with this version and Spitfire Vs provided the backbone of Fighter Command during 1941/2.

Like Armstrong Whitworth's works at Baginton, Castle Bromwich also attracted its share of VIPs. On 26th September 1941 Winston Churchill, accompanied by Eleanor Roosevelt, the wife of the US President, came to the factory. A display of flying was given by the test pilots, including amongst others Alex Henshaw, the celebrated pre-war racing pilot who had won the prestigious King's Cup Air Race in 1938 and who was chief test pilot at Castle Bromwich. Henshaw is reputed to have test flown one in ten of all Spitfires produced, more than any other pilot. Churchill's secretary, Sir John Colville, later recalled this day and recorded in his diary: 'Their performance was so daring as to be positively frightening and we shuddered as Henshaw flew over us upside down, some 40 feet from the ground.' It is interesting to note that Spitfire Vs of the US Eighth Air Force first went into action with the 31st Fighter Group on 26th July 1942.

The Spitfire was continually modified during the war to improve the performance and operational range as well as adapting it for various operational roles and theatres of war. These modifications to the airframes, the use of different engines and various types of armament, provision for carrying bombs and the other numerous minor refinements complicated production lines. During 1942 there was an urgent priority placed on the production of spares and in this year Castle Bromwich also became engaged in producing the Mark IXs, which had been developed in April to counter the *Luftwaffe*'s Focke-Wulf Fw 190A, which was markedly superior to a Spitfire V. The Mark IX was powered by a 1,600hp Merlin 61 engine driven by a four-blade propeller, giving a top speed of just over 400mph, and the first were delivered to No 80 squadron in May 1942. Some 5,660 Mark IXs were built – the second most numerous Mark – operating in ninety squadrons even after 1945. During 1942 the Castle Bromwich factory produced on average fifty Spitfires each week. Of course this figure reduced once the factory became engaged in producing Lancaster bombers.

In late September 1941 Vickers Armstrong received an order for the production of two hundred Avro Lancaster IIs. This was changed to Mark IIIs in February 1943 but were completed as Mark Is. To cope with these heavy aircraft, short concrete runways were laid at Castle Bromwich and the first production Lancaster III was tested there by Alex Henshaw on 16th October 1943. Another two hundred Mark Is were ordered in July 1943 but one hundred were cancelled and actually only ninety-nine were delivered. In December one hundred Mark IVs and Vs were ordered, followed in June 1944 by another one hundred,

Lancaster III of No 97 squadron: 299 Lancasters were produced at Castle Bromwich. (RAF Museum)

and fifty in December, but both contracts were cancelled. The factory's Lancaster production peaked in December 1944, when twenty-five were produced, in total two hundred and ninety-nine Lancasters were built at Castle Bromwich. Also, from the end of July 1943, Castle Bromwich repaired some seventy Wellingtons for the Brooklands Repair Organisation in Surrey.

What was happening at the neighbouring RAF airfield seemed to pale into insignificance against this frantic pace of aircraft production, but it should be remembered that some 34,000 Spitfire test flights took place from the airfield up until the end of November 1945 as well as Lancaster trial flights. Nevertheless, in March 1943, another AACU – No 6 – arrived with a mixture of Oxfords and Magisters. In June the airfield was passed back to Fighter Command, and on 1st December three AACUs, Nos 6, 7 and 8, were amalgamated to form No 577 squadron, which continued with anti-aircraft co-operation duties. As with all such squadrons and units, many of its aircraft were dispersed to other airfields – twelve in total – Sealand, Flintshire, Wrexham and Ipswich, Suffolk, to name just a few. The squadron was originally equipped with Hurricane IXs and Oxfords but later received some Spitfire VBs, Beaufighters, as well as a rather unusual and fairly rare

Vultee A31 Vengeance operated with No 577 squadron.

aircraft – Vultee A31 Vengeance IV. This was an American-built two-seater dive-bomber and some four hundred had been purchased by the British Purchasing Commission in 1940. The RAF found them highly unsuitable for operations in Europe and they subsequently equipped four squadrons in Burma. The remainder were converted to target tugs and served as such in nine squadrons. No 577 squadron soldiered on at Castle Bromwich until it was disbanded in June 1946.

Spitfire production at Castle Bromwich continued unbounded. The demand for this fighter and its spares seemed insatiable. On 1st June 1944 there were over five thousand six hundred Spitfires in service with the RAF, and during that month Castle Bromwich produced three hundred and twenty Spitfires along with twenty Lancasters, the highest output of any aircraft factory in the country. Mark IXs were built alongside yet another new Mark – XVI. This version was the last to be powered by a Merlin engine, albeit the American-built Packard Merlin 226 (equivalent to the British low altitude Merlin 66). Over seven thousand IXs and XVIs were finally produced, the latter mark operating with forty-four squadrons and remaining in service until July 1951.

Earlier in January Castle Bromwich had received an order for fifteen hundred Mark 21s, which were powered by a Rolls-Royce Griffon 61 engine driven by a five-blade propeller. Back in 1942 it was recognised that the Merlin engine had been developed to its full potential and the Air Ministry asked Rolls-Royce to resuscitate their Griffon engine that dated back to 1939, when it had been shelved because of the intense

Fifty-three Spitfire IXs and a couple of Lancasters on the apron outside Castle Bromwich Flight Shed in the spring of 1944. (Imperial War Museum)

development of the Merlin engine. The evolution of the Mark 21 had been a rather prolonged affair as the larger and more powerful Griffon engine required a number of airframe changes, and the wing had been redesigned and strengthened. The test flying of the prototype had disclosed handling problems and when it was trialled by the Air Fighting Development Unit, the verdict was not promising to say the least: 'although the Spitfire 21 is not a dangerous aircraft to fly, pilots must be warned of its handling qualities ... in its present state it is unsatisfactory both for air-to-air gunnery and ground attack ... and compares most unfavourably with other modern fighters.' However, its control problems were resolved and the Mark 21, now powered by a Griffon 65 engine, managed to attain a top speed of 450mph at 19,000 feet. One hundred and twenty Spitfire 21s were built; the first went into service with No 91 squadron in April 1945. This version did at least lead to the last two Spitfire marks – the 22 and 24 – and their Seafire equivalent 46 and 47.

During the last twelve months or so of the war, the Castle Bromwich factory received a number of orders for various Marks of Spitfires – IXs, XVIs and 22s – but these were often amended at short notice and some were cancelled. At this stage of the war the RAF was in the fortunate position of having an adundance of Spitfire squadrons and their future was somewhat uncertain with the arrival of the turbojet-powered Gloster Meteors in July 1944. However, during this period the factory produced some six hundred Spitfires for the Soviet Union. The last Spitfire (PK614) – a Mark 22 – left the factory on 30th November 1945 and in the following month the factory closed. Ultimately, most of the Castle Bromwich factory was purchased by Fisher & Ludlow Ltd and was acquired by the British Motor Corporation in 1953.

It seemed highly appropriate, considering the number of Spitfires that had been built at Castle Bromwich, that the RAF station hosted an 'At Home' on 15th September 1945 to commemorate the fifth anniversary of the Battle of Britain, which established the universal fame of this legendary fighter. Castle Bromwich was one of ninety-three RAF stations that opened their gates on the first 'At Home' day. These occasions, held at RAF stations up and down the country,

The de Havilland Chipmunk: the most numerous aircraft to be seen at Castle Bromwich during the 1950s.

128

became an increasingly popular feature of the post-war years attracting large crowds. It was estimated that over 145,000 attended the Castle Bromwich 'At Home' and air display on 17th September 1955. The last occasion that Castle Bromwich was 'At Home' to the public was on 14th September 1957.

After the war, Castle Bromwich reverted to a training station of the Reserve Command, which was re-named the Home Command in July 1950. On 1st November 1947 No 44 Reserve Centre was formed, along with No 5 Reserve Flying

The station badge of RAF Castle Bromwich. (RAF Museum)

School; the school, operated by Birkett Air Services Ltd, used Avro Ansons, Tiger Moths, a handful of Percival Prentices, and more latterly de Havilland Chipmunks. The Chipmunk had first flown in May 1946 and became the RAF's standard elementary trainer, a fine replacement for the beloved Tiger Moth. Indeed Chipmunks were the most numerous aircraft using Castle Bromwich during the 1950s, as they also equipped the Birmingham University Air Squadron, which was based at Castle Bromwich until March 1958. No 5 RFS, like all such schools, was disbanded in June 1954.

The sixty-acre British Industries Fair site at the south-west corner of the airfield, convenient for Castle Bromwich railway station, attracted a number of civil aircraft to the airfield. In 1955 royal approval was granted for an official badge for RAF Castle Bromwich. It portrayed a sprig of broom in a bricked crown with a motto 'Supra Urbem Alae Nostrae Volant' or 'Our Wings Rise Over the City'. Two years later

(August 1957), HM Queen Elizabeth II arrived at Castle Bromwich in a Heron of the Queen's Flight en route to an official engagement elsewhere in the county.

From March 1955 No 1955 (AOP) Flight of No 663 squadron operated British Taylorcraft Auster AOP (Air Observation Post) 6s and 7s along with Chipmunks from the airfield until the Flight was disbanded on 10th March 1957. It was rather fitting that a Spitfire IX (ML427) at Castle Bromwich was displayed as 'a gate guard' at the entrance to the airfield. However, the last scheduled flight left the airfield on 14th March 1958 – a Chipmunk flown by the Station Commander – and at the end of the month RAF Castle Bromwich finally closed down; the RAF ensign was lowered for the last time, thus bringing to a close some forty-four years of military flying – a historic day indeed. In September 1960 the airfield site (350 acres) was sold to the city corporation and a massive new housing development – Castle Vale – finally covered the old airfield. However, on 8th October 1965, a memorial to RAF Castle Bromwich, sited on a green in the Castle Vale estate, was unveiled by Alex Henshaw. This memorial has as its centrepiece a large RAF badge in bronze that had been in place over the Officers' Mess at Castle Bromwich since 1938; the memorial has since been removed to the grounds of St Cuthbert's Church, Tangmere Drive.

6
CHURCH LAWFORD

It was perhaps a little ironic to discover, whilst searching for the site of this airfield in September 2003, that there was a plethora of notices and placards in the nearby villages exhorting the local residents to say 'No to Rugby Airport'. This was certainly a climate change from sixty-three years ago when probably not a single soul complained about the wartime airfield that was being hastily constructed on Lawford Heath by the road to Long Lawford, a couple of miles due south of the village and three and a half miles west-south-west of Rugby.

Church Lawford, like neighbouring Bramcote, was planned as a bomber station. However, unlike Bramcote, it had been provided with three concrete runways covered with tarmac: two were 1,400 yards in length, with the third shorter at 1,200 yards. At the time of the airfield's construction – 1940 and early 1941 – the Air Ministry had not yet settled on standard runway lengths considered essential for bomber airfields, although the runways would be later lengthened. However, because no hard-standings had been laid down, it seemed most unlikely that heavy bombers would ultimately use the airfield. Nevertheless, Church Lawford was supplied with ample hangarage, one large 'aircraft shed', six Bellmans and later ten Blisters (four 'Over' and six 'Extra Over'). The presence of the latter was a sure sign that a considerable number of training aircraft would operate from Church Lawford; these were invariably of wooden construction and thus they really needed to be stored in hangars for protection against the elements. The only possible flying hazard was the close proximity of the Rugby wireless masts, but at least they also provided a good landmark for trainee pilots.

The airfield was finally completed in the late spring of 1941. The main Technical and Training sites were immediately to the east of the airfield proper, with two dispersed sites for the living quarters of the officers and airmen further to the east and over the other side of the Long Lawford road. On 1st May an advance party of officers and airmen arrived from RAF Cranwell to prepare the new station for occupation. It ultimately housed about 1,600 permanent staff, including some 400 WAAFs. The airfield had been placed under the control of No 23 Group of the Flying Training Command, which then had its headquarters at Grantham. The unit destined to serve at Church Lawford was No 2 Central Flying School that had been newly formed in the previous year.

At the outbreak of the war the RAF college at Cranwell formally closed and almost immediately reopened as the RAF College Service Flying School. In 1940 numerous and various new courses and schools were established at Cranwell, including an additional school for training flying instructors. As has already been noted, the Central Flying School had long been responsible for the training of flying instructors. Since the school's move from Wittering to Upavon, Wiltshire, in 1935, it had been given many additional tasks and responsibilities. It was now fully recognised that there would be a major requirement for flying instructors; thus in September 1940 No 2 Flying Instructors' School had been formed under Wing Commander Darvell; in November it became known as No 2 Central Flying School, a proud name steeped in the rich traditions and history of the Service.

The reason for the school's move to Church Lawford in May 1941 was perhaps a matter of sheer logistics. Cranwell was crammed with training aircraft. Indeed, in the following year it became the largest RAF station in the country, with some 7,000 service and 3,000 civilian personnel. Such was the pressure on the crowded airspace around Cranwell that a number of smaller airfields were sought to ease the situation. So the presence of a new airfield was a heaven-sent opportunity to alleviate the situation and No 2 CFS moved into Church Lawford on 30th May, just eighteen days after the airfield had been formally opened. It would take another fortnight or so before the school's move was finalised – at the completion of its No 11 course. However, two of the school's flights remained at Cranwell, but in October they moved to two airfields in Scotland – Montrose and Dalcross.

Originally the school was designed to train flying instructors for both Elementary and Advanced Flying Schools. The intake of students – all experienced pilots – was forty to forty-five each fortnight and the course was planned to last eight weeks. The majority were trained for

Church Lawford was 'awash' with Airspeed Oxfords.

instruction on multi-engined aircraft, as they were needed in a far greater number than those for single-engined aircraft. The proportion was about 3:1, such was the requirement for Bomber and Coastal Commands pilots.

The school was equipped with fifty Airspeed Oxford Is and IIs, twenty-eight Avro Tutors and a General Aircraft Monospar. Indeed, throughout the Second World War Church Lawford was 'awash' with Oxfords, and, because of the number of small landing grounds used by Church Lawford's Oxfords and their manufacture at Ansty, Oxfords rivalled or maybe surpassed Wellingtons as the most numerous aircraft to be seen in the wartime skies over Warwickshire.

For its time, the Oxford was quite a remarkable aircraft with dual controls as standard. Although normally manned by three crew, it also provided six crew stations for various training duties. It was primarily intended for advanced flying training for pilots, but also provided facilities for pupil navigators, bomb aimers, air gunners, and radio and camera operators, without doubt the most complete training aircraft yet produced for the RAF. Moreover, the relatively small but sturdy aircraft had been specially designed to have handling qualities similar to those of far larger and heavier aircraft and was never intended to be an easy aircraft to fly. It was generally accepted that 'if you can handle an Oxford with reasonable competence, you could tackle almost anything in the way of recalcitrant twins and multis'; they were mainly used to train pilots for service on multi-engined aircraft.

The Mark I Oxford was provided with an Armstrong Whitworth turret amidships armed with a single .303 inch Lewis-type machine gun, whereas in the Mark II the turret had been removed. Both were powered by two Armstrong Siddeley 375hp Cheetah radial engines, and perhaps flat out an Oxford could be nursed to 185mph but cruised at a more leisurely pace of about 140mph. They were used for a number of roles besides flying training – air ambulances, radio calibration work, beam approach training, and target-towers. Oxfords also equipped countless flying schools abroad under the Empire Air Training Scheme.

Almost in direct contrast, the school's other training aircraft – Avro 621 Tutor – recalled a far different age of flying – the days when the RAF was still a biplane air force. As a two-seater biplane, it had first appeared in December 1929, following in the long tradition of Avro trainers for the RAF. It underwent service trials against other aircraft and was selected to replace the Avro 504N as the standard elementary

Avro 621 Tutors of the Central Flying School demonstrating inverted flying. (RAF Museum)

trainer, and an Air Ministry order was placed for twenty-one. The standard Tutors began to arrive at the CFS in 1933 and were powered by a 215hp Armstrong Siddeley Lynx IVC engine, giving a top speed of 120mph and a cruising speed of maybe 97mph. Pilots said that they were 'a delight to fly' and they proved to be ideal aircraft for aerobatics. Tutors first made an impression and impact during the RAF Hendon Display in June 1933, when six Tutors of the CFS gave a magnificent exhibition of 'inverted' formation flying, which then became a most popular feature of these displays over the next four years. Just under eight hundred Tutors had been built when production ceased in May 1936. Although to a large extent Tutors were replaced by the Magister monoplane trainer, they could still be found in AAF and university air squadrons and they remained in service until officially withdrawn in October 1947. The solitary Monospar also dated back to the early 1930s. General Aircraft Ltd produced a series of small twin-engined airliners for both civil and private owners. Their most famous was the ST-25 or so-called *Jubilee*, as it was produced in 1935 – King George V's Silver Jubilee year. This rather squat aircraft carried up to six passengers and could cruise at about 130mph; it was possibly used by the school as a communication aircraft.

The sheer intensity of flying training of whatever description placed a heavy strain on the flying resources and facilities at the parent airfield and no stone was left unturned to provide Relief Landing Grounds (RLGs), which could be used for the innumerable practice take-offs, landings and circuit flying. In this respect No 2 CFS was quite fortunate as it so happened that in June 1941 a small grassed airfield at Sibson, about seven miles south-west of Peterborough, which had up until then been used by Oxfords of No 14 SFTS, based at Cranfield, Bedfordshire, became available. Thus, from 15th June, Sibson was used by the school. In fact, on 21st August, one of the school's Oxfords was written-off at Sibson when it struck a water tank on the landing approach. The school had to share the facilities at Sibson with Tiger Moths of No 17 EFTS, stationed at nearby RAF Peterborough. However, when Sibson passed under the direct control of Peterborough, No 2 CFS was forced to find suitable alternatives. In July the school's Oxfords started to use another small grassed RLG at Southam, which was already being used by Tiger Moths of No 9 EFTS based at Ansty. In January 1942 an RLG at Warwick was brought into use by the school and the RLG remained in constant use by training aircraft from Church Lawford

The spacious cabin of an Oxford with the second pilot's seat moved to allow room for use with a folding chart-board. (via L. Henderson)

until the end of the war. Later in 1942 a rather 'up-market' RLG at Hockley Heath, ten miles south-south-east of Birmingham, was brought into use for Church Lawford's Oxfords and Tutors. But it would be another nine months (May 1943) before Church Lawford was allocated a genuine satellite airfield at Snitterfield, about three miles to the north of Stratford-upon-Avon. Details of all these landing grounds will appear later.

January 1942 brought some changes, at least in the designation of the five schools engaged in training flying instructors. On the 19th No 2 CFS was renamed No 1 Flying Instructors' School. Despite the new name, though, most of its staff still considered that they belonged to the 'real' Central Flying School because of its long history and traditions. This was especially so in March when the CFS, still based at Upavon, also lost its identity and became known as the Empire Central Flying School, moving to Hullavington, Wiltshire. This change of name was intended to reflect the vast experience gained by the RAF's worldwide training organisation and to establish standardised training procedures and ensure that they were maintained in all training schools throughout the world. The Central Flying School, as such, was not reactivated until May 1946.

Despite a different name very little else had changed at Church Lawford. The school continued training instructors for the Elementary and Service Flying Schools but it was now additionally training instructors for the Advanced Flying Units, the first of which had recently formed. The Air Ministry had finally accepted that pilots posted to Operational Training Units as flying instructors after completion of their operational tours should receive instruction in 'the standard methods of flying training procedures' and the finer arts of instruction. Many of these battle-hardened pilots were firmly convinced that these courses were mainly to eradicate the bad flying habits they had acquired during their time on operational squadrons! The operational training instructor's course was scheduled to last for four weeks, and these courses became an increasingly important aspect of the type of flying instruction conducted at Church Lawford.

In April, No 1509 BAT Flight was formed at Church Lawford, which inevitably brought an increase in the number of Oxfords based at the airfield. Because the school was solely instructing experienced pilots, there was no need for Beam Approach training to be part of the course syllabus; therefore, the Flight left for Dyce in Scotland during May. However, No 1 School, itself, had a relatively brief existence. In late October it was disbanded and immediately re-formed as No 18 (Pilots) Advanced Flying Unit.

These units had been set up to bridge the gap between the advanced flying training schools undertaken overseas under EATS and the numerous and various OTUs. It had been recognised that some kind of 'refresher' flying training was needed, especially as the newly-qualified pilots had completed all their flying training in the clear, bright and open skies found in Canada, Australia, etc., but now they had to cope with the highly congested and grey skies of blacked-out Britain and acclimatise themselves to a very different and far more dangerous flying environment. The course lasted between three and four weeks, depending on the weather, and was planned to include about thirty hours of flying time with the greater emphasis placed upon night exercises, circuits and landings, for obvious reasons. By the close of 1942 there were thirteen AFUs in operation, the majority engaged in training pilots for subsequent service flying twin or multi-engined aircraft. By 1944 the course had been extended to eight weeks, with the newly-qualified pilots completing double the number of flying hours, or even more if the weather conditions allowed. Operational commands and more especially Bomber had pressurised Flying

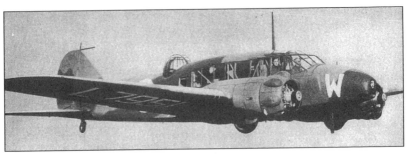

Avro 652A Anson on navigational duties. L7951 was an early production model.

Training Command to produce more *experienced* pilots in an attempt to reduce the high accident rate that was prevalent at OTUs.

Perhaps it is needless to mention that No 18 (P)AFU was almost entirely equipped with Oxfords, although a solitary Avro Tutor had been retained at Church Lawford (for sentimental reasons?). The Unit was also supplied with a handful of Avro Ansons, which were used for communication duties but of course they also doubled as navigation and radio trainers. The Anson, like the Oxford, owed its origin to a small but fast four-passenger and mail carrying airliner, although only two were actually built and operated with Imperial Airways. The prototype military version – 652A – made its maiden flight on 24th March 1935 and was named Anson in honour of Lord George Anson, Admiral of the Fleet in the eighteenth century. This resulted in a slight fracas with the Admiralty, as they considered they held the sole right to use names of famous sailors; the Air Ministry agreed that such a faux pas would not happen again! When the Anson entered the RAF almost exactly a year later, on 16th March 1936, it became the Service's first monoplane and also the first to be fitted with a retractable under-carriage. They were originally designed as a twin-engined coastal reconnaissance aircraft, armed with a manually operated turret, a forward firing Lewis gun and capable of carrying 360 pounds of bombs. Ansons successfully served in Coastal Command until replaced by the American Lockheed Hudsons. In the late 1930s its worth as a trainer for all types of aircrew was fully recognised and in December 1939 the Anson was selected as one of the standard training aircraft for EATS and orders were placed for over two thousand three hundred.

The Anson's reliability and proven low accident rate gained it the nickname the 'Faithful Annie' and furthermore, like Oxfords, Ansons were powered by Armstrong Siddeley Cheetah engines, which made life somewhat simpler for the ground crews at Church Lawford. The aircraft enjoyed one of the longest production runs of any RAF aircraft and four short of eleven thousand (in more than twenty versions) were built between 1935 and May 1952. At their peak production during 1943/4 one hundred and thirty-five were flowing off Avro's assembly lines each month. Six Ansons, or 'Flying Greenhouses', so called because of the array of windows along the fuselage, made their farewell RAF flight with a ceremonial formation flypast over their final RAF base at Bovingdon, Hertfordshire on 29th June 1968.

The formation of the new Advanced Flying Unit meant that Beam Approach training was now back on the course agenda. The majority of the pilots, having trained overseas, had scant knowledge or experience of SBA. Therefore, a new BAT Flight, No 1533, was formed at Church Lawford and yes, of course, it was equipped with Oxfords. This Flight mainly confined its flying training to the shorter runway.

Since 1941 the *Luftwaffe* had attempted to target operational and training aircraft by making intruder raids at night and attacking as the aircraft were entering or in an airfield's circuit. As one German General of its *Fernnachtjager* (Night Intruder force) commented, 'When I want to kill wasps. I smoke them out of their nest. I don't swat the insects in the air one at a time. I go to their nest when they are in'! The various training units in Warwickshire were situated a little too far west to experience many problems during the early years, although both Gaydon and Wellesbourne Mountford did suffer an occasional attack. However, during March to June 1944 the *Luftwaffe* greatly increased the number of night intruder raids over operational and training airfields

Messerschmitt 410A-1: one collided with an Oxford near the airfield on 26th/27th April 1944.

139

D.H. 89B Dominies used for navigational and wireless training.

in East Anglia and eastern England, with, sad to say, more than a modicum of success. For these intruder raids the *Luftwaffe* used its much-vaunted Messerschmitt 410As, a heavy two-seat fighter. On the night of 26th/27th April an Oxford I (LX196) collided with a Me 410A-1 whilst in the landing circuit above Church Lawford and sadly Pilot Officer C. G. W. Moore, a Canadian airman, and two crewmen were killed; the Oxford crashed at Frankton near Rugby, the two German airmen were also killed. This was the twenty-fifth and last Allied aircraft to be lost to enemy intruders during April. It was the only fatality on that specific night but it might have been far worse because at this period the airfield was experiencing its busiest time of the war; by the end of September over one hundred and seventy Oxfords were operating from Church Lawford. This total had been boosted by Oxfords of Nos 1514 and 1546 BAT Flights, which had taken up temporary residence.

In March 1945 No 21 Group's Communication Flight moved into Church Lawford, the Air Ministry had decided that the airfield would remain in operational use by Flying Training Command, certainly at least for the foreseeable future. This Flight brought a few different aircraft to the airfield and amongst them – a de Havilland D.H.89B Dominie. This was the military version of the company's most successful small Dragon-Rapide passenger biplane, which dated back to July 1934. However, the first Dominies did not enter the Service until

No 20 SFTS was equipped with North American Harvards for advanced flying training.

September 1939 and were used as 8/10 passenger aircraft. They were also employed on wireless and navigation training. When the production of Dominies ceased in July 1946, over five hundred and twenty had been built for the RAF, some three hundred and thirty by Brush Coachworks Ltd of Loughborough. The Flight also had a couple of Percival Proctors, which were of a similar vintage to the military Dominies, having first flown in December 1939; they were also used mainly for radio training and communications.

By this latter stage of the war the demand for refresher pilot training had rapidly declined and Flying Training Command sought a new temporary home for No 18 (P)AFU; Ashbourne and Darley Moor, both in Derbyshire, were under active consideration, but in early April the Unit moved away to Church Lawford's satellite airfield at Snitterfield. The reason for the Unit's departure was the formation of a new Service Flying Training School – No 20 – at Church Lawford, which used North American Harvards for advanced flying training along with some Tiger Moths. This, of course, meant that No 1533 BAT Flight was no longer needed and it was disbanded; with its demise the last Oxfords left, on what was possibly a rather sad day for those airmen stationed there, as they had acquired a real affection for the trusty and reliable 'Ox-boxes'.

In the post-war years Church Lawford was destined to have a fairly brief existence. No 20 Service Flying Training School was re-numbered No 2 in July 1947 and was still training pilots with its Tiger Moths and Harvards; but in the following March the school was transferred to South Cerney, Gloucestershire, which since 1936 had been involved in various types of flying training. With the school's departure, all flying ceased at Church Lawford and the airfield was placed on a Care and Maintenance basis. It finally closed and was sold in the mid-1950s. The airfield itself is now partly a landfill site and there are a number of commercial companies occupying buildings at the Lawford Heath Industrial site. On 16th December 2003, a contentious debate over a proposed new Rugby airport was resolved with the publication of a Government White Paper on aviation. This ruled out the construction of another Midlands airport between Rugby and Coventry.

7
ELMDON

Today, when one visits Elmdon – the very busy Birmingham International Airport – it is almost impossible to visualise a time when the airfield was crowded with Tiger Moths. These rather elegant and deceptively delicate looking biplanes appeared even more diminutive when compared with the Stirling and Lancaster heavy bombers that had been produced at Austin's factories at Longbridge and Marston Green and were awaiting their trial flights. But nevertheless this was the scene at Elmdon for most of the Second World War.

Elmdon opened for flying on 1st May 1939 and on the same day Air Work Ltd established there a new Elementary and Reserve Flying Training School, numbered forty-four, although in fact it was the thirty-sixth such school to be formed since 1935. Thus arrived the ubiquitous Tiger Moths along with some Miles Magisters and Hawker

A de Havilland Tiger Moth II – 1942. (RAF Museum)

143

Hinds. The latter aircraft had first appeared in September 1934 as a day bomber, although most considered it nothing more than an operational trainer. Three years later, as they were being superseded by the Battle and Blenheim monoplanes, it was decided to officially adapt the some five hundred Hinds as training aircraft. The armament was removed, dual controls and full instrumentation installed and the rear cockpit accommodated a flying instructor. Very few pilots serving at the outbreak of the war had not flown Hinds at some time in their pre-war RAF service. With a top speed of 160mph it was markedly different from a Tiger Moth. Group Captain Hugh Dundas described it as 'like driving a Bentley after pottering around in an old Austin tourer'.

No 44 School had a relatively brief existence because at the outbreak of the war it was disbanded and amalgamated with two similar schools, Nos 14 and 20, to form a new Elementary Flying Training School – No 14 – at nearby Castle Bromwich. It was placed in No 51 Group of Flying Training Command, then based at Leeds. However, on 10th September the new school moved into Elmdon, where it remained and was active until February 1946 training pilots for both the Royal Air Force and the Fleet Air Arm. On the previous day Wellington IAs of No 99 (Madras Presidency) squadron arrived at Elmdon from Mildenhall, Suffolk, under Bomber Command's Scatter Plans. It must be said that during the first few weeks of the war the dispersal of bomber squadrons from their operational stations resulted in a considerable number of wasteful aircraft movements, which frustrated crews and placed an unnecessary burden on ground crews responsible for strict maintenance and servicing schedules. These plans certainly reduced Bomber Command's capabilities as an strike force for most of September. On 15th September the squadron departed for Newmarket Heath, where it remained until March 1941.

On the following day the Air Ministry formally requisitioned Elmdon. The school's civilian flying instructors had also been seconded into the RAF and given appropriate ranks and the school's Tiger Moths began to resemble military aircraft: their upper fuselages were camouflaged, RAF roundels were applied and their wing undersides and tips were painted in training yellow. It is thought that over one hundred and twenty-five Tiger Moths were operated by No 14 EFTS during some six and a half years but the total number could have been more.

The young and enthusiastic student pilots were on the first step of the ladder to their cherished ambition – the award of their wings – the

Student pilots with their flying instructor, a Tiger Moth in the background.

hallmark of professional competence. They would discover that the path would not be easy; indeed, many fell by the wayside at this elementary stage. The most dreaded news for any student was that he had to undertake a Backward Progress Test, conducted by the Chief Flying Instructor. Most of these resulted in the student being failed and given a 'Bowler Hat' – RAF slang for being seconded to ground duties. The failure rate at EFTS averaged about 30%.

The course comprised as much practical flying experience as possible – cross-country exercises, countless take-offs, circuits and three point landings, forced and cross-wind landings and aerobatics, the latter considered very necessary to improve the student's confidence in the air and his ability to control his aircraft. They were expected to accomplish rolls, tail glides, spins, loops, figures of eight, and side slips until they were completely in tune with their aircraft.

The students' ground training included many hours spent 'flying' on the ground in the covered cockpit of the Link trainer, so named after its American inventor – Edward Albert Link. This was effectively a miniature aircraft, complete with instruments, miniature tails and wings and a hooded fuselage. It was able to move from side to side, and up and down, and fairly accurately simulated flying. The pupils were required to respond to instructions from the Link instructor, with the appartus's automatic recorder, known as the 'crab', faithfully tracing all the student pilots' reactions and errors. As the Air Ministry official hand-out stated, 'The Link Trainer saves valuable hours of

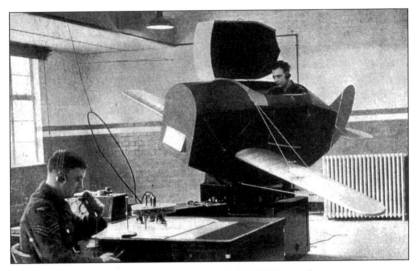

A Link trainer – learning to fly on the ground. (RAF Museum)

instruction in the air, as well as lives and aircraft.' From such humble beginnings came the highly sophisticated aircraft simulators of today. This introduction to instrument training came later on in the course when the trainee pilots had completed a fair amount of flying and their visual judgement had developed. Now they had to put all this ground experience into practice in the rear cockpit of their Moths, suitably covered with blind flying hoods. Many pilots remember this as one of the most frightening and exacting parts of the course.

Considering that the school operated for over six years with literally thousands upon thousands of training flights, circuits and landings both by day and night, it is quite remarkable that only twenty-seven Tiger Moths were *known* to have been written-off in flying accidents. Like most EFTSs the highest incidence of accidents occurred during the compulsory forced landings, which were normally executed on rough and uneven fields with hedges and trees offering other additional hazards to the inexperienced pilots. High-tension and barrage balloon cables also provided particular dangers in low flying practice. Indeed, the first two accidents suffered by the school were so caused. On 12th November 1939 a Tiger Moth crashed about a half a mile from Ansty whilst the pilot was attempting a forced landing, and on New Year's Day 1940 a Moth hit high-tension cables near Tamworth. Of course, weather conditions and poor visibility were other contributory factors but inexperience and pilot error probably accounted for a number of accidents due to stalled engines at low altitudes, when the margin of error was insufficient to recover control of the aircraft. But, because of the relatively slow speeds and the fairly robust construction and forgiving nature of Tiger Moths, fatalities were mercifully far fewer than at SFTSs and OTUs.

Of the sixteen Elementary Flying Training Schools operating in the United Kingdom during 1944, all but three used grassed airfields, which in truth were more than adequate for Tiger Moths. Therefore Elmdon with its two concrete runways, which had been constructed for the test flying of the heavy bombers, was a rare bonus for the school and its endless stream of trainee pilots, and provided them with valuable experience of the different braking effect of concrete rather than grass. The two runways were of almost equal length – 1,420 and 1,390 yards – both were 50 yards wide. Furthermore, there were no natural or man-made obstructions in the vicinity of the airfield to pose additional threats for the young pilots. In fact, Hamshall power station, about $5\frac{1}{2}$ miles north-east of the airfield, was recorded as a prominent landmark and it provided the students with a valuable navigational guide.

The airfield's brand new terminal building, duly clad with camouflage netting, was brought into use but the necessary accommodation blocks and classrooms for the three hundred and forty or so officers and men of the school and its trainee pilots were all of prefabricated construction and of a temporary nature. The airfield's original large hangar, which had been erected in early 1939, was quickly augmented by another two, along with two Bellman and nine Blister hangars.

The fever of aircraft production that was taking place at Austin's factory at Longbridge hardly impinged on Elmdon until late 1940. Since October 1938 the company had been producing Fairey Battles, and by August 1940 over eight hundred and sixty had been delivered; a proportion of these had been supplied in a 'knocked-down' state for ultimate transportation to Canada, Australia and South Africa. Since February 1940 the Battles had been transported to RAF Worcester for test flying and delivery. The three hundred Hurricane IIBs that were built by Austin during 1940/1 were flown from their small grassed airfield at Crofton Hackett to Elmdon for testing. The first Hurricane left there on 8th October 1940. From then onwards Elmdon was used for the test flying of Hurricanes, Stirlings and Lancasters.

Short Stirling I awaiting delivery at Elmdon – July 1941: over 500 Mark Is and IIIs were test flown and delivered from Elmdon.

In January 1939 Austin Motor Company had became part of what was known as the Stirling Group, which also comprised Short Brothers and the Rootes Group, and was formed to organise the production of various components of the new heavy bomber; Stirlings were ultimately produced in more than twenty different factories, and a countless number of sub-contractors produced component parts. In late 1939 Austin was given a contract for the production of one hundred and ninety-one Short S.29 Stirling Is – the RAF's latest (and first four-engined) heavy bomber. The first prototype had flown in May 1939 but unfortunately it crashed on landing when its undercarriage collapsed, which delayed the test flight programme. Nevertheless, the first production aircraft appeared twelve months later and in August 1940 No 7 squadron received its first Stirlings, which went into action on the night of 10th/11th February 1941.

Of the three major four-engined bombers, the Stirling was the highest off the ground (22 ft 9 ins to the cockpit), the longest at 87 ft 3 ins but with a relatively short wing-span of 99 ft (deliberately restricted on the express orders of the Air Ministry to ensure that the bomber fitted inside the normal RAF hangar!). With four 1,650hp Bristol Hercules XVI engines, it had a cruising speed of under 200mph and an operational ceiling of about 17,000 feet, and as a result it suffered proportionally heavier losses than either the Lancaster or

Halifax – 3.39% against 2.20% and 2.28%. There is no doubt that the Stirling looked rather ungainly on the ground and, at first sight, could be quite daunting to new crews. In flight it proved to be very manoeuvrable, gaining the name of the 'fighter bomber' by *Luftwaffe* fighter pilots, not because of its eight .303 inch machine guns in three turrets but rather because by repute it could turn inside a Spitfire. Famously, a Stirling of No 218 squadron returning from a night raid in June 1942 suffered continual attacks from four enemy night fighters but its gunners destroyed three and the aircraft returned to its home base, very heavily damaged but safely. The Stirling was a very sturdy aircraft, able to sustain considerable damage and reputed to be 'built like a battleship but it flew like a bird'. The aircraft had a maximum bomb load of 14,000 pounds with a range capable of delivering what Winston Churchill called 'the shattering strikes of retributive justice'. The RAF's *Official History* considered its performance 'disappointing' and Air Chief Marshal Harris held little regard for the bomber, but it served his command well, equipping thirteen squadrons at its peak and making 18,400 operational sorties until early September 1944. Stirlings also served as transports, glider towers and troop carriers, with over 2,360 being produced in four versions.

The Stirling contract necessitated the use of Elmdon for test flying, and thus the provision of concrete runways. Another requirement was the means to transport the aircraft from the factory at Marston Green, where the final assembly of the Stirlings and later Lancasters was completed. A concrete track was laid down from Marston Green, situated to the north-west, to the airfield and along this track the heavy bombers were towed. By October 1944 six hundred and twenty Stirlings had made their way to Elmdon for test flights. The only crash during test flying occurred on 10th January 1943, when a Stirling III (BK660) stalled at 1,000 feet and crashed on the Coventry road not far from Elmdon, but the crew were safe. Mark IIIs had been provided with the more powerful Bristol Hercules VI or XVI engines and new dorsal turrets; they were the most numerous of all Stirling marks. The last Stirlings built by Austin were converted to Mark IVs, specially adapted for use with airborne forces; the nose and dorsal turrets were removed and glider towing equipment installed. In total five hundred and twenty Sirling Is and IIIs were built by Austin.

From late 1943 the Austin factories were also engaged in building Lancaster Is. The Avro Lancaster was undisputedly the finest British, if

Avro Lancaster: the most famous RAF heavy bomber of the war. Some 330 were delivered from Elmdon. (Imperial War Museum)

not to say Allied, heavy bomber of the Second World War. Air Chief Marshal Harris could hardly find adequate words to praise the aircraft sufficiently, 'It was easy to handle ... had the lowest accident rate ... its efficiency was almost incredible – in performance and bomb capacity ... I continually pressed for its production at the expense of others.' As has already been noted, it was directly developed from the twin-engined Manchester, which due to the unreliability of its Rolls-Royce Vulture engines had failed to live up to expectations. Rather than waiting for Rolls-Royce to improve the engine, Avro went ahead with a four-engined Merlin version of the Manchester purely as a private venture. This prototype Manchester III (BT308), only later to be named Lancaster, was powered by four Rolls-Royce Merlin X engines and first flew in January 1941, followed four months later by the second prototype, with Merlin XX engines. The bomber was sent for service trials in August and the first production Lancaster (L7527) took to the air at the end of October. Lancasters entered the Service with No 44 (Rhodesia) squadron in late December, and the first operational sortie was made on 3rd March 1942 to lay mines, followed on the night of the 10th/11th, when just two Lancasters were in operation over Essen.

Another 156,190 operational sorties (40% of Bomber Command's total) were made by the end of the war by fifty-nine Lancaster squadrons, and most of the epic bombing operations of the war – the breaching of the Möhne and Eder dams and the sinking of *Tirpitz* – were conducted by Lancasters; they figured large in the Pathfinder Force and 3,431 were lost in action and another 246 in operational crashes.

The Mark Is were powered by a variety of Merlin engines, from XXs to 224s, which gave a maximum speed of about 287mph and a cruising rate of some 200mph. The Lancaster was originally designed to carry 4,000 pounds of bombs but this figure rose steadily to the 12,000 pound (Tallboy) bomb and ultimately to the 22,000 pound (Grand Slam) bomb; it was the only Allied bomber capable of carrying such massive bombs. The second most numerous version was the Mark III, which was virtually identical except for an enlarged bomb aimer's 'bubble' in the nose, and they were powered by American-built Packard Merlin 28, 38 and 224 engines. These two Marks accounted for over 87% of the total production of 7,374 Lancasters, which were built by five major United Kingdom manufacturers, known collectively as the Lancaster Manufacturing Group – A. V. Roe, Armstrong Whitworth, Austin Motors, Metropolitan Vickers and Vickers-Armstrong – and Victory Aircraft in Canada. However, in 1942 Austin was called upon to build a number of Mark VIIs, which proved to be the final production version. They were equipped with an American Glenn Martin dorsal turret with two .50 inch guns in place of the normal Frazer-Nash turret and located slightly further forward.

From October 1942 until late 1943 the relief landing ground at Hockley Heath was used by the school's student pilots for practice landings and circuits, although it is possible that this small airfield was still used intermittently well into 1945, despite the fact that during this period other flying training units were in residence at Hockley Heath. Certainly, on 22nd May 1945, one of its Tiger Moths came to grief when it struck a Blister hangar whilst making a landing approach. Perhaps it is a little ironic that in 1945 when pressure to produce trained pilots had lessened the school suffered more Moths written-off in training accidents and other incidents – eleven – than in any previous year.

In 1944 the elementary flying training course had undergone some changes. Although it still lasted about ten weeks, it was now scheduled to provide the students with more flying experience. Depending on the weather, they were now expected to complete up to eighty flying hours before passing on to their advanced flying training. Flying Training Command had been deeply concerned with the high wastage rate at EFTSs and as a result it had introduced a grading system at the Initial Training Wings and some EFTSs in order to assess a student's aptitude for flying duties. Another concern was the higher accident rate at the advanced training stage and an attempt to counter this resulted in an increase in the number of flying hours to be completed at EFTSs. This should, in theory, produce a higher calibre of student pilots progressing to the more complex training aircraft they would encounter at the SFTSs. The desperate urgency to train pilots in the shortest available time had now passed; in fact, in 1945 the RAF found itself in the enviable position of possesing a surfeit of trained pilots.

Lancaster production at the Austin factories peaked in June 1945 when thirty-five Mark VIIs were delivered. The company had also been engaged in producing over three hundred and sixty wooden fuselages for Airspeed A.S.51 Horsa Mark I and A.S.58 Mark II gliders, which were the main British assault gliders of the war. Horsas were manufactured in no fewer than thirty sections and many sub-contractors were involved in producing some 3,790. Wing sections were also built for Miles Magisters and Bristol Beaufighters. But with the celebration of VJ-Day on 12th August 1945 existing orders for Lancasters were cancelled and the last one was delivered from Austin in December 1945, making a grand total of three hundred and thirty Lancasters. Over the previous seven years Austin had produced some 2,860 military aircraft – a remarkable achievement considering the heavy raids suffered by Birmingham during 1940/1.

When No 14 EFTS finally closed down on 1st February 1946, Birmingham City Council firmly believed that Elmdon would fairly soon be returned to their control. It was therefore quite a shock when, on 13th June 1946, the airfield was handed over to the Ministry of Civil Aviation. Early in July (8th) Elmdon once again opened for civil flying after a lapse of seven years, although scheduled passenger services did not commence until 8th April, with a British European Airways flight to Paris. In the summer Elmdon was chosen by the Royal Aero Club to host the National Air Races, which took place from 28th July to 1st August – a Bank Holiday weekend. The meeting was the largest yet staged at any British airport and attracted over 120,000 visitors.

The growth and development of Elmdon into the United Kindom's fifth largest airport over the next fifty-five years can only be briefly

Outside the Millennium Link at Birmingham International Airport. (Birmingham International Airport)

traced in this account. From 1949 when a mere 18,200 passengers used the airport, the numbers steadily increased in the following decade as flights to the continent became more frequent. Finally on 1st April 1960 Elmdon was returned to Birmingham City Council and on the following day it was officially renamed Birmingham International Airport (BIA). One year later, on 28th April, HRH The Duchess of Kent returned to Elmdon to officially open the terminal extension known as the International Building. It was almost twenty-years since she had formally opened the original terminal. The main runway was subsequently lengthened to accommodate turboprop and jet airliners, and in 1973 some 1.1 million passengers passed through BIA. In 1974 control was passed to the West Midlands County Council and plans for the expansion of the airport were considered. On 16th September 1980 an Air France Concorde arrived from Paris – a far, far cry from the diminutive Tiger Moth biplanes that had lorded over the airfield thirty-five years earlier.

A new passenger terminal was formally opened by HM The Queen on 30th May 1984, and three years later the airport's status was altered to that of a public limited company. During the 1990s the number of passengers rose steadily each year, and in 1997 development plans were agreed for the expansion of the airport over the next ten years. Some eight million passengers used Birmingham International Airport in 2002 and it now proudly claims to be 'Serving the Heart of England'.

8
GAYDON

Gaydon is one of the easiest wartime airfield sites to locate in the county. It is to be found just off junction 12 of the M40 motorway, alongside the B4100 to Banbury and about 7½ miles south-south-east of Royal Leamington Spa: just follow the signs to The Heritage Motor Centre. The centre's most impressive art-deco-style buildings are set in sixty-five acres of landscaped parklands and are built on part of the airfield. Unfortunately, what remains of the old airfield is securely screened from public gaze because it is now used as a vehicle proving ground.

Although for over thirty-two years Gaydon was an RAF station, it really had two separate and distinct existences. For the majority of its first four years or so it was a satellite airfield deeply engaged in operational training for crews of Bomber Command, and then rather briefly the airfield was used for glider pilot training until August 1946. Then there was an interval of almost eight years and during the latter stages the airfield was virtually reconstructed before re-opening in March 1954 as a V-bomber crew training base. Gaydon finally closed twenty years later, after it had also been involved in far more basic flying training. But it is fair to say that its fame resides with its ten-year period as a V-bomber training station, when it was known as 'the birthplace of the RAF's V-bomber force'.

The airfield was built during 1941/2 as a standard bomber station with three concrete runways of normal lengths but, somewhat unusually, they were also covered with tar and sand. Twenty-seven hard-standings were provided, with just two hangars – Types 'B1' and 'T1'. Originally the control tower was of the normal two-storied construction but towards the end of the war a third storey was added, after the style found at most Fleet Air Arm airfields. Subsequently a 'glasshouse' or Visual Control Room was added to the roof; VCRs were

155

octagonal in shape with angled windows to reduce reflection; they became familiar sights at RAF airfields during the post-war years.

By the end of 1941 most bomber and indeed fighter stations had been supplied with a quite complex system of airfield lighting, universally known as Drem Lighting. The system had been devised in early 1941 by the Mechanical and Engineering Division of the Air Ministry's Works Directorate in conjunction with the RAF. In very *simple* terms the lighting system comprised five essential parts – the runway lighting, the flarepath, the angle of approach lighting and indicators, the circuit lighting (maybe some twelve miles in diameter) and the taxiing lights along the perimeter track. Many wartime pilots have vividly recalled the spectacular sight of all these airfield lights on a clear and moonlit night, especially over areas of the country where the airfields were relatively close together. One pilot later wrote, 'These airfields were like close-cut necklaces of pearls ... England gleamed with all its fires like a woman wearing her diamonds.' They must have been an impressive sight, especially as the neighbouring towns and villages were completely 'blacked-out'.

The airfield opened officially on 13th June 1942 as a satellite for No 12 OTU, which had been operating from Chipping Warden, Northamptonshire, since the previous August. Like the majority of OTUs, the unit was equipped with Wellingtons and was controlled by No 91 Group at Abingdon. However, two days later Gaydon along with its parent station was transferred into the newly formed No 93 Group. Hardly had things settled down into the normal and prescribed pattern when, on 1st September, Gaydon was transferred to No 22 OTU at Wellesbourne Mountford, which is about six miles due west; so the airfield returned to No 91 Group's control. The reason for this move was that No 12 OTU had recently acquired a new satellite airfield at Turweston, Buckinghamshire. At this time the main runway at Wellesbourne Mountford was out of commission undergoing urgent remedial and strengthening work, thus the Unit's 'A' and 'B' Flights were moved into Gaydon, along with their Wellington 1Cs. The parent station, which had been operating since April 1941, already had use of another satellite airfield near Stratford-upon-Avon, making No 22 then one of the busiest OTUs in the country. The Unit was almost solely devoted to training bomber crews for the Royal Canadian Air Force (RCAF).

At the outbreak of war the RCAF had a solitary bomber squadron – No 10 – equipped with the out-moded Wapiti biplanes. The Canadian

Wellington III (of No 12 OTU). The first Mark IIIs arrived in late 1942. (RAF Museum)

bomber force slowly increased in size and by the end of 1941 four squadrons, all numbered in the RAF's 400 series, were serving in Bomber Command. The Canadian Government had requested that a special RCAF Group should be established within Bomber Command as and when there was a sufficient number of RCAF squadrons, and the Air Ministry readily agreed to the proposal. Thus on New Year's Day, 1942, an all-Canadian group – No 6 (RCAF) – was formed under the command of Air Vice-Marshal G. E. Brookes; he was a Yorkshire-man who had emigrated to Canada after service in the RFC/RAF and had transferred to the RCAF in 1921. No 6 Group would ultimately comprise fourteen squadrons, with another squadron serving in the Pathfinder Force.

The new trainee crews at Gaydon were not sufficiently advanced in their training courses to be involved in the several '1,000' bomber raids mounted in late May and June, but their time to experience live bombing operations came in September. On the night of 10th/11th, Düsseldorf, a major industrial centre in the Ruhr, was the target for over four hundred and seventy bombers. Sadly, it was a costly operation with thirty-three aircraft lost (7.1%); No 16 OTU from Upper Heyford, Oxfordshire lost five of its thirteen trainee Wellington crews. No 22 OTU lost two crews missing in action, both from Stratford-upon-Avon. Two nights later Bremen was targeted once again by a force of four hundred and forty-six bombers. Of the fifteen Wellingtons missing in action, thirteen were flown by trainee crews, and No 22 OTU

Boulton Paul Defiant T.T.Mk1: one of the 140 target-towers ordered in July 1941.

suffered three losses, one of which had left Gaydon; the five-man crew (four RCAF airmen) were 'lost without trace'. The official report of the operation stated: 'Bremen's industry suffered further considerable damage ... including the Focke-Wulf factory'. Certainly Bremen was not targeted by Bomber Command for another five months.

It was fairly common practice for OTUs to locate the Armament flight at satellite airfields, and, as the name of the Flight suggests, it was responsible for the additional training of gunners. For this purpose a number of target-towing aircraft were allocated to each Unit. In the early years the RAF utilised suitably adapted redundant front-line aircraft for this task, such as Lysanders and Battles, and it was the former aircraft that were originally used by No 22 OTU. Within the Service it was fully recognised that the pilots and winch operators of these target-towers were more than a little intrepid. As one trainee pilot remarked, 'You wouldn't get me up in one of those when I think of the shooting accuracy of some of the gunners on our course!'

By mid-1941 the Air Ministry had decided to convert a number of Defiant fighters into special target-towers designated Defiant T.T. Mk.1s. The turret had been removed and a fixed canopy fitted over the winch mechanism, and a total of one hundred and ninety were ultimately produced. On 17th October 1942 one of the Unit's Defiant T.T. Mk.1s came to grief at the south-east of the airfield, but fortunately the pilot escaped with minor injuries. This was the first of several mishaps to training aircraft operating from Gaydon.

The following month proved to be the worst month of the war for flying accidents involving the Unit's Wellingtons based at Gaydon. On the 8th, Pilot Officer T. D. Withington and Sgt. C. W. Milton were engaged on a solo practice when their Wellington III stalled at a low altitude and crashed at Harbury, a village some four miles from the airfield, and both RCAF airmen were killed. Pilot Officer Withington had previously flown with No 208 squadron in the Middle East and his award of a Distinguished Flying Medal (gained with No 208) was not officially gazetted until 22nd January 1943. On this same night another six OTU aircraft crashed and were written-off, just one example of the high accident rate that prevailed in all OTUs throughout 1942. On the next evening a Wellington III had just left Gaydon when its starboard engine failed and the aircraft crashed at the village of Lighthorne on the northern edge of the airfield; all five RCAF airmen were killed. The final day of November brought yet another fatal accident. A Wellington III left Gaydon for a night navigation exercise but as the weather conditions quickly worsened the trainee crew was promptly recalled. However, whilst the pilot was making his landing approach, the aircraft struck some trees and all six crewmen (three RCAF) were killed – a harsh month indeed.

Although by the end of September Bomber Command had decided not to use training crews on bombing operations over German targets, there were other methods of introducing trainee crews to more 'realistic' operational flying. Since the early days of operational training, crews in their last week of training were sent out on 'Nickel' operations, which became known to the trainee crews as 'Graduation flights'; Nickel was the RAF's codename for dropping propaganda or information leaflets over mainly France and Holland. In the early days the method of distribution was rather crude. It involved sending bundles of leaflets down flare chutes, there to be scattered by the aircraft's slipstream. Later, the leaflets were enclosed in bomb-shaped casings which were opened by the automatic detonation of an explosive cord. These 'Nickel' operations were considered a valuable and essential part of the psychological war and had been accorded a high priority by the Air Council, although the forthright Viscount Trenchard described it as 'a monstrously ineffective means to a useless end'! Nevertheless, these 'Nickel' operations really fulfilled two objectives. Firstly they enabled Bomber Command to maintain a regular despatch of such leaflets without seriously impinging on the activities of operational squadrons, but perhaps more importantly, they

Early example of 'Nickel' operations – dropping leaflets down the flare chute. (RAF Museum)

provided the trainee crews with valuable navigational and operational experience over enemy-occupied territory.

Normally four crews per Unit were sent to selected areas in enemy occupied France, such as Paris, Brest, Nantes, Rennes and Rouen. The operations were initially controlled from Group headquarters but later

Unit Commanders were allowed a certain discretion to mount their own operations with the strict proviso that only one such operation be authorised per week. Each aircraft usually carried about twenty packs of leaflets which measured 8½ ins by 5½ ins and perhaps a couple of live bombs, which could only be dropped providing the crews had clearly established the military nature of the target, to minimise the risk of French civilian casualties. The leaflets were dropped from a height of about 15,000 feet, so the crews had to keep their wits about them to avoid enemy anti-aircraft batteries flying at such a relatively low altitude.

In late August and early September 1943 about one hundred and twenty trainee crews were engaged in bombing ammunition dumps known to be sited in several forests in northern France. Because of the difficulty in locating such targets, each operation was led by a handful of Pathfinder Force aircraft, which would find and then mark the targets. Besides the strategic value of these operations they also afforded the trainee crews experience of bombing on target markers. Since its formation in August 1942 the PFF target marking had become quite sophisticated, following the precedent set by the *Luftwaffe's* pathfinder force in late 1940. It became normal practice for the top three or four crews of each course to be invited to volunteer to serve in the Pathfinders. All PFF crews were volunteers. The members of this elite force proudly wore the famous gilt hovering eagle below their medal ribbons. They were required to complete sixty operations, although on joining the Pathfinders they were immediately upgraded one rank above that which they already held.

The first of these bombing raids was conducted on the night of 30th/31st August and proved very successful; thirty-three OTU Wellingtons took part and two were lost in action. The third raid despatched on 2nd/3rd September was directed at ammunition dumps in the Forêt de Mormal and the Forêt de Raisnes near Valenciennes. One crew from Gaydon failed to return; on the homeward flight the aircraft's port engine caught fire and it crashed near Wantage, Berkshire. The pilot, Pilot Officer W. I. St Johns, who died in the crash, was actually an American from Los Angeles, as was another member of the crew.

1943 saw the highest number of training accidents and fatalities. It was, of course, the peak year for operational training, with twenty-three bomber OTUs in full swing. The Units' commanders were continually exhorted by Group headquarters 'to do all within your

Wellington X (of No 75 squadron); Mark Xs equipped many OTUs from early 1943.

powers to reduce the number and burden of needless and costly accidents'; all very laudable sentiments but it was not made clear just how this could be achieved. One obvious way to reduce accidents would be to provide newer and more reliable training aircraft. When Wellingtons were finally removed from the Command's front-line squadrons, the majority of those coming off the production lines were supplied to OTUs and more especially the final bomber variant – Mark X.

This mark, directly developed from the Mark III, was provided with the more powerful Bristol Hercules VI and XVIII engines and the internal structure was strengthened. They went into production in mid-1942 and began to filter their way into OTUs by January 1943, although not in any appreciable numbers until later in the year; 3,800 Wellington Xs were produced by October 1945. At the end of the war, with hundreds of surplus Mark Xs available, conversions were undertaken to provide trainers for the peacetime RAF and many of these survived in the service until the 1950s.

On 2nd January 1943 a Wellington X (L4379) was returning to Gaydon after a cross-country flight when it crashed on landing because of a faulty undercarriage; both crewmen escaped unharmed but the aircraft was declared a write-off; the first Mark X to be lost by a training unit. Perhaps the most tragic accident in 1943 came on 19th April when a Wellington III crashed at Withington, about seven miles south-east of Cheltenham, during a night cross-country exercise. All five crewmen were killed, as were two Belgian paratroopers of the Belgian Special Air Service who were also on board. I believe that a memorial plaque to these airmen was dedicated at Withington church in April 1998.

Although the number of training accidents reduced somewhat during 1944, the Flights operating from Gaydon managed to achieve a

162

quite exceptional safety record, far superior to its parent station. During the year there were just three accidents. A seven-man RCAF crew disappeared without a trace over the North Sea whilst engaged on a navigation exercise during the night of 31st August/1st September. The last fatal accident occurred almost three months later (20th November), when a Wellingon X was engulfed in flames from an engine fire and only three airmen managed to escape by parachute. The other three RCAF airmen, including the captain, Pilot Officer D. McK. Roy, were killed when the aircraft crashed about four miles south of Evesham, Worcestershire.

Four days earlier Gaydon was used as an emergency airfield by Boeing B-17s of the US Eighth Air Force because of deteriorating weather conditions. The B-17s (Flying Fortresses) were returning from Operation *Queen*, a combined Allied bomber assault on road and rail communications at Düren, Jülich and Eschweiler behind the German front-lines. The US 1st and 9th Armies' advance had been halted by stout German resistance. Although some 2,380 Allied aircraft bombed the area, the American advance was not immediately successful and proved to be a prolonged and costly affair. The ten B-17s that landed at Gaydon belonged to Nos 306 and 384 Bomb Groups of the 1st Division operating from Thurleigh, Bedfordshire and Grafton Underwood, Northamptonshire, respectively.

In the New Year (22nd January) a Wellington III overshot the runway when the crew were returning from a night bombing practice; although the aircraft was written-off, all of the crew escaped unharmed. To show how sturdy these Wellingtons were, this particular Mark III (HF609) had been on the unit's complement for almost two years and had already been repaired after suffering another accident back in September 1943. Over the next five months, as operational training was winding down, there were no further accidents at Gaydon, and on 1st July 1945 No 22 OTU closed.

Gaydon, along with Wellesbourne Mountford, was passed over to No 23 Group of Flying Training Command and towards the end of July No 3 Glider Training School (GTS) moved in from Exeter, Devon. The school was still using General Aircraft Hotspur gliders, which had been the standard wartime training glider, with Miles Master IIs as glider-tugs. The course normally lasted twelve weeks and the trainees were predominantly RAF pilots as the Service now had a surfeit of trained pilots. After completion of the course the pilots would pass into an Operational Conversion Unit equipped with Horsas and

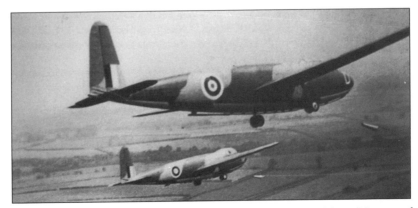

General Aircraft Hotspurs were the standard wartime training gliders. (Museum of Army Flying)

Hamilcars – the main operational gliders. In May the Glider Instructors' Flight arrived from Croughton, Northamptonshire for a very brief stay. No 3 GTS closed down on 15th August, and towards the end of the month Gaydon was placed under Care and Maintenance in the nominal control of No 12 (P) AFU and its first existence came to a close.

The next chapter in the Gaydon saga will, perforce, be unfortunately brief, as it relates to another type of war – the Cold War. Less than seven years after the airfield was closed to flying, the Air Ministry decided that Gaydon would be redeveloped and virtually reconstructed to enable it to accommodate the planned V-bombers. It was one of ten airfields to be brought up to 'Class One' standard, although another twenty-six dispersal airfields were also upgraded. For security reasons it was the Air Ministry's intention to move V-bomber squadrons fairly frequently.

In the spring of 1953 John Laing & Son Ltd began construction work at the airfield. Perhaps the most striking feature was the long runway, 3,000 yards and over 66 yards wide, and strong enough to accept a 200,000 pound aircraft, such was the requirement for the V-bombers; this was double the length of the original main runway. The runway stretched far to the south-west and was also provided with parallel taxi and access tracks. Sixteen hard-standings were provided and large fuel storage tanks with the requisite piping were installed. Two large hangars were erected. Similar to the wartime 'J' type hangars but with a door entrance of 160 feet, they became known as 'Gaydon' hangars. The modernised airfield reopened on 1st March 1954 under No 3 Group of Bomber Command and was ready to receive its first V-bombers.

It was in late 1945 that the concept of developing a four-jet bomber materialised with Operational Requirements (OR) 229 (Medium Range) and 230 (Long Range). The Air Ministry's draft Specification B.35/46 was issued in January 1947 and called for a four-jet bomber capable of carrying the 10,000 pound atomic bomb of the day up to a height of 50,000 feet, with a range of 3,600 miles, at a speed exceeding 550mph and with the provision of radio countermeasures. Thence the RAF's V-bomber force originated.

The Vickers Valiant was the first V-bomber to arrive on the scene, making its maiden flight on 18th May 1951 from a *grass* airfield at Wisley, Surrey, and finally entering the Service in January 1955 at Gaydon. It was followed by the delta-winged Avro Vulcans, which first flew on 30th August 1952 and which were ready for crew training with No 230 Operational Conversion Unit at Finningley, Yorkshire in May 1956. To my knowledge, no Vulcans operated from Gaydon. The last of the triumvirate of V-bombers was the crescent-winged Handley-Page Victor; it first took to the skies on 1st February 1956 from Radlett, Hertfordshire, and five early production Victors arrived at Gaydon in November 1957. A Valiant of No 49 squadron was the first to drop an operational atomic bomb over Maralinga range, South Australia in October 1956. Valiants equipped ten squadrons and they remained in service until February 1965. Various marks of Vulcans served in nine squadrons and they survived until 1984. In fact three Vulcans operated in the Falklands War in 1982. Victors had the longest service life, equipping eight squadrons from April 1958 until being retired from RAF Strike Command in October 1993.

On 1st January 1955 the first Valiant B.1s arrived at Gaydon for use by the newly formed Operational Conversion Unit and also to equip No 138 (Bomber) squadron, which had reformed at Gaydon under the command of Wing Commander R. G. Oakley, and thus was given the honour of becoming the RAF's first V-bomber squadron. This squadron had gained lasting wartime fame for its operations on behalf of the Special Operations Executive. The OCU, which was designated No 232 on 4th July, converted existing Bomber Command crews onto Valiants. The normal five-man crew comprised two pilots, a tactical navigator, a radio operator and an air electronics operator. No serving officer could

Valiants of No 138 squadron at Gaydon – March 1956. (RAF Museum)

apply to join the V-bomber force; appointment was by selection only, which proved to be a most rigorous process. Pilots were required to have at least 1,750 hours in command, with jet and four-piston engine experience; moreover they were not considered for selection unless they were marked 'above average' in flying ability. Navigators had to have completed at least one tour in English Electric Canberras. It was obvious that the Air Ministry intended to create an elite force. But, over the years, the various restrictions were slowly reduced and were finally abandoned.

The second Valiant squadron, No 543, was formed at Gaydon on 1st April, under Wing Commander R. E. Havercraft. For just twelve months during 1942/3 the squadron had operated Spitfires on photographic reconnaissance duties. The re-formed squadron was now allocated a similar role, that of Strategic Reconnaissance, and was equipped with the first Valiant variant – B (PR)1 – provided with a wide range of reconnaissance cameras. On 6th July No 138 squadron moved to its operational station at Wittering, Cambridgeshire, whereas on 16th November No 543 moved out to its permanent station, Wyton, also in Cambridgeshire. The Operational Conversion Unit continued to train crews for the other eight Valiant squadrons formed over the next two years.

166

In early November 1957 'A' squadron of the 232 OCU received its first five Victors, followed in the New Year by another four, which were specially equipped with Yellow Aster reconniassance radar. These Victors were used to train some No 543 (Strategic Reconnaissance) crews on the new aircraft and equipment, and they formed the Radar Reconnaissance Flight at Wyton. Gaydon's OCU continued to train Victor B.1 crews alongside Valiant crews. No 10 squadron at Cottesmore, Derbyshire was the first bomber squadron to receive Victor B.1s in April 1958. During 1961, the new improved Victor B.2 was being prepared and a Victor Training Flight at Cottesmore trained some of the B.2 crews, although in 1962 a Victor B.2 Conversion Unit was established at Wittering.

By 1964 the RAF's V-bomber force was at its optimum strength, although No 138 squadron had been disbanded in April 1962. There were now one hundred and fifty-nine V-bombers operating with eighteen squadrons and the days of crew training at Gaydon were numbered, especially as Valiants were shortly to be withdrawn from the Force. On lst June 1965, No 232 OCU was disbanded. Another major factor was the change in the Government's defence policy. The country's nuclear deterrent was transferred to the Royal Navy and this brought about a slow but steady reduction in the RAF's V-bomber force.

The old control tower at Gaydon as it is now. (British Motor Industry Heritage Trust)

However, Gaydon did not close but still maintained its flying training role, albeit of a much more leisurely and sedate nature. On 1st September 1965 the airfield was passed over to Flying Training Command, and No 2 Air Navigation School arrived from Hullavington, Wiltshire with its Vickers Valettas ('Flying Classrooms') and Vickers Varsitys, the latter a replacement for the doughty Wellington T10 crew trainer. The school provided instruction in elementary or basic navigation and it remained at Gaydon until May 1970, when it was transferred to Finningley. For the second time Gaydon was placed under Care and Maintenance, until it was formally closed on 31st October 1974.

In 1978 British Leyland acquired the site and proceeded to develop a new car testing and development ground. The Heritage Motor Centre occupies only a small area of the original site. Since 1983 it has been managed by the British Motor Industry Heritage Trust and its remarkable museum holds nearly three hundred vehicles. The museum faithfully records the growth and development of the British motor industry and has become a mecca for motoring enthusiasts.

9
HONILEY

For most, if not all, of its seventeen years as an RAF station, Honiley was a veritable paradise for plane-spotters, and quite possibly the inspiration for many a future airman. During that time it played host to such famous fighters as Defiants, Hurricanes, Spitfires, Beaufighters, Typhoons, Mosquitos, Meteors, Vampires and Sea Attackers, as well as a number of more 'mundane' wartime aircraft – Blenheims, Lysanders, Ansons, Beauforts, Hudsons, Oxfords, Harvards, Wellingtons, etc. Certainly, few, if any, more famous RAF airfields could equal or surpass such a rich and remarkable array of celebrated aircraft.

Whilst the airfield was under construction during 1940/1, it was known, for some unaccountable reason, as Ramsey but by the time it formally opened on 3rd August 1941 it had been named RAF Honiley from the neighbouring village. The airfield was situated off the A4177 road, about seven miles south-west of Coventry, and was originally intended to house a bomber OTU. The increasingly regular and heavy night raids during the winter of 1940/1 and the paucity of fighter airfields in the Midlands decided the Air Ministry to re-allocate Honiley to Fighter Command to serve as a Sector Station within No 9 Group.

The airfield had been provided with three tarmac runways in the typical triangular layout and conforming to the standard lengths, but as in many wartime airfields they were later extended; Honiley's main runway ultimately measured 2,350 yards. It was amply supplied with hangars – fifteen – three Bellmans and the rest Blister types. The Operations Block, where the flying operations were controlled and monitored, was situated almost a mile away from the main airfield for safety reasons on a remote site along Bree's Lane. The airfield also had sufficient temporary technical and living blocks to accommodate over

2,150 personnel, including almost 600 WAAFs. Indeed John Laing & Son Ltd, responsible for the airfield's construction, estimated that these sectional huts, if placed end to end, would measure over one mile. The company also reported (almost proudly?) that 1¾ miles of hedging had been uprooted, along with 5,000 trees – no vociferous environmental lobby to protest in those wartime days!

Prior to the official opening, Boulton Paul Defiant Is of No 96 squadron, then based at Cranage to the south of Manchester, had used the airfield during May for night patrols, as had other squadrons based at Baginton. Even as far back as October 1940, a Blenheim from No 27 Maintenance Unit when caught in severe weather attempted an emergency landing at the partially completed airfield. The Blenheim struck a newly constructed drain and was severely damaged, although the crew escaped unharmed.

The first squadron to use the new airfield, albeit fleetingly, was No 457 (RAAF) with its Spitfire Is, which had formed at Baginton earlier in June. The Australian pilots soon moved on to Jurby on the Isle of Man. Then on 4th September the Sector headquarters staff moved in from Baginton, followed by Nos 605 (County of Warwick) and 132 squadrons; both were operating Hurricane IIs. Neither squadron would remain in residence for very long, although No 135 did manage to be declared operational whilst at Honiley; its pilots flew their first operational sorties on 3rd October. The eighteen pilots of No 605, along with their Hurricanes, embarked on the aircraft carrier HMS *Argus* at Glasgow on 1st November, bound for Gibraltar.

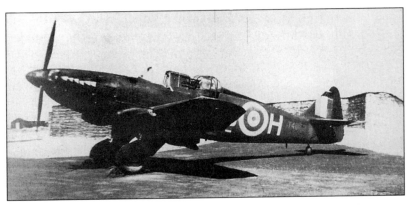

Boulton Paul Defiant of No 96 squadron.

In the following month the squadron's ground personnel left Gourock, Scotland on the *Warwick Castle* (a highly appropriate vessel?) for an unknown destination, which turned out to be the Far East. Also in November (10th), No 135 Squadron departed for the Far East – ultimately to operate from an airfield at Zayatkin, Burma.

By a strange coincidence the squadron had been immediately replaced by one of the RAF's two 'Burma' squadrons – No 257 – so named in recognition of the financial support for aircraft received from that country – sufficient to provide fifteen Hurricanes. The squadron's badge carried a motto in Burmese, which when translated read *Death or Glory*, and certainly during the Battle of Britain its pilots had tried to live up to it. In fact, they became known as the 'Death or Glory boys'. Since those times the squadron had been commanded by two famous Battle of Britain pilots – Squadron Leaders Robert Stanford Tuck, DFC and H. P. Blatchford, DFC – and had latterly served at Coltishall, Norfolk. It was now transferred to night fighter duties and equipped with Hurricane IIBs under a new commander, Squadron Leader R. E. Drake, AFC. During the seven months that the squadron stayed at Honiley, its pilots were involved in a most frustrating, prolonged and ultimately unsuccessful tactical experiment in night fighting, which perhaps illustrates just how stretched Fighter Command was in the desperate battle in the night skies.

This experiment involved the establishment of 'Turbinlite' Flights. No 1456 was formed at Honiley on 24th November 1941 under Squadron Leader I. E. Chalmers-Watson, AFC. The concept of these flights was that American-built Douglas Havocs would be equipped with a large airborne Helmore searchlight (the originator was Wing Commander W. Helmore) of 2,700 million candlepower, which was capable of throwing a wide beam of light for a distance of about one mile. The 'Turbinlite' Havoc would be guided onto an enemy contact by Ground Control Interception (GCI) and its own AI (Airborne Interception) radar, and at a distance of about 3,000 feet its crew would pass the code-word 'Hot' to its following 'parasite' aircraft, in this instance a Hurricane II of No 257 squadron. Once the enemy target was firmly locked on, the code-word 'Boiling' would be passed and when the accompanying fighter was within about 900 feet of the enemy aircraft, the 'Turbinlite' Havoc would illuminate the target for the 'parasite' fighter to move in to destroy – well, at least that was the theory. This most bizarre idea is said to have originated with Winston Churchill, and it was largely because of his enthusiasm for the project

Douglas Havoc modified with a Turbinlite and used by No 1457 Flight.

that the ten Turbinlite Flights were so quickly formed. Despite a conspicious lack of success and a high number of accidents by the Flights and associated squadrons (it is believed that only one enemy aircraft was destroyed along with one probable and a couple damaged by this method), the Flights were made up to full squadrons in September 1942, No 1456 becoming No 535 squadron. However, by that time, both the Flight and No 257 squadron had moved to High Ercall near Shrewsbury. All the 'Turbinlite' squadrons were disbanded on 27th January 1943, and with the benefit of hindsight this experiment can be viewed as a sorry waste of valuable resources – both in terms of aircraft and airmen.

The 'Turbinlite' Havocs and their 'parasite' Hurricanes shared the airfield with a detachment of No 96's Defiants; the rest of the squadron was based at Wrexham. This two-seater fighter with its unique four-machine-gun-powered turret had first flown in August 1937 and came into service in December 1939. Although originally successful over the Dunkirk beaches in May 1940 because of its unusual armament, its weaknesses – lack of speed, poor manoeuvrability and a vulnerability to frontal attack – were grievously exposed during the Battle of Britain, and they were withdrawn after suffering heavy losses. Defiants were then hastily adapted to carry the Mark I AI radar equipment and brought into the Command's meagre night fighter force. In fact during the winter of 1940/1 Defiants recorded more 'kills' than any other night fighters, and ultimately thirteen squadrons were equipped with them.

In March 1942 Blenheim Is, Lysander IIIs and the odd Hudson of 'B' Flight of No 285 Anti-Aircraft Squadron, also based at Wrexham, used

Honiley as its base. During March there was also a brief appearance of the Command's latest fighter – the Hawker Typhoon; No 56 squadron had been the first unit to receive these remarkable, heavy and pugnacious aircraft in the previous September. Its pilots, under Squadron Leader (later Group Captain Sir Hugh) Hugh Dundas, DFC, were attempting to work up their aircraft to operational readiness. They were experiencing countless teething problems and Sir Hugh later recalled that at this time 'the sole purpose of flying around the country was to flog the bugs out of the Typhoons as quickly and thoroughly as possible'. These were slowly resolved and the 'Tiffy' (as it was nick-named) became a superlative low-level ground attack aircraft, which revealed its full and devastating potential with the 2nd Tactical Air Force over Normandy after D-Day and beyond.

For a brief period during April/May, No 257 received a handful of Spitfire VBs but the squadron, now under Squadron Leader P. G. Wykeham-Barnes, DFC, Bar, was never fully equipped with Spitfires. Early in June (6th), as the Havocs and Hurricanes departed for High Ercall, they were replaced on the same day by Bristol Beaufighter VIFs of No 255 squadron, which had been operating from High Ercall since March. These solid and very reliable night fighters had entered the service in September 1940 and they had already fully proved their worth in the night skies during 1940/1. The Mark VIFs had first entered Fighter Command in March and were powered by two 1,670hp Hercules VI or XVI radial engines, giving them a top speed just in excess of 330mph, and they were heavily armed with four 20mm Hispano cannons and six .303 inch Brownings in the wings; the latest AI Mk VIII radar had been mounted in the so-called 'thimble nose'. One pilot – the legendary Guy Gibson – described the Beaufighter as 'sturdy, powerful and fearsome'. Over 1,850 Mark VIs were produced for both Fighter and Coastal Commands, ultimately equipping fourteen night fighter squadrons until they were gradually replaced by de Havilland Mosquito night fighters.

No 255 squadron was commanded by a Wing Commander rather than a Squadron Leader, mainly due to Group Captain (later Air Chief Marshal Sir Basil) Embry, whilst Station Commander at Wittering. Embry had stoutly maintained that the responsibilities of commanding AI night fighter squadrons were just as arduous and onerous as those of bomber operational squadrons, which had for some time been commanded by Wing Commanders. He continually petitioned the Air Ministry on the subject and finally it was agreed to upgrade the post to

Hurricane IIBs of No 257 squadron at Honiley in late 1941.

Wing Commander with the Flights placed under Squadron Leaders. No 255 squadron, under Wing Commander D. Kelly, remained operational until August, when it began to prepare for an overseas posting, and on 15th November the squadron left for its overseas assignment – Maison Blanche in Algeria.

Hurricane IIB & Cs returned to Honiley on 10th September when No 32 squadron moved in from West Malling, where it had been engaged on intruder raids over northern France as well as operating in the ill-fated Dieppe landings in mid-August. Like No 255 squadron, it was also destined for overseas service as part of the RAF force for Operation *Torch*. On 19th October the squadron moved across to Baginton to prepare for its move abroad. The following day saw the arrival of Honiley's longest serving wartime squadron – No 96 – with its new Beaufighter VIFs. In May the squadron, whilst based at Wrexham, had exchanged its doughty Defiants for Beaufighter IIFs and had only recently received the newer marks. The squadron was commanded by Wing Commander R. J. Burns and operated from Honiley for about ten months. During this period, as the *Luftwaffe's* night bombing raids were lessening, some of the crews were detached to Tangmere and Ford in Sussex for them to try their hand at night intruder and rangers raids. The latter was the code-name for operations at either squadron or wing strength of freelance intrusions over enemy occupied territory with the primary objective of depleting the German fighter force.

Towards the end of October the remainder of No 285 squadron arrived to join its detached 'B' Flight. It had now been augmented by

Bristol Beaufighter VIF: they first operated from Honiley in June 1942.

Oxfords and some Defiant IIs, and when it moved away to Woodvale in August 1943 a number of Miles Martinet target-towers had also been added to its complement. In November a Flight of No 287 squadron was detached to Honiley to undertake anti-aircraft co-operation duties in and around the Midlands; Honiley was just one of thirteen airfields used by the squadron's aircraft.

On 11th January a Spitfire VB squadron, No 91 (Nigeria), moved in from Hawkinge, Kent, where its pilots had been engaged on 'Jim Crows' and Air-Sea-Rescue patrols in the English Channel. 'Jim Crow' was the code-name for coastal patrols to intercept any enemy intruders crossing the coasts. The squadron was commanded by Squadron Leader R. R. Harries, DFC and was a most cosmopolitan unit with French, Belgian, Dutch, Norwegian, Australian and British pilots. In April it was re-equipped with a very rare Spitfire Mark – XII. This Mark was powered by a Rolls-Royce Griffon III or IV engine, with clipped wings to provide increased speed at low altitudes and a strengthened fuselage which gave it an even greater rate of roll. It had been developed to provide a more effective counter to Focke-Wulf Fw 190As, the speedy fighter-bombers that were causing considerable mayhem with their low-level bombing raids on towns along the coasts of south-east and eastern England. By repute, the XIIs had better handling qualities than any previous Spitfires and almost reached 400mph at 18,000 feet; they were regarded 'as something of a "hot ship"'; only one hundred were built and they served in just two operational squadrons – Nos 41 and 91. When the squadron moved back to Hawkinge on 21st May (via a brief spell at Wittering), within

175

A rare Spitfire mark – XII – operated by only two squadrons, Nos 41 and 91. These are with No 41 squadron.

days its pilots destroyed five Fw 190As over the English Channel in a single encounter. During the summer of 1944 Spitfire XIIs proved their mettle against the VI flying bombs until being phased out in September of that year.

On 5th July the distinct and dulcet tones of Rolls-Royce Merlin engines (different from the harsher Griffon engines) heralded the arrival of yet another Spitfire squadron, No 130 (Punjab), with its VBs. Since its formation in June 1941, the squadron had seen a frequent change of pilots and had served at nine different fighter stations, mainly in the West Country; but the squadron had previously been operating from Ballyhalbert near Londonderry, Northern Ireland. Three days later it was joined by another Spitfire VB squadron, No 234. This squadron had also spent much of its time in the West Country, but had now been given a highly secret task. It would appear that intelligence sources had revealed that Germany was preparing to invade Portugal and the Air Ministry wanted to undertake a series of fuel consumption tests to decide what aircraft would be suitable to equip a force to quickly combat such a threat. It was for this reason that a number of North American Mitchell IIs of No 98 squadron were detached from Foulsham, Norfolk to assist in the trials. This American twin-engined light bomber had entered No 2 Group, Bomber Command in September 1942, primarily as a replacement for Blenheim IVs. The aircraft had gained early fame with the USAAF in April 1942, when General 'Jimmie' Doolittle led a formation of Mitchells from an aircraft carrier to bomb Toyko for the first time. As it turned out the Mitchells remained at Honiley for only about two weeks, as the invasion scare had proved to be groundless. On 5th August both Spitfire squadrons left Honiley, bound for the same airfield – West Malling, Kent. Then, on the following day, No 96's Beaufighters disappeared to Church Fenton, Yorkshire.

With the airfield suddenly devoid of operational aircraft, it was ready to take on a new role. In May No 9 Group had assumed the control of all of Fighter Command's OTUs and it was decided that Honiley should become the home of the Command's new fighter OTU – No 63. The Unit would be devoted to the training of crews in the skills of Airborne Interception. For this task it was supplied with a mixture of aircraft – Beaufighter IIs, Beaufort IIs and Blenheim Vs. The Bristol Beaufort had entered the service in December 1939, as a land torpedo-bomber with Coastal Command. Many of the Mark IIs had been completed as purpose-built trainers with dual controls, and the two-gun dorsal turret had been removed. The Blenheim Vs were also specially adapted for training, with the provision of dual controls.

The first course commenced on 17th August and by October the Unit had received a couple of Wellington XIs. They had originally been developed to operate in Coastal Command on anti-submarine duties and were provided with ASV (Air-Surface-Vessel) radar. However, a number of XIs had been converted for crew training with an array of

Bristol Beaufort II modified for use as a trainer, several were employed by No 63 OTU.

special equipment for night flying training. The Unit's life was relatively short because on 21st March 1944 it closed down and the special Wellington XIs were transferred to No 51 OTU at Cranfield, Bedfordshire. I suspect that one of the reasons for the relatively short existence of the OTU was the acute shortage of trained and experienced instructors, especially those with a wide knowledge of AI procedures. In any case No 51 OTU was fully experienced in providing a range of specialised night fighting instruction.

For a period of just eleven days in March perhaps the most famous, exciting and versatile wartime aircraft – the de Havilland Mosquito – made its first appearance at Honiley. They were Mark NFXVIIs of No 219 squadron under the command of Wing Commander A. D. McN. Boyd, DFC. The squadron had recently returned from service in North Africa, where it had operated Beaufighter VIFs. Since its return the crews had recently received their new Mosquito night fighters at Woodvale. The squadron left Honiley for Colerne, Northern Ireland, on 26th March but within days it was sent to Bradwell Bay, Essex, from where it would operate night patrols over the Normandy beaches from D-Day.

With the closure of No 63 OTU, Honiley reopened briefly as a Sector airfield. But things had changed now. No 9 Group of Fighter Command no longer existed, it had been disbanded. Indeed Fighter Command *per se* had also ceased to exist from 15th November 1943 owing to the loss of thirty-two squadrons to the 2nd TAF. In a much reduced state, it now rejoiced under the name Air Defence of Great Britain (ADGB) – echoes of the early 1930s. In May a detachment of Typhoons of No 3 Tactical Exercise Unit of the 2nd TAF used Honiley as a temporary base for mock Army support exercises. The Typhoons moved off to Acklington, Durham during June and returned briefly to Honiley before joining No 84 Group Support Unit of the 2nd TAF at Aston Down, Gloucestershire in mid-July.

Honiley was now transferred out of ADGB, its days as a wartime fighter station had come to a close. On 15th July the airfield was handed over to No 26 (Signals) Group of Bomber Command at Langley Hall, under the control of Air Vice-Marshal O. G. W. Lynwood, CB, CBE, who was responsible for a variety of operational signals units and the extensive ground communications network that had been developed at service airfields throughout the country. At the end of the month one of the command's more important units, the Signals Development Unit (SDU) under Wing Commander C. C.

McMullen, moved into Honiley from Hinton-in-the-Hedges, Northamptonshire.

The SDU operated with a rather strange mixture of aircraft – Ansons, Oxfords, Beaufighters, Wellingtons, Hudsons, Spitfires, Mosquitos and the odd Whitley and Stirling. It was engaged in checking the various electronic airborne landing and navigational aids, as well as installing radio transmitters in aircraft and ground vehicles; another task was testing the calibration and accuracy of the various defence radars and similar equipment then in use at airfields. One Flight was engaged in the trialling and development of a new beam approach system – the American-devised Signals Corps System, which the USAAF considered was more accurate and far safer.

The Air Ministry had agreed to trial and test the American system, which had been abbreviated to ILS or Instrument Landing System. In simple terms, this system was based on two ground transmitters, which provided an approach path for the aircraft's exact alignment and it also produced the correct angle of approach for the aircraft's final descent onto the runway. The Ground Approach Flight was also trialling and developing 'talk-down' approach and landing procedures, particularly for use by the fast-growing Transport Command. Of course, highly developed and very sophisticated ILS and talk-down procedures are now in universal use at commercial airports and military airfields throughout the world. However, the ILS was not introduced into Transport Command airfields until after the end of the Second World War.

The Signals Development Wing, as it had been redesignated, also used Stratford-upon-Avon as a satellite airfield during 1945. The Wing remained at Honiley until the summer of 1946, when it was transferred to Watton, Norfolk, which was the home of the Radio Warfare Establishment, later evolving into the Central Signals Establishment, and ultimately, in November 1958, into Signals Command. With the departure of the Signals Development Wing, the control of Honiley was passed over to Reserve Command, which had been formed on 1st May 1946. The airfield was now prepared to host the re-formation of the county's Auxiliary Air Force squadron – No 605.

The Auxiliary Air Force had been disbanded on 15th August 1945, and considerable pressure was placed on the Air Ministry to reconsider what many in the RAF felt was an abrupt and imprudent decision. In early 1946 the Air Ministry relented and announced the re-introduction of the Auxiliary Air Force, to comprise twenty squadrons – sixteen fighter and four fighter-bomber – and all were allowed to retain their former territorial titles. Thus on 10th May 1946 No 605 (County of Warwick) squadron was re-formed at Honiley under Squadron Leader R. J. Walker, DSO. It was one of the three AuxAF night fighter squadrons.

Since the squadron had previously served at Honiley back in late 1941, its pilots had operated briefly in Malta and Palemberg, Sumatra before the squadron was disbanded in February 1942. Four months later No 605 was re-formed in Fighter Command at Ford, Sussex, under Wing Commander (later Group Captain) Peter W. Townsend, DSO, DFC for intruder raids over the Continent, equipped with Havocs and Bostons. Then, in February 1943, the squadron re-equipped with Mosquito IIs and later Mark VIs, serving with distinction in the 2nd TAF until it was disbanded on 31st August 1945 and renumbered No 4 on the following day whilst operating from Volkel in Holland.

Local recruitment for the AuxAF had to be introduced, and the process proved to be a lengthy affair: many months passed before the various AuxAF squadrons began to take shape. In April 1947, No 605 squadron received its operational aircraft, the ubiquitous Mosquito NF36s, along with a couple of Harvards for training. All AuxAF squadrons were, to all intents and purposes, manned by 'weekend airmen'. Ground crews were required to serve for twelve weekends and undertake one hundred hours of training per annum, whereas the pilots were obligated to complete at least one hundred and twenty-five flying hours each year. Flying and ground personnel were also expected to attend the fifteen days summer camp (as in the pre-war days). Part-time airmen or not, the AuxAF squadrons did provide a considerable proportion of the country's fighter strength in the early post-war years. On 16th December 1947 the Auxiliary Air Force was accorded the right by King George VI to use the prefix 'Royal', a recognition of the sterling service made by these squadrons during the Second World War.

Perhaps No 605's proudest moment came in the following April, when it was nominated as the first RAuxAF squadron to receive jet aircraft – de Havilland Vampire F.1 day fighters. The Vampire had first flown on 29th September 1943 but it was too late to see service in the Second World War. It was powered by de Havilland's own developed turbo-jet engine – Goblin I – which gave it a maximum speed of 540mph; indeed, in 1943, it was the first British aircraft to exceed 500mph in level flight. The Vampire was armed with four 20mm

D.H.100 Vampire of No 605 (County of Warwick) squadron on display at the Midland Air Museum. (Midland Air Museum)

Hispano Mk.5 cannons. The squadron's identification code throughout the Second World War had been UP but its Vampires now carried the letters RAL, at least until June 1950, when the code was changed to NR. It was also provided with a couple of Gloster Meteor T.7s for jet-conversion training, which was the RAF's first jet-trainer when it entered the service in December 1948. In June 1951 the squadron was re-equipped with the fighter-bomber version of the Vampire – FB.5 – which ultimately equipped forty squadrons, including eleven of the RAuxAF.

In June 1953 HM Queen Elizabeth II was present at RAF Odiham, Hampshire for the Coronation Review of the RAF, in which six hundred and forty various aircraft flew past in precisely twenty-seven minutes. The aircraft taking part in this remarkable display had been fed from airfields all around the country, including twenty-four Gloster Meteor F.8s that had left from Honiley. In the following March HRH Princess Margaret visited Honiley to present the squadron with its Royal Standard, which lists its battle honours and portrays its Royal badge (approved in April 1944) with the squadron's motto *Nunquam dormio* 'I never sleep'.

A year later No 605 squadron shared the airfield with No 1833 (RNVR) squadron then based at Bramcote. Because this airfield was not really suitable for jet operations, the Naval Reserve pilots used Honiley for their conversion onto Sea Vampires and ultimately to Supermarine Sea Attacker FB.5s. However, the days of Auxiliary and Reserve squadrons were now numbered. In late 1956 the decision was taken to disband such squadrons, partly, it was said, for cost considerations, but mainly because of the various complications involved in the training of 'part-time' pilots to operate the more complex aircraft then entering both Services. The two squadrons were therefore disbanded, and, on 11th March 1957 No 605 (County of Warwick) squadron ceased to exist after thirty-one years of operational service. In 1990 the Squadron Memorial and Rose Garden was dedicated at St Cuthbert's church, Castle Vale, Birmingham. In October 2004 the Royal Auxiliary Air Force commemorated the 80th anniversary of its formation, and, as part of the celebrations, a memorial, to be dedicated to all Auxiliary Air Force personnel, is to be commissioned at the National Memorial Arboretum at Alrewas, Staffordshire.

No 605 (County of Warwick) squadron badge (officially approved April 1944) (Midland Air Museum)

The somewhat premature demise of these Auxiliary and Reserve squadrons heralded the end of Honiley's operational days. In April the airfield was placed on Care and Maintenance under the nominal control of Bramcote before it was finally closed on 1st March 1958. Three years later the airfield was sold and is now owned by Prodrivelive Ltd. Like many Midland wartime airfields, it is now used as a vehicle development ground, but the old control tower has survived, as have parts of the runways.

10
LONG MARSTON

Sixty-three years after it opened as an RAF station, Long Marston is one of the two wartime-built airfields in the county still being used for private flying. Indeed, this airfield only just manages to be included in Warwickshire; its southern perimeter is barely two miles from the county boundary with Gloucestershire. Long Marston was yet another wartime airfield to be constructed by John Laing & Son Ltd and is located immediately to the west of the B4632, some four miles to the south-west of Stratford-upon-Avon.

The airfield was under construction from late 1940 through most of 1941 and from the outset was intended to operate as a satellite station for a new bomber OTU planned to be formed in late 1941. In December 1940 the Air Ministry decided that Long Marston would be allocated to Honeybourne, about four miles further to the south-west, which was then also in the throes of construction. Indeed, there was yet another airfield in the close vicinity that was also nearing completion, at Atherstone on Stour, about three miles to the north-east of Long Marston. So much for the Air Ministry's cherished precept that airfields should be no less than six miles apart.

As a planned bomber OTU, albeit as a satellite airfield, Long Marston was provided with three tarmac runways in the standard A configuration, with the main one measuring 1,500 yards and the other two 1,100 yards each; in due course they were extended, with the second runway becoming the longest and effectively the main runway, at 2,400 yards. Twenty-seven hard-standings were laid down and three hangars erected – two Type T2s and a single B1. Temporary living and technical huts were installed to accommodate the 1,000 or so permanent staff and the relatively small number of trainee crews that used the satellite airfield during certain periods of their courses.

Long Marston was a little different from most wartime airfields in the respect that the main technical and training buildings were set down in an almost ribbon design along the eastern perimeter. A large communal site, along with four dispersed sites and a separate WAAF domestic site, were well away to the east of the airfield and across the other side of the B4632. The distances involved would suggest that bicycles were fairly essential, if only to obviate a long daily walk. Another aspect of the airfield that was slightly unusual and appeared to contravene another of the Air Ministry's hallowed principles was the presence of a significant natural obstruction – Meon Hill, which is 764 feet above sea level and was less than two miles south of the main runway. This high ground could pose a formidable obstacle for inexperienced trainee crews, and I suspect this might be one of the reasons why the second runway was later lengthened to become the main runway. However, it does show the considerable pressure that was placed on the Air Ministry, especially during 1940/1, to find airfield sites in certain areas, which certainly in other less fraught and extenuating times would not have even been considered, let alone developed.

The airfield was finally ready for occupation in November 1941; its parent station had formally opened in the previous month. However, instead of the two airfields being allocated to No 6 (Training) Group of Bomber Command as was expected, they were placed under the control of No 44 Group of Ferry Command. This Command had been formed on 20th July 1941 under Air Chief Marshal Sir Frederick W. Bowhill, KCB, CMG, DSO, one of the RAF's 'veteran' airmen. He had qualified as a pilot with the Naval Wing of the RFC in January 1913 and since 1937 had been in charge of Coastal Command. The original *raison d'être* for Ferry Command was as a result of the requirement to move large numbers of American aircraft across the Atlantic and then to fly the ferry crews back across to Canada. This task had previously been the responsibility of the Atlantic Ferry Organisation, based in Montreal, Canada, and Ferry Command was formed to replace this organisation. In its early days the Command, working closely with British Overseas Airways Corporation, was almost exclusively engaged in flying military personnel and courier services to North and West Africa and the Middle East via Gibraltar; by mid-1942 Ferry Command was flying at least sixty thousand hours each month.

No 44 Group included a crew training unit, which was known as the Service Ferry Squadron and had hitherto been based at Kemble, Gloucestershire until its move to Honeybourne and Long Marston on

16th November. The squadron was formally reconstituted as the Ferry Training Unit, comprising three Flights; two days later the first training course commenced. The unit instructed experienced pilots and navigators in the techniques and skills of long-distance flying and long-range navigation; many of its instructors had previously flown with Imperial and British Airways and thus were well experienced in the field of long-distance flying.

The Unit was supplied with quite an unusual assortment of aircraft – Wellingtons, Beauforts, Dominies, Hudsons, Marylands and Bombays. The American-built Martin 167 Maryland had originally been designed as a twin-engined light and speedy reconnaissance bomber. The French Air Force had ordered over two hundred, seventy-five of which were diverted to the RAF after the fall of France, followed by an order for another seventy-five. The reason Marylands were seconded to the Unit was on account of their relatively long operational range – some 1,300 miles. However, Marylands were used for a number of other roles such as target-towers, transports and trainers but only as operational bombers in North Africa and the Middle East.

Perhaps the Unit's most interesting aircraft was the Bristol Bombay. It had originated way back in 1931 as a result of an Air Ministry's specification (C.26/31) for a troop and carrier transport that could also double as a long-range bomber. The prototype made its maiden flight in June 1935, and, although the Air Ministry ordered fifty, the first production Bombay did not appear until March 1939 and entered service in October with No 216 (Bomber Transport) squadron, by

The Ferry Training Unit was equipped with a few Bristol Bombays.

185

Consolidated Liberator 1s were operated by No 1425 Communications Flight.

which time it was considered almost obsolete, although the squadron used them for bombing in North Africa during 1942. The Bombay was a twin-engined high-wing monoplane with a cruising speed of 160mph and could carry twenty-four troops. But its most significant attribute, as least for Ferry Command, was its operational range – 2,230 miles – with additional fuel tanks carried in the fuselage. Bombays were used mainly to transport ground crews and their supplies and spares when operational squadrons moved stations and were still being used as carriers until late 1943; as such, the ponderous Bombays were evident at many wartime airfields throughout the country.

Another of Ferry Command's Flights arrived at the two airfields in mid-November – No 1425 Communications Flight. It had formed at Prestwick at the end of October and been equipped with Armstrong Whitworth Albermarles and some American-built Consolidated Liberator 1s. The LB.30A had been first developed in January 1939 but did not make its maiden flight until 29th December. As a B-24 four-engined heavy bomber, it operated with great distinction in the USAAF throughout the war, possibly most notably and successfully with the US Eighth Air Force, from airfields in East Anglia. The first Liberators (named by the Air Ministry) arrived in the United Kingdom in April 1941 and were planned to operate on the return ferry service to Canada, but some, on account of their long operational range, found their way into Coastal Command, where later marks operated successfully on anti-U-boat patrols. The paramount features of the aircraft were its operational range – 2,100 miles – and its four very reliable Pratt & Whitney Wasp engines. The Air Ministry originally ordered over one hundred and thirty, to be known as Liberator IIs, and many of these were used as RAF transports as well as with BOAC. Maybe the most famous RAF Liberator was AL504, named *Commando*, which was fitted out to a high VIP standard to become the personal transport aircraft for Winston Churchill.

No 1425 Flight's objective was to establish and maintain a regular and reliable transport service to Gibraltar and the Middle East. Of course the acquisition of the early Liberators and the increasing number due to enter the Service meant that both the Flight and the Training Unit had to introduce a crew conversion course not only for RAF airmen but also BOAC crews. Although the Training Unit made good progress during the early weeks when it fully utilised the facilities at Long Marston, a spell of rather severe weather and heavy snowfalls in January 1942 delayed the training programme and the month of February showed only a little improvement. Furthermore, it was also fairly clear that the Air Ministry considered Honeybourne as a purely temporary or stopgap base until a larger and more suitable permanent station became available. Thus it was towards the end of March when the Ferry Training Unit moved to Lyneham, Wiltshire, which had recently been vacated by Flying Training Command; No 1452 Flight followed in early April. Lyneham then developed into a major RAF transport base. Ferry Command immediately relinquished Honeybourne, along with Long Marston, to Bomber Command and on 13th March 1942 a new OTU was formed at Honeybourne – No 24.

The new Unit was originally placed in No 7 Group but when No 92 Group was formed in May, No 24 was transferred into the new Group, but only until 15th November when it was moved into No 93 Group. Like No 22 OTU at Wellesbourne Mountford the Unit was mainly devoted to training crews for RCAF bomber squadrons. Perhaps the biggest surprise for the Unit's instructors and ground crews was the news that the Unit would not be equipped with Wellingtons but rather Whitley Vs. Of the fifteen heavy bomber OTUs then in operation, only two (Nos 10 and 19) were using Whitleys for operational training, although another OTU – No 81 – was provided with Whitleys when it opened in July. In fact, the redoubtable Whitleys were fast approaching

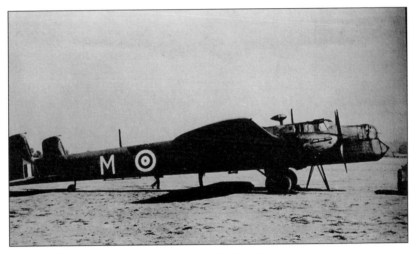

No 24 OTU was originally equipped with Whitley Vs.

the end of their operational life as front-line bombers, the last Whitley bombing operation conducted by an operational squadron was made on 27th/28th April 1942. Nevertheless No 24 OTU would soldier on with Whitley Vs for the next two years.

The demand for trained bomber crews was reaching a peak during 1942. On 22nd February Air Chief Marshal Arthur Harris had been appointed AOC-in-C of Bomber Command and he will forever be associated with the history of Bomber Command. Under his leadership the Command's fortunes dramatically changed and with a grim and ruthless determination he prosecuted an increasingly strong and forceful bombing offensive, which, although it showed signs of success, also proved costly in aircraft and crews. During late 1942 and early 1943 aircrews had about a 13% chance of completing a tour of thirty operations – a grim statistic for trainee crews. Furthermore, new heavy bomber squadrons were being formed, especially during the latter months of 1942, another factor that only increased the urgent demands for even more trained crews.

The objective for OTUs during 1942 was to produce fourteen crews each fortnight. Although this ambitious target figure was not really attainable for No 24 OTU until it had received its full complement of Whitleys, in July the Unit was almost there with fifty-four Whitleys and five Ansons on its strength. The hectic pace of operational training inevitably brought in its wake a marked increase in the number of training accidents. Although the Unit lost eight Whitleys due to accidents and another six in operations during 1942, Long Marston experienced a most remarkable run of good fortune, not a single accident to any aircraft operating from the airfield during the year.

Most of the initial conversion training was conducted at Long Marston and normally one of the oldest training aircraft was retired from flying duties to be used as a ground instruction machine. It was normal practice for satellite airfields to instruct crews on basic handling skills. These were more especially conducted during the hours of darkness, for obvious reasons, as Bomber Command was then almost solely devoted to night bombing. In November an Armament Flight was formed at Long Marston, with several of the older and less reliable Whitleys set aside for gunnery instruction, along with a few Battles and at least two Lysanders, each operating as target-towers. The gunners were instructed in the theory and technical nature of their trade – hydraulics, pyrotechnics, control of the Nash and Thompson turrets, especially the tail turret with its four machine guns, sighting, correct deflection firing and live practice with the Brownings. They were also instructed on diagnosing the reasons for gun stoppages and practised continually to clear their guns until they could perform the task 'almost blindfold'.

The problem of simulating enemy fighter attacks had taxed the minds and ingenuity of Bomber Command since the inception of operational training. In the early days both operational fighter squadrons and fighter OTUs had on occasions been called upon to make mock attacks on training aircraft, but the sheer logistics in mounting such exercises, allied to the increasing operational and training demands, meant that OTUs had to fall back on their own very limited resources; the Units' smaller aircraft – Ansons, Lysanders, Battles, and Defiants – were called upon to double as enemy fighter aircraft. At least these exercises brought a welcome change for their pilots, some relief from the hazardous business of being fired at by not-too-accurate gunners!

In June 1943 Bomber Command attempted to improve this aspect of operational training with the formation of the Bomber (Defence) Training Flights; the first six were numbered from 1381 to 1386. These Flights were originally equipped with Curtiss Tomahawks, the American-built fighter that had not quite made the grade operationally, although the Flights would later be re-equipped with 'out-dated'

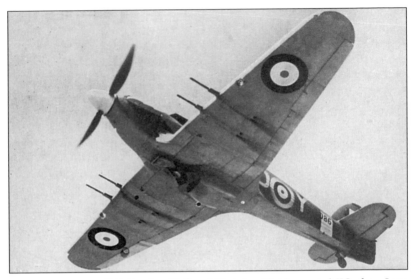

Hurricane IIC. No 1381 Bomber (Defence) Training Flight operated IICs from Long Marston.

Hurricanes. The Flights made regular tours of OTUs and Heavy Conversion Units. Nevertheless, it was freely acknowledged that it was virtually impossible to replicate the enemy fighter attacks that the crews would face in live operations. However, these exercises did afford the gunners the opportunities to practise and perfect evasive instructions to their pilots whilst desperately attempting to keep the attacking aircraft in their sights and make allowances for the correct deflections. In March 1944 No 1381 Flight moved into Long Marston from Pershore, Worcestershire and made the airfield its operational base. Not long after the Flight's arrival, its Tomahawks were exchanged for Hurricane IICs, which by now had ceased to be used operationally. They had been mainly superseded by IIDs and IVs.

If 1942 had passed by as a remarkable accident-free period for Long Marston, 1943 proved to be somewhat different. The first accident at the airfield occurred on 16th March, when a Whitley V crashed on take-off as its undercarriage collapsed. The crew were fortunate to escape unharmed. The pilot, Sergeant A. E. Evans completed his course and was posted to a Halifax squadron – No 158. Whilst on his ninth operational sortie to Cannes in the south of France on 11th/12th November, his Halifax was shot down by a night fighter on the

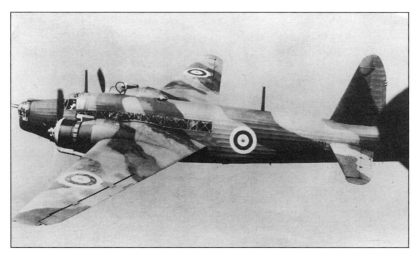

No 24 OTU was re-equipped with Wellingtons in April, 1944.

homeward flight. Evans and another crewman were killed; the other five airmen escaped by parachute, three of whom managed to evade capture. Then, on 28th June, a Wellington III of No 22 OTU, which had taken-off from Gaydon, was attempting to make an emergency landing at Long Marston after suffering a loss of engine power. It crashed into two parked Whitley Vs. Four Canadian airmen in the Wellington were killed and another injured, and the three aircraft were written-off as beyond repair – an expensive accident. During October, in two fatal accidents ten RCAF airmen from Long Marston were killed.

For a short period during 1943 Wellingtons of No 23 OTU, based at Pershore, also made use of Long Marston's facilities but there is no record of any of these Wellingtons being involved in accidents whilst flying from the airfield. These Wellingtons were really the forerunners of the Unit's own Wellingtons; the first Mark IIIs and Xs began to appear in April 1944, although Whitleys continued to operate with another OTU until late August. The last Whitley V to be lost by the Unit took-off from Long Marston on the night of 22nd/23rd May 1944. It was one of six detailed for a 'Nickel' operation; each crew had been given a different target area. The Whitley crashed near Alençon, France, and all six RCAF airmen are buried at the Canadian war memorial at Bretteville-sur-Laize. No radio messages were received that the crew were either under attack or, indeed, that they were experiencing technical problems with the aircraft. This particular Whitley had been operating with the Unit since September 1942 and had already flown a total of 652 hours, which even for a training aircraft was inordinately high; it was assumed that the likely cause of this accident was engine failure. Sadly, it was not long before the first Wellington from Long Marston was lost in a fatal accident. On the night of 3rd/4th July a trainee crew returning from a cross-country exercise crashed their Wellington on landing. It careered into the bomb dump and burst into flames; the seven RCAF airmen were killed.

The last trainee crew from Long Marston to go missing left the airfield on 23rd/24th September 1944, bound on a long cross-country night exercise, and part of their planned route took them out over the North Sea. At 1.20 am the crew reported their position as just off the Norfolk coast, and nothing further was heard from them. Over the next two days six Wellingtons were sent to the area to make an extensive search for any signs of wreckage or survivors but sadly to no avail. The five RCAF airmen were presumed dead and their names appear on the panels of the Runnymede Memorial.

From mid-February 1945, with the closure of No 93 Group, the Unit's two airfields had been placed back under the control of No 92 Group. Although No 24 OTU continued to suffer training losses, no crews from Long Marston were involved. It could be said that the airfield's safety record was far better than most OTU satellite stations, especially when it is compared with its near neighbour at Atherstone (or Stratford-upon-Avon as it was now called). No 24 OTU was one of the last Units to be disbanded; it finally closed down on 24th July 1945. Both Honeybourne and Long Marston were placed under the control of No 8 Maintenance Unit at Little Rissington, Gloucestershire, and they were mainly used for the storage of the large number of redundant Wellingtons.

Then followed a period when Long Marston, like several hundreds of airfields, was placed under Care and Maintenance. The Air Ministry subsequently decided that a number of airfields could be 'modestly' refurbished and then used for flying training purposes. In the Midlands, Halfpenny Green and Lichfield, Staffordshire were included along with Long Marston. So, once again, flying returned to Long Marston, in the shape of Airspeed Oxfords, the steady and reliable 'Ox-box', which was still going strong. The Oxford Vs belonged to No 10 Advanced Flying School, operating from Pershore, and the school used Long Marston purely as a Relief Landing Ground. The school was

The entrance to the present airfield.

mainly engaged in training 'National Service' pilots and closed down in 1954. The school's closure also heralded the demise of the well-loved Oxfords. They finally disappeared from the RAF after seventeen years of sterling service. Long Marston finally closed as an RAF station in 1954 but nowadays it is still active with a variety of private flying including a couple of microlite flying clubs and Freedom Sports Aviation uses the old control tower as its base. The entrance to the present airfield is in fact the wartime emergency entrance at the end of the third runway.

11
SNITTERFIELD

During 1942 there was a quite frantic urgency and rush to build as many airfields as were then considered necessary for the operational and training needs of both the RAF and the USAAF. It was perhaps inevitable that a number of these hastily selected sites would be completed to a far higher standard of specification than their ultimate use justified; in fact, a couple were barely used at all. Without doubt Snitterfield fell into this category. It was constructed as a standard bomber station; yet, during its brief three or so years as an RAF station, the airfield was only used by a variety of small training aircraft, and then only in a purely satellite role.

Snitterfield was completed and ready for occupation in early 1943. At that time all but four of the twenty-seven bomber OTUs were up and running and well into their operational training, and the next two Units to be formed during the year had already been allocated to new airfields. Furthermore, those OTUs operating in a fairly close proximity to Snitterfield were already well provided with satellite airfields. Therefore, Snitterfield, which had cost close to £3/4 million, appeared to be surplus to requirements, certainly as far as Bomber Command was concerned.

The airfield was situated about three miles to the north of Stratford-upon-Avon, to the west of the A46 to Warwick. The land was some 375 feet above sea level and made Snitterfield one of the highest airfields in Warwickshire. The airfield also straddled the minor road from the village of Snitterfield to Bearley, about one mile away to the west, where there was a rather convenient railway station. Three concrete runways covered with tarmac had been laid down: the main one, running almost due north to south, measured 2,000 yards, with the other two at 1,350 and 1,250 yards, respectively. Perhaps not surprisingly, considering the airfield's subsequent use, the runways

194

were not further extended. A total of thirty circular hard-standings were sited in three corners of the airfield and two 'T1' type hangars erected but because of the number of training aircraft using the airfield, six Double Blister hangars were later supplied and placed on the unused dispersal pans.

I suspect that Flying Training Command gladly accepted the offer of this pristine new airfield and it was allocated to No 23 Group; an ideal satellite airfield for one of its flying training units in the area. Although Church Lawford was about seventeen miles away to the north-east as the crow flies, No 18 (Pilots) Advanced Flying Unit based there certainly needed another airfield to alleviate the pressure of the large number of training aircraft using its runways. Thus the first aircraft to use Snitterfield's new runways were Airspeed Oxfords and for the next two years or so they would be the most familiar aircraft at Snitterfield and in the skies above.

However, in January 1944, the airfield suddenly acquired a distinctive continental atmosphere when the RAF (Belgian) Initial Training School arrived. The school had been recently formed to produce both pilots and ground crews for the proposed Royal Belgian Air Force, which was planned to re-form after the war ended. The RAF had also formed a similar Flying Training School of airmen of the Royal Norwegian Air Force. There had always been a number of Belgian airmen serving in the RAF; during the Battle of Britain twenty-nine pilots served in RAF squadrons and six were killed during the battle. Indeed, No 131 squadron later had two Flights manned solely by Belgian fighter pilots. In November 1941 these two Flights were formed into the first RAF (Belgian) squadron – No 350 – followed by a second squadron, No 349, in January 1943: another example of the cosmopolitan make-up of the wartime RAF.

The Belgian school was equipped with the inevitable Tiger Moths, along with a number of Miles Master IIs – advanced flying trainers. The Master was probably the best designed single-engined advanced trainer of the war. It possessed similar handling characteristics to both the Hurricane and Spitfire and provided the student pilots with their first real taste of high-speed flying, as it had a maximum speed of about 240mph. The first Master had flown in March 1939 but a mere handful had entered the service by the outbreak of the war. It was constructed of wood and covered with plywood with a sliding canopy. Masters proved to be most reliable training aircraft, with over 3,200 being produced in three Marks. All had an instructor's seat in the rear

Miles M.9A Master – advanced trainer – first flew in March 1939.

cockpit, which could be raised to provide better vision over the head of the pupil in front and was especially beneficial during practice landings and take-offs. In October the school moved away to Snailwell in Cambridgeshire, where it remained until mid-October 1946, when the Royal Belgian Air Force was re-formed.

Snitterfield's concrete runways were heaven-sent for many a trainee crew which might be having difficulty finding their home base at night or maybe experiencing mechanical or engine faults. With so many OTUs in the area, Snitterfield was frequently used for emergency landings. The airfield seemed to be used more often by trainee crews of No 22 from nearby Wellesbourne Mountford and Stratford-upon-Avon. Indeed, on 14th February 1944, a trainee crew from Wellesbourne Mountford engaged on night circuits and landings tried to land at Snitterfield. The pilot, Sergeant Shields, RCAF, made an error on his landing approach and the Wellington III crashed short of the runway at Comyns Farm; the aircraft caught fire and the four RCAF airmen were killed. Five months later (24th/25th July) another Wellington III of No 22 OTU crashed on landing when the starboard undercarriage failed to lock. All the crew escaped unharmed. During late 1944, like most training airfields in the Midlands, Snitterfield was used as an emergency airfield for operational bombers based in Nottinghamshire or Yorkshire.

In early April 1945 No 18 (P)AFU moved into Snitterfield en bloc from Church Lawford with its full complement of Oxfords, although at this stage of the war refresher flying training was nearing its end. On 29th May the Unit was disbanded, and the Oxfords were despatched to other flying training schools or placed under the care of Maintenance

North American Harvards: student pilots receiving final instructions.

Units. Nevertheless, the airfield continued to be controlled by Church Lawford and was used as a Relief Landing Ground for No 20 Flying Training School, which had recently formed at Church Lawford. The school was equipped with another famous Second World War advanced trainer, the American-built North American Harvard.

The Harvard was the most universally used military training aircraft of all time. The original protoype, designated NA-16, had first flown back in April 1935. Two hundred were ordered in June 1938 by the British Air Purchasing Commission in Washington, and the first Harvards arrived in the RAF in the following December. By the outbreak of the war over two hundred and twenty were on the strength of flying training schools. The Harvard was the RAF's first all-metal advanced trainer and it was used in great numbers by the RAF, USAAF and EATS training schools. It was a rather squat and compact aircraft and was never considered particularly graceful. Both cockpits were quite commodious and comfortable, but it was said to be 'noisy and unpleasant to fly'. Many flying instructors considered it to be inferior to the British-built Master trainer, and it was certainly slower, at 205mph.

Snitterfield is now providing pleasure for many gliding enthusiasts.

Nevertheless, over 17,000 were finally produced and they were still training pilots well into the 1950s.

The airfield closed down in 1946 and since those days part of the site has disappeared under a golf course. However, the remainder of the old airfield that lies to the south of the Bearley/Snitterfield road is now a busy centre for members of the Stratford-upon-Avon Gliding Club. It is very reassuring to see a windsock flying from the old airfield site, and that almost sixty years later Snitterfield is now providing pleasure for many gliding enthusiasts.

12
STRATFORD-
UPON-AVON

In the summer of 1940, when the fate of the country hung delicately in the balance, the Air Ministry sanctioned, along with many more, the final approval for the construction of a bomber airfield on farmland close to the village of Atherstone on Stour, about three miles to the south of Stratford-upon-Avon and directly east of the A34 to Oxford. The necessary land had been requisitioned from the Alscot Park estate, and all too soon the building contractors moved in and for the next twelve months everyday life for the villagers became a good deal more intolerable.

The fate of the airfield that was slowly taking shape at Atherstone had already been decided: it was to act as a satellite airfield for an Operational Training Unit destined to be formed at a larger airfield at Wellesbourne Mountford, which was also in the process of construction about 3½ miles further away in a north-easterly direction – another example of wartime airfields being sited far too close to one another. When both airfields were fully operational, it was not unusual for aircraft taking-off from Wellesbourne Mountford to pass directly over the main runway at Atherstone, which was particularly unsatisfactory from a safety viewpoint.

Atherstone, as it was known in its early days, was provided with all the standard features of a bomber airfield – three concrete runways (1,600, 1,350 and 1,210 yards in length), although one runway was uniquely completed half in concrete and half in tarmac, I presume for experimental reasons, twenty-three hard-standings, a perimeter track, two large hangars (B1 and T1 types), control tower, fuel storage tanks, a water tower, a bomb dump, shelters and defence emplacements, and so on. However, because it was intended to operate as a satellite, there were far fewer temporary buildings and huts, as the planned station complement was to be in the region of 1,650 personnel.

Wellesbourne Mountford opened in April 1941, and almost immediately No 22 OTU was formed. Equipped with Wellingtons, the unit was almost exclusively devoted to the training of crews for bomber squadrons of the Royal Canadian Air Force. Three months later, on 5th July, an advance party of officers and men from the unit arrived at Atherstone to prepare the new airfield for occupation. They ensured that all the vital services and communications networks were in place and functioning and that the necessary stores had arrived. A week later the first Wellington 1Cs of 'C' Flight appeared, along with the trainee crews. This now meant that No 22 was officially recognised as a full strength OTU and would ultimately receive the full complement of aircraft: a total of fifty-four Wellingtons and maybe sixteen Ansons. However, Wellington ICs were still in relatively short supply because priority was given to the eighteen front-line Wellington

Wellington III (of No 419 squadron): there were always plenty of Wellingtons to be seen at the airfield.

squadrons, and Ansons were also not particularly plentiful as they were still serving operationally with Coastal Command besides their major training commitments.

With Atherstone up and running, the Unit was now fully expected to produce at least six fully trained crews every two weeks. In order to maximise the number of flying hours the training regime at OTUs was strict and rigorously regulated. The flying day started at 08.00 hours, and maybe an hour earlier during the summer months, with exactly an hour's break for lunch, and daylight flying ceased at dusk. The night flying, which was the most important part of the flying programme, normally commenced at 20.00 hours and continued well into the early hours of the morning. One of the critical factors that impinged heavily on the flying programme, besides the weather conditions, was the availability of serviceable Wellingtons. It was estimated that on average only about 60% of a Unit's Wellingtons were engaged on training at any given time, despite the fact that each Unit was allocated a number placed in the 'immediate reserve'. The older training aircraft had already completed a considerable number of flying hours before being allocated to the Units and thus were more prone to mechanical failures, requiring regular inspections, maintenance and servicing checks. It was soon made abundantly clear to the trainee crews that one of the most heinous crimes they could commit was to land their Wellingtons at another airfield without a good reason. This meant that the aircraft was effectively 'lost' for a day or so whilst it was being recovered and brought back to the Unit. For the harrassed Flight Commanders attempting to maintain the maximum number of flying hours, good weather and a ready supply of reliable aircraft were priceless commodities which helped to make their lives a little easier.

Not long after the airfield had opened it was renamed Stratford-upon-Avon. There is, of course, another and larger Atherstone in Warwickshire to the north-west of Nuneaton, and in all probability the understandable confusion between the two places brought about the name change. The first three months of flying training progressed without any serious mishap. However, as has already been noted, flying accidents were an unfortunate part of operational training. The first fatal accident occurred on 8th November: a Wellington piloted by Warrant Officer J. A. Rich, DFM, was making a landing approach, when the port engine failed and he attempted to increase speed to go around for a second approach. Unfortunately, the aircraft stalled and

Accidents were an unfortunate part of operational training. This Wellington III (of No 21 OTU) was written-off in August 1944. (Via J. Adams)

crashed at Alscot Park, barely a mile from the airfield. The aircraft burst into flames and W. O. Rich, along with another crewman, was killed; the other three airmen escaped with injuries. W. O. Rich, a flying instructor, was an experienced Wellington pilot, having recently completed an operational tour with No 142 squadron.

Most, but not all, of the flying instructors at OTUs were similar to Rich in that they had already completed an operational tour, which in March 1941 had been set at thirty operations. The airmen would then be given a well-earned spell of leave and many were awarded the DFC (for officers) and the DFM (for NCOs). After leave they proceeded to a flying instructors' school to be inculcated into 'the standard methods of flying instruction' before being posted to an OTU. On average they would remain on flying training duties for eighteen months or so, and many instructors found it somewhat difficult to adjust to the rather mundane and monotonous regime of a training unit after the drama, excitement and more relaxed discipline of an operational squadron. They sorely missed the close camaraderie of an operational bomber crew, and some quickly volunteered for a second operational tour. However, Bomber Command had to maintain a fine balance between the need to retain their expertise on operational training duties and the constant demand for experienced and battle-hardened airmen to serve in operational squadrons and those that were being newly formed. One instructor described his time at an OTU as 'a tour of circuit bashing with "sprog" [recruit] crews ... it was like a living hell'! Not all instructors subscribed to this view; the majority felt

The rear turret of a Wellington.

One hundred and twenty airmen are buried in the RAF plot at Stratford-upon-Avon cemetery.

that anything was better than constantly facing enemy flak and fighters night after night.

Until mid-November 1942 Stratford-upon-Avon remained an integral part of No 22 OTU. Along with the Unit's other satellite airfield (Gaydon) Stratford-upon-Avon was called upon to take on extra flying training commitments whilst the runways at the parent station were under repair. This increased pace of flying training did, of course, come with a heavy price to pay: there was a marked rise in the number of accidents at the airfield. In ten months twenty-nine airmen, mainly RCAF airmen, were killed in accidents at the airfield or whilst engaged on flying exercises. Another twenty-five airmen went missing in action whilst engaged in the several bombing operations that were mounted from the airfield during September.

The cost in human terms of operational and conversion training in Bomber Command was quite staggering. It is recorded that over 8,190 airmen (more than double Fighter Command's total fatalities in the Second World War) lost their lives either in flying or ground accidents. This figure is about 15% of Bomber Command's total fatal losses during 1939/45. Several cemeteries and churchyards in Midland towns bear a silent and poignant testimony to the sacrifice of so many young airmen, especially those from Commonwealth countries; perhaps of these none more so than the cemetery at Stratford-upon-Avon. One hundred and twenty airmen are buried in the RAF plot; ninety-seven of them served with the Royal Canadian Air Force. It is a most moving experience to visit this cemetery with all those neat white headstones arrayed in serried lines, which really registers the immense sacrifice made over sixty years ago by a generation of young men, many of whom are laid to rest so far from their homelands.

The first serious accident at the airfield in 1942 came on 25th May; a Wellington was awaiting clearance to take-off on a night exercise, when it was struck by another Wellington as it landed in a strong cross-wind, and nine airmen were killed. Tragically, Sergeant C. R. Whitworth, who had escaped with minor injuries from the first accident at the airfield back in November, lost his life in this unfortunate accident. September proved to a very black month indeed. On the first day a Wellington crashed heavily and was so badly damaged that it was beyond repair, but fortunately the crew escaped with injuries. Six days later a five-man Canadian crew were killed when their aircraft lost power and crashed near Bicester, Oxfordshire. The crew's captain, Flight Sergeant P. N. Templeton, was only nineteen years old. He was an American, who had travelled from Texas to Canada to volunteer for the RCAF, one of the many Americans who enlisted in the RCAF before the USA entered the war. On the 10th/11th two Wellingtons from the airfield were shot down over Düsseldorf; ten RCAF airmen were killed, including an American from Montana. Two nights later another two crews went missing on the operation to Bremen. One Wellington was shot down by a night fighter, the other was presumed to have been lost over the North Sea.

The last major bombing operation involving trainee crews was scheduled for the 16th/17th, with Essen as the target. Every operational and training aircraft detailed for the operation was required to undergo an air test before being cleared for operations. In addition to the Canadian crew, two RAF ground fitters were on board a Wellington 1C which left Stratford during the afternoon for an air test. When the aircraft reached an altitude of 800 feet it lost power and suddenly went into a dive, the force of which tore off the port wing and tail section; the aircraft crashed about six miles south-west of the airfield, with no survivors. On the Essen operation that night one Wellington failed to return to the airfield; it had been shot down by anti-aircraft fire. The pilot and navigator – Flight Lieutenant J. Dawson, DFC and Warrant Officer P. S. O. Brichta, DFM – were instructors with the Unit. Brichta had recently survived an operational tour in Handley Page Hampdens with No 49 squadron.

The final accident in September occurred on the 24th, when a Wellington returning from a night cross-country exercise landed with only the aid of floodlights and the aircraft careered into the control tower, killing one of the crew. Thirty-eight airmen had been lost during the month, along with nine Wellingtons. It was a difficult task for the Station and Flight Commanders to restore the morale of trainee crews as well as the permanent personnel after such a traumatic month. Nevertheless, throughout the war Bomber Command's commanders and crews suffered heavy losses at certain periods and their unofficial motto could well have been 'Press on regardless' – a resolute and steely determination probably best epitomised by its Commander-in-Chief, Air Chief Marshal Harris.

On 15th November the control of Stratford-upon-Avon was passed over to No 23 OTU, based at Pershore, Worcestershire, which had also been operating since April 1941. Very little changed at the airfield: it remained in the same Group – No 91 – and No 23 was also equipped with Wellingtons. A greater number of Mark IIIs were filtering into OTUs. The first Mark IIIs had been delivered to No 9 squadron in July 1941, although they would not really appear in any appreciable numbers until early 1942. They were powered by the larger 1,500hp Bristol Hercules XI engines, which produced an improved performance. Wellington IIIs were the first to be specially designed to carry the 4,000 pound 'Blockbuster' bomb. Their armament had been slightly increased with two manually operated Browning .303 inch guns in the beam position. Although over fifteen hundred were produced in twenty-seven squadrons, they were quickly overtaken by the much improved Mark Xs.

It would be quite natural for the staff at Stratford to hope that with a different OTU, the station's fortunes might also change for the better. There was some justification for this view, considering the arrival of the Wellington IIIs and, in the spring, the first Xs. In the fourteen months that the airfield remained under the control of No 23 OTU, a total of thirteen training aircraft were written-off, with the loss of twenty-eight airmen. One particularly disastrous accident occurred on 29th January 1943, when five crews were despatched on a long cross-country navigation exercise. Two Wellingtons collided in heavy

The Armament Flight of No 23 OTU was equipped with Miles Martinet target-towers.

cloud over Suffolk and both crashed near RAF Honington. All ten airmen were killed.

Exactly four months later (29th May), a Wellington III from the airfield was detailed to take part in the 'Wings for Victory' fly-past over Pershore. Air Chief Marshal Sir Edgar Ludlow-Hewitt, GCB, GBE, CMG, DSO, MC attended to take the salute at a ceremonial march-past led by the bands of the RCAF and the Worcestershire Regiment. Sir Edgar had been the AOC-in-C of Bomber Command from September 1937 to April 1940 and was now the Inspector-General of the RAF. The Wellington piloted by Flying Officer G.S. Hynam, DFC, RCAF, an American from Ohio, left Stratford at 18.25 hours, and forty-five minutes later it crashed over Pershore, when for some unaccountable reason the port wing sheered off. The five airmen were killed and a civilian was injured; it was a tragic conclusion to the celebrations.

During 1943 No 23's Armament Flight regularly used the airfield. The days of the make-shift Lysander target-tower had virtually disappeared and in their place the RAF had a specially designed target-tower – the Miles Martinet. The prototype M.25 had made its first flight on 24th April 1942 and was largely based on the successful

Master advanced trainer but with a longer nose section to compensate for the weight of the target-towing equipment. Like all Miles' aircraft, it was of wooden construction and covered with plywood. The two-seat Martinet cruised at just under 200mph, and over seventeen hundred were produced. Martinets continued to operate for some years after the war until replaced by faster aircraft. They were also used by training units to operate as enemy fighters in fighter affiliation exercises.

In early 1944 it was clear that major reconstruction work was required at Pershore, and furthermore the throughput of RCAF crews for RCAF bomber squadrons was being adequately covered by No 22 OTU. It was therefore decided to close No 23 OTU with effect from 15th March. Another OTU (No 15 at Harwell) was also disbanded on the same day, but both were replaced by new OTUs in June. Stratford-upon-Avon had returned to the control of No 22 OTU in the first week of March and most of No 23's Wellington Xs were transferred to No 22 to operate mainly from Stratford. For some months they retained the old Unit's codes – BY, FZ and WE – rather than No 22's codes – DD, LT, OX and XN.

Just over a month after the airfield had returned to No 22 OTU, the 'fold' so to speak, a Wellington III, whilst making a landing approach lost power in one of its engines. The trainee pilot, Sergeant J. G. M. Savard, RCAF attempted to make a single-engined landing, not a particularly easy procedure even for an experienced pilot. It crashed after over-shooting the runway but all on board escaped unhurt. The crew was returning from a bombing practice over the Prior Hardwick bombing range. Sergeant Savard was killed in action in mid-August whilst engaged on mine-laying in the Baltic Sea with No 433 squadron. At the age of nineteen he was one of the youngest RCAF pilots to be killed in action with Bomber Command.

Such bombing practices were one of the most important aspects of the last few weeks of the training course. The Wellingtons were loaded with about six $10\frac{1}{2}$ pound practice bombs and the bombing practice was carried out in a strict clover-leaf pattern, close radio contact being maintained with the observers in the high towers overlooking the range. Time at the bombing ranges was always at a premium, and the timings over the range were precisely regulated. Most trainee crews spent far more time carrying out simulated bombing runs over selected targets using a special camera, which provided the trainee bomb aimers with some valuable practice, as well as providing photographic evidence for their instructors back at the airfield.

The number of accidents at OTUs reduced quite markedly in 1944. This was largely because of the newer Wellington Xs, now almost exclusively equipping the training units. Another important factor was that the trainee crews were gaining more actual flying training and experience. By May most had completed eighty or more flying hours by the time they left the Units, almost double that of two years previously. In fact, from May to December, only four Wellingtons were lost from Stratford-upon-Avon and one of these could most probably be attributed to faulty aircraft rather than to human error.

On 11th June a Wellington III crash-landed at the airfield after a cross-country navigation exercise. One of the engines had cut out and the undercarriage failed to engage, despite all the crew's efforts to pump it down manually. The aircraft had originally been delivered to No 23 OTU in September 1942; in 1943 it had survived a mid-air collision with a Spitfire and after extensive repair the Wellington had flown almost continuously, logging over 1,273 flying hours, which was considerably above the norm for a training aircraft. Five days later, there was no doubt that human error was the cause of a fatal accident when a Wellington X flew into a hill in the Lake District, killing all eight RCAF airmen. Then, in July (29th/30th), a Wellington X returning in the early hours of the morning crashed at Coombe Farm, about 1½ miles from the airfield, when one of the engines burst into flames. Only one member of the crew escaped. The other five airmen were buried at Stratford-upon-Avon cemetery; the last RCAF airmen to be interred there.

As far as I am aware, the last accident at the airfield occurred on 8th December, when a Wellington X from No 11 OTU based at Westcott, Buckinghamshire, made an emergency landing late in the evening. The pilot, Flight Sergeant Wagstaffe, RNZAF, landed about a third of the way along the runway, and because of the downhill gradient the aircraft careered on until it came to a stop with the nose section overhanging the railway line that formed the eastern boundary of the airfield. The Wellington was hardly damaged and the crew were able to climb down unharmed but no doubt badly shaken by this alarming experience! The station master at Stratford-upon-Avon was alerted to the situation and he ordered a train with some gangers to go and investigate the problem. Inexplicably, the engine driver failed to apply the brakes early enough and the engine crashed into the aircraft

The old control tower has survived at Stratford-upon-Avon airfield.

causing so much damage that the aircraft was subsequently written-off. It is not clear whether the engine was also damaged! This railway line has long since been dismantled.

A week after this accident operational training ceased at the airfield. The Unit's Wellingtons left on 15th December. Stratford-upon-Avon was transferred to No 26 (Signals) Group of Bomber Command and allocated as a satellite airfield for the Signals Development Unit based at Honiley. Until November 1945, when the airfield finally closed for flying, assorted aircraft of the SDU and the Signals Flying Unit – Whitleys, Wellingtons, Spitfires and Hudsons – used the airfield purely as a Relief Landing Ground.

Like so many wartime airfields, Stratford-upon-Avon has long since returned to farming: Ailston Farm covers most of the existing airfield site. There are a few surviving buildings that still manage to evoke some strong images of the old airfield's wartime existence – the control tower, a bomb shelter and a pillbox – all adjacent to the farmhouse. I would stress that these disused buildings are on private farmland and therefore permission to view them would be required from the present owners.

13
WELLESBOURNE
MOUNTFORD

Although Wellesbourne Mountford appears alphabetically as the final airfield in this account, it was, in fact, the first of Warwickshire's wartime airfields to open – on 14th April 1941. Over sixty-three years later the airfield is still being used by aviators, with an inevitable windsock proudly proclaiming that fact. It is situated to the south of the B4086, about five miles to the east of Stratford-upon-Avon and just a stone's throw from the village of Wellesbourne, where the unfortunate villagers found themselves on the north-eastern edge of the new airfield. John Laing & Son Ltd was responsible for its construction and like most of the Warwickshire airfields, it was built to accommodate a Bomber Command OTU.

Three concrete runways, in the conventional 'A' pattern, were laid down along with thirty-nine hard-standings; these were spaced out around the airfield and lead from the long perimeter road. Rather unusually, a large type 'J' hangar was erected, with four 'T1' types behind it set out in pairs. Although an extra Over Blister hangar had also been provided to the south-east corner of the technical site, it was used as 'a free gunnery trainer'. The technical site was set out immediately to the east of the hangars, and beyond that and across the perimeter road was the Communal or Domestic site. There were also five dispersed sites to the east and south of the airfield, with hutted accommodation for officers, NCOs and airmen. The Bomb Stores were placed to the south of the airfield, on the edge of Wellesbourne Wood, with the Wireless Transmission site positioned to the west of the wood. Little House in the village of Wellesbourne had been requisitioned and

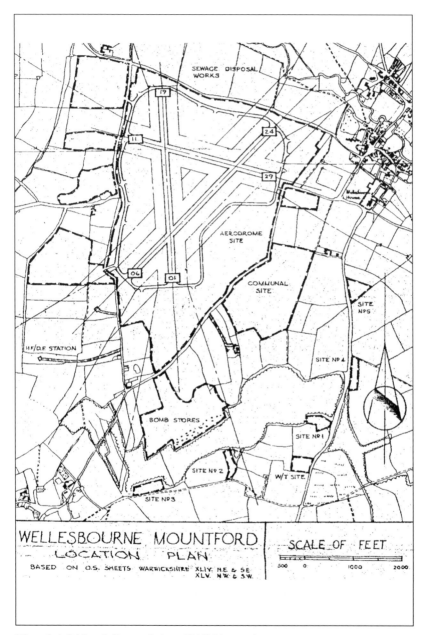

Plan of airfield and dispersed sites. (RAF Museum)

was utilised as the WAAF officers' quarters and mess, while the airwomen were housed in nearby Wellesbourne House, where even the gardener's cottage was brought into use as the sleeping quarters for the WAAF sergeants, an indication of how comprehensively a wartime airfield could impinge on the local scene and community.

It could be argued that the airfield site was far from ideal. Its two satellite airfields – Atherstone and Gaydon, already under construction to the south-west and east, respectively – were within a distance of five miles, below the Air Ministry's prescribed limit for adjacent airfields. Also the presence of high land, Long Hill (420 feet) at Loxley, just a mile or so to the south of the main runway, could present a flying hazard, certainly for trainee crews. To my knowledge, several wartime airfields with similar neighbouring high land were not authorised for any type of flying training.

Nevertheless, a new OTU – No 22 – was formed at Wellesbourne Mountford on 14th April and was placed under the aegis of No 7 (Training) Group at Abingdon. It was the thirteenth OTU to be created in the previous twelve months, and, like the majority, the Unit was equipped with Wellington 1Cs, along with several Avro Ansons. No 22 had been selected to train bomber crews for squadrons of the Royal Canadian Air Force. The first RCAF bomber squadron – No 405 (Vancouver) – commenced operations with Bomber Command on 12th/13th June 1941. This was the onset of a four-year bombing offensive, during which fifteen RCAF squadrons completed 46,700 operational sorties (12% of the Command's total), losing one thousand and twenty-six aircraft and over nine thousand, nine hundred airmen in action, by far the largest contribution in men and machines made by any Commonwealth country.

The Unit had hardly settled down to its regular training regime before the *Luftwaffe* paid several visits to the airfield during May and June. The bombing caused slight damage to several buildings and heavily damaged two Wellingtons and an Anson. On 10th May a Heinkel III attacked the active runway, but fortunately its bombs were off target and fell harmlessly on a field close to the village. Despite this enemy action, the Unit managed to exceed four hundred and ten flying hours during May, a most commendable total, considering that it had only been operating for six weeks.

The various categories of aircrew – pilots, air observers, wireless operators/gunners, bomb aimers and air gunners – arrived at the OTU after the normal spell of leave granted on successful completion of their specialised courses, all proudly wearing their newly acquired wings or half-wings. At this stage of the war they were really unaware of just what to expect during their ten weeks at the Unit no horrendous tales of life at the OTUs had yet filtered down through the service. Of course, they fully anticipated that a considerable amount of their time would be spent flying at night. One pilot later remembered, 'I was scared stiff ... taxi around at nightfall, literally praying that we hadn't forgotten some essential part of the cockpit drill ... take-off, go round and land and the same thing again and again ... followed by those seemingly interminable cross-country night flights when we thought we were lucky to have found the airfield in the dark ... If you passed through the OTU training you were bound to get through operations ... In the time I was at an OTU twenty-two Wellingtons crashed owing to the inexperience of the pilots and engine failure.'

The Unit's instructors continually impressed on their trainees the sobering fact that operational flying training could be a most hazardous business unless they rigidly adhered to the correct procedures. This harsh truth was brought home to them in the early hours of 26th June, when a trainee crew took-off for night circuit practices, and their Wellington crashed close to the airfield at Loxley after losing power and stalling. The five-man crew were all killed, and the three Canadian airmen were the first to be buried with full military honours at Stratford-upon-Avon cemetery. Many of the trainees were required to attend the funeral parade and often some were detailed to act as pall bearers. This practice was common to all OTUs, which used local cemeteries and churchyards for the interment of Commonwealth and Allied airmen. Perhaps the Unit Commanders felt that their attendance at such distressing ceremonies would further concentrate their minds on the attendant perils of operational flying training. As a gunner later grimly recalled, 'Funerals were commonplace events at OTUs'.

Before the novice crews were allowed to take their first flight in a Wellington, they underwent up to two weeks of ground instruction interspersed with the inevitable parades, drills, inspections and seemingly endless physical training exercises. It was clearly emphasised that operational flying was not only a mentally draining task but was also physically demanding. They would have already organised themselves into crews, and from now on during the course they mainly received their ground and flying instruction as an entity. The parent station of an OTU had been provided with a number of specialised

Ground instruction in the art of bomb aiming.

instructional buildings not normally present at the satellite airfields. Amongst these were Celestial Navigation training rooms, Link trainer blocks, Turret and W/T Instructional buildings, an AML Bombing trainer and a Crew Procedure Centre. Most of these buildings, certainly those at Wellesbourne Mountford, were sited quite close together in the technical site.

Perhaps the most important buildings in the ground training regime were the last three. The AML Bombing Trainer was two-storeys high and this method of ground bombing instruction dated back to 1925. A film projector was housed on the first floor, which projected an image of a slowly moving landscape on the ground floor below, the image was intended to simulate an aircraft flying at an altitude of about 8,000 feet and it could be adjusted to replicate the effect of different wind directions and speeds. The trainee crew, with a bomb sight and navigation instruments, gathered around an observation space above the image, and bomb runs on selected targets were simulated. The bombsight was devised to instruct the crew at which point, usually some distance from the target, the bombs should be released. All the crew had to take part in this exercise, as a bomb aimer might be injured or killed on operations and another crew member would have to take over the duties. The Mk IX Course Setting Bombsight was in general use in Bomber Command at this time, although an improved version – Mk XIV – was later introduced, which automatically accounted for any evasive action the pilot might take during the bomb run. An American-built copy, known as 'T1', was brought into use on Wellingtons towards the close of 1943.

The Turret Trainer (there were two at Wellesbourne Mountford) used similar photographic techniques, but with the image projected onto a curved wall. The Frazer-Nash turrets on Wellingtons were armed with .303 inch machine guns and the gunners were expected to learn how to strip down a machine gun in the shortest possible time with their eyes open as well as closed! The rear gunners in their remote turrets had the coldest and most dangerous position of any crew member, cramped for hours upon end on a hard seat with no heating, and often the perspex turret misted over and then quickly froze. Without doubt, it was the most vulnerable position in any bomber. Night fighters invariably made their attack from the stern, and for the whole of the operation the rear gunner had to remain constantly on the alert, searching the night skies for the merest hint of an ominous shadow. Few, if any, crewmen envied the lot of the 'tail-end Charlies', as they were known. However, for most of the time on the flying exercises at the OTU, the rear gunner was merely a passenger in his lonely turret.

The largest instructional building was the Gunnery and Crew Procedure Centre, which at Wellesbourne Mountford was situated on the edge of the communal site. This type of ground training had been devised by Air Vice-Marshal Arthur Harris, when he was AOC of No 5 Group during 1939/40. Harris had utilised the fuselages of a couple of old bombers to place the trainees in a simulated operational environment. He later recalled, '... the whole crews were put through this 'hoop' time and time again *ad nauseum* if necessary and certainly until they were procedure perfect.' An old Wellington had been specially adapted at Wellesbourne Mountford and the crews were expected to be thoroughly conversant with the aircraft's lay-out and equipment. The various emergency crash positions and ditching stations were endlessly practised as well as dealing with different types of operational emergencies. The Wellington was boarded and exited from the nose and the crews were continually warned about the dangers of the propellers, which revolved at about shoulder height and could result in a fatal accident to any unwary airman turning too quickly either to the right or left!

The Procedure Centre or the Grope, as the test was known to the trainees, basically attempted to replicate the navigational and other problems a crew might encounter during an operation. The exercise was conducted in a large hall that was divided at the rear into a half-a-dozen two-level studios, each housing a different crew member. The noise of the aircraft's engines was amplified so that each crew member was forced to communicate by intercom and, as an added complication, the large clock controlling the test was set faster than normal, thus giving the trainees less time to undertake their normal tasks, let alone to react to any emergency which had been artifically created – icing, engine or radio failure, internal fires, crew injuries, emergency landings, ditchings in the sea and dinghy procedures. Most trainees remembered 'the Grope' as a most stressful occasion but the lessons learnt in this building eventually saved the lives of many crews when confronted with the real thing.

Now commenced the actual flying part of their course and they were duly kitted out with their flying clothes and their necessary equipment. Crews operating in Bomber and Coastal Commands had to operate in aircraft that had very little effective cabin heating. One Wireless

A Wellington crew putting on their flying clothing. (via J. Adams)

Operator/Gunner said that he liked the Wellington especially because his seat was just behind the pilot, with 'a heater outlet right there'. The sheer and utter cold experienced on operations is a constant thread running through so many wartime memories by 'bomber men'. Over their battledress the crew members wore off-white knitted woollen pullovers along with the Irvin insulated flying suits with electrically heated separate linings; thick woollen sea-socks under the brown-suede zip-up boots; two pairs of gloves – silk, woollen – under the leather flying gauntlets; and flying helmets with goggles and oxygen masks. Life jackets, more commonly known as Mae Wests and either chest or seat parachute harnesses completed their ensembles. Those airmen that went to war in the heavy bombers looked rather cumbersome in all this clothing and equipment as the countless wartime photographs vividly portray. Another new experience for these fledgling 'bomber men' was their introduction to the briefing room, which figured so large and importantly in their future operational life with all its attendant stresses, and the fears and excitement the briefings engendered. Before any flying training exercise the trainee crews were closely and carefully briefed in all aspects of the operation, and on their return they were debriefed just as if it had been a real live operation.

With the opening of Atherstone (Stratford-upon-Avon) as a satellite airfield in July, No 22 attained the status of a full OTU and the Unit managed to improve on the nine hundred flying hours it had achieved during June. This was just as well because during the last three months of 1941 there were prolonged spells of bad weather which curtailed the flying programme. Indeed the weather conditions were so severe that Bomber Command did not mount any operations during 5th to 10th October and 10th to 15th November. The conditions did not greatly improve in December, although operational flying training continued in quite unfavourable weather. Sadly, on 7th December, two of the Unit's Wellingtons were lost in a snow storm whilst returning from evening exercises. One crashed about a mile from the runways and the other flew into Long Hill at Loxley. One of the five airmen killed was a flying instructor, Pilot Officer W. J. Turner, DFM, who had previously served with No 405 RCAF squadron.

Since mid-July 1941 'Nickel' operations had been mounted as the main means of providing trainee crews with some experience of live

Wellingtons of No 22 OTU at Wellesbourne Mountford. The distant Wellington clearly shows one of the Unit's codes – DD. (via H. Raymond)

operational flying. The busiest year for Nickels was 1943, when over 1,470 crews were called upon for such operations, but there was a marked increase during May 1944, when over two hundred and thirty sorties were flown, really to inform the French people that the long-awaited invasion of Europe was near at hand. By the end of the war Bomber Command crews had dropped over 1,500 million leaflets, over 90% of these from June 1941 and mostly by OTU crews, although the chiefs of Bomber Command were never convinced that the wholesale despatch of propaganda leaflets warranted the risk of valuable crews. Air Chief Marshal Harris, in one scathing attack, thought all they achieved was 'to supply the continent's requirement for toilet paper for the long five years of war'!

There were however other ways of replicating operational flying – 'Bullseyes' and 'Erics'. The former were conducted at fairly regular intervals and were organised and controlled at a Group level. They involved trainee crews from many OTUs flying, invariably at night, over certain designated areas or towns where the crews would face opposition from the ground defences – anti-aircraft and searchlight batteries. 'Erics', on the other hand, were exercises, perhaps less frequently mounted and mainly by day, where the crews were confronted by operational fighter squadrons from either Nos 10 or 11 Groups of Fighter Command.

In retrospect 1942 proved to be an eventful twelve months for the Unit in several respects. For a brief period from 1st September until 15th November, with the opening of Gaydon and until the loss of Stratford-upon-Avon, it was upgraded to a 1½ OTU. It was then one of the busiest OTUs in the country. The year also brought the heaviest toll of training accidents: nineteen aircraft from Wellesbourne Mountford, without those lost at the satellite airfields; fifty-three airmen killed and another sixteen seriously injured. Virtually all these accidents came in the first nine months of the year with just one in December, almost completing three months accident-free – quite an achievement considering the hectic pace of flying training during this period.

One particularly horrendous accident occurred on 5th May, when a Wellington IC returning from a night exercise stalled whilst in the airfield circuit and crashed, bursting into flames. The Station Medical Officer, Squadron Leader F. G. Mogg, was one of the first at the crash scene. Despite the intense heat, he managed to locate one of the trapped airmen, Flight Sergeant D. A. Blue, RCAF, and with great difficulty rescued him from the burning aircraft. Sadly, F/S Blue later died from his injuries, but Squadron Leader Mogg was awarded the George Cross for his heroism.

The year was also a difficult time for the Unit because two runways at the airfield were undergoing repair and extension. One had been found to be critically short for night flying, and the other needed re-alignment because of the adjacent high ground. Therefore the Unit's staff were constrained to juggle with flying training schedules. Besides relying heavily on its satellite airfields, the Unit briefly used the facilities at Wing, Buckinghamshire and Elsham Wolds, Lincolnshire; indeed, for the first bombing operation to Cologne on 30th/31st May the Wellesbourne Mountford crews were detached to Elsham Wolds. In the event two crews were forced to return early owing to mechanical problems and four were lost in action: nineteen airmen killed, including four instructors.

In early October the first Wellington IIIs were received and were quickly followed by Mark Xs. In theory, their arrival should have brought a marked improvement in the Unit's safety record but in practice this turned out to be only marginally better. Seventeen Wellingtons were lost during 1943, May being a particularly hard month when in two weeks four Mark Xs were lost along with fourteen airmen. During September some of the Unit's Mark Xs were modified.

Wellington X (of No 10 OTU) with faired-over nose turret.

A hood was fitted over the front turret and the Hercules VI engines were adjusted to slightly increase their power boost. Although the modifications were considered a success, it was decided that just the front hoods should be introduced, and on a minor scale; some ninety hoods were finally ordered and about one third fitted to the Unit's Mark Xs.

No 91 Group had commenced Nickel operations at the end of 1942, and in the first six months of the following year the number of operations had steadily increased until seven per month were mounted by July. At the end of August the Group became involved in Operation *Starkey* – bombing operations against selected targets (mainly ammunition dumps) in the Pas de Calais region of northern France. These operations were undertaken in an attempt to convince the enemy that the impending invasion of Europe would take place along that stretch of coast. On four nights (30th/31st August to 3rd/4th September) a total of one hundred and twenty-five OTU crews led by PFF Halifaxes and Mosquitos bombed these dumps. No 22 OTU's crews took the lion's share, despatching thirty-six crews, and all returned safely to Wellesbourne Mountford. On the night of 8th/9th September a number of OTU crews joined a main bomber force in attacking enemy gun positions at Boulogne and not a single aircraft was lost. This operation was notable, as it was the first occasion that B-17s (Flying Fortresses) of the US Eighth Air Force flew a night operation with Bomber Command.

With the runways now back in a fully operational condition, they were very active with training Wellingtons, more especially from 11th July when No 312 Ferry Training Flight was formed at Wellesbourne Mountford in order to train crews prior to ferrying aircraft out to North Africa and the Middle East. This Flight also used Wellingtons and it remained at the airfield until mid-December. In January 1944 No 22 Unit managed to complete over 2,200 flying hours and when Stratford-upon-Avon returned as a satellite airfield in March, the Unit was once again approved as a 1½ OTU, with over eighty Wellingtons, six Ansons and six Martinet and Defiant target-towers. It was now producing on average forty-six trained crews each month who were still predominantly RCAF airmen.

During 1944 the incidence of training accidents finally began to fall. In total eleven aircraft were lost and twenty-nine airmen killed. This figure equated to about 3% of the total OTU accidents in the year. When one considers the size of the Unit and the hundreds of

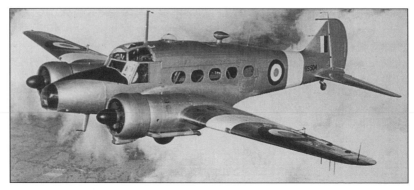

Avro Anson T Mark 20 Navigational trainer: Ansons operated from the airfield for many years.

flying hours completed, it was a remarkable record. Unfortunately, three experienced pilots were killed during the year – Flying Officer L. W. Matthews, DFM, RCAF, Flight Lieutenant R. A. G. Turner and Flying Officer D. C. F. Parker, DFM. The latter officer had previously completed a tour with No 424 (RCAF) squadron and was killed in May when flying a Martinet I on a fighter affiliation exercise; his aircraft spun out of control and crashed near Wellesbourne.

A feature of the operational flying training during the later stages of the war was the number of OTU crews that were sent out on a variety of diversionary operations. These were usually routed over the North Sea, some to within ninety miles of the German coast. They were really attempts to divert enemy fighters away from Bomber Command's main force when it was attacking Berlin and other targets in eastern Germany. Sometimes diversionary flights were made over northern France with a similar object. However, such operations were also mounted on nights when no major bombing operations were taking place. In these instances the diversions were intended to attract enemy fighters and thus help to deplete the enemy's fast dwindling reserves of valuable aviation fuel.

The first such operation was made on 20th/21st February 1944 when one hundred and thirty-two OTU crews flew far out into the North Sea as the preliminary diversion before the main bomber force left to attack Stuttgart. But it was after D-Day and after the return of Bomber Command to German targets in July that these large-scale operations became almost weekly occurrences at OTUs. By and large they replaced Nickel operations as the trainee crews' 'graduation flights'. These diversionary exercises continued to be flown well into April 1945. Thus, training Wellingtons were still being used 'operationally' several months after Bomber Command's final Wellington sortie (47,000+) on 7th/8th January 1945 – a Radio Counter Measures flight over the North Sea. As well as these operations, trainee crews were also engaged on Air/Sea Rescue patrols over the North Sea. On nights when the Command had launched major operations, the trainee crews were ready to respond to Mayday signals from crews that had ditched in the sea.

Like all operational training airfields in the Midlands, Wellesbourne Mountford was used on a number of occasions by operational aircraft returning from bombing raids which had been diverted to other airfields because of poor weather conditions at their home airfields. The occurrence of these emergency landings increased quite markedly during 1944, which is not really surprising considering the vast armadas of Allied heavy bombers operating both by night and day. Perhaps it is no mere coincidence that it was mainly RCAF squadrons based at Yorkshire airfields that used Wellesbourne Mountford. After all, most of the RCAF crews were familiar with the airfield, having completed their operational training there, and they could be well assured of a friendly welcome from their Canadian colleagues. For example, on two occasions in June (7th and 14th), Halifax IIIs of No 420 (Snowy Owl) RCAF squadron landed there, followed in August by ten RCAF Halifax IIIs. The last emergency use of the airfield came on 15th April 1945, when fifteen Halifax IIIs of No 415 (Swordfish) squadron landed. At least the Canadian trainees had their first opportunity to inspect Handley-Page Halifaxes, the heavy bomber that the majority would fly when they were posted to an operational RCAF squadron.

At the end of 1944 the Unit had once again lost Stratford-upon-Avon as a satellite but Gaydon was still going strong. During 1945 there was a considerable decrease in the requirement of trained crews and although three Wellingtons were lost in accidents, fortunately there were no casualties. However, on 28th May, a Wellington X engaged on a night cross-country exercise failed to return. The crew's last recorded position was over St George's Channel, between Eire and Wales. Early the following morning six trainee crews were sent out to search the area for survivors, but alas in vain; the five-man RCAF crew was declared missing, the last fatalities suffered by the Unit.

Almost two months later, on 24th July, No 91's course was

Miles M.19 Master II glider-tug operated with No 3 GTS.

completed and the Unit was closed down after training well in excess of two thousand bomber crews. In the previous four years or so, No 22 OTU had lost a total of one hundred and eighteen aircraft (sixteen in action), which was about 5% of the total OTU aircraft (2,354) lost during the war. On the face of it, this figure appears a high cost to pay for operational training; in fact, it was about equal to 23% of the *total* aircraft lost by Bomber Command in action and operational crashes in the United Kingdom. But it should be recognised that without all the skill, dedication and patience of the flying and ground instructors, along with the courage and determination of the trainee crews who strove to achieve the high standards demanded from them, Bomber Command would have been a much poorer and far less effective bomber force. The contribution made by its twenty-seven OTUs was immense.

From the end of July 1945 Wellesbourne Mountford and Gaydon were transferred to Flying Training Command and, as has already been noted, No 3 Glider Training School with its Miles M-19 Master II glider-tugs and Hotspur gliders arrived from Exeter. In 1942 Miles Aircraft Ltd were asked by the Air Ministry to produce a glider-tug, with the intention of replacing the existing Hawker Audax and Hector biplanes then in service. Within weeks Miles adapted their Master advanced trainer by incorporating a towing hook in the rear fuselage with a release mechanism in the cockpit. The trial was successful, and numerous Master airframes were suitably adapted. The Masters and Hotspur gliders remained at the airfield until early December 1947 when Wellesbourne Mountford was passed over to

Oxfords of No 9 Advanced Flying Training School in June 1952. (RAF Museum)

Technical Training Command to continue in a training role, albeit mainly the ground variety. In the following spring the School of Photography moved in from its hitherto temporary base at Farnham, Surrey. The school remained at the airfield until 1963, when it left for Cosford. Aerial photo-reconnaissance had been an essential aspect of

View of the airfield as it is now.

the Service since First World War days; indeed, the Army had considered photo-reconnaissance one of the main reasons for the formation of the Royal Flying Corps. During the Second World War the school, then based at Farnborough, had trained over six thousand, five hundred RAF photographers. The school now had the use of a few Ansons, mainly Marks 20 and 21, along with the odd Spitfire XI and Mosquito XVI for aerial photography training.

In the fifteen or so years that it was in residence at Wellesbourne Mountford, the school was required to share the airfield's facilities, first with the School of Education, from 1948 to 1950, and then, from May 1950, with No 9 Advanced Flying Training School. This school was equipped with the indomitable Oxfords and provided advanced flying instruction up to wings standard for largely National Service airmen. The course lasted ten/twelve weeks, and on successful completion the newly qualified pilots passed on to an operational training course. In the Queen's Coronation Review of the RAF at RAF Odiham, Hampshire in June 1953, twelve Oxfords from Wellesbourne Mountford were part of the impressive line-up of aircraft, which reflected all Commands of the Service, from the 'lowly' Chipmunk,

Prentice and Oxford trainers right up to the new jet fighters and V-bombers. However, in the following year, like other similar AFTSs, No 9 closed down.

The School of Photography remained as sole resident until 1963 and three years later the airfield was sold. Another fifteen years passed by before flying finally returned to Wellesbourne Mountford when in 1981 HRH the Duke of Edinburgh formally opened the private airfield. This is now confined mainly to the west of the old wartime airfield and has two concrete runways, one just below 1,000 yards and the other at 644 yards. The airfield is at present managed by Radamoor Ltd and there are several flying schools in residence along with the Touchdown cafe. Wellesbourne Wartime Museum, housed in the old Battle Head-quarters building and operated by the Wellesbourne Aviation Group, is open every Sunday from 10am to 4pm.

14
LANDING GROUNDS

Brinklow

Brinklow, about 5½ miles due east of Coventry, was the site of one of just fifty Satellite Landing Grounds (SLG) that were developed and used during the Second World War. They should not to be confused with the many more operational or training satellite airfields; these fifty SLGs were predominantly used for the storage, preparation and repair of operational aircraft. They owe their existence to Sir Alan Cobham, who in the autumn of 1940 was asked by the Ministry of Aircraft Production to search for possible sites that were not too distant from operational stations and were suitable for the storage of aircraft. Even at this early stage of the war, RAF Maintenance Units had already become rather congested and overcrowded, and, as aircraft production was rapidly increasing, this situation was likely to worsen considerably in the immediate future.

Sir Alan, accompanied by a chartered surveyor and a small team of RAF pilots, scoured the countryside for likely sites. Ultimately, he and his team indentified over one hundred locations, although less than a half were actually approved and developed. A firm of consultant engineers, Rendell, Palmer & Tritton, was given the task of managing their preparation and construction. All these SLGs were rather primitive grassed landing areas provided with a few basic facilities and the minimum of buildings in order to afford the maximum camouflage from the air. Usually, existing farmhouses were requisitioned to accommodate the small number of Service personnel based there. At many of the sites almost miniature hangars, known as Robins, were provided and they were often camouflaged to resemble farm buildings. Originally SLGs were forbidden to be used as emergency

Handley Page Hampdens could be seen at Brinklow and Leamington. This one of No 455 (RAAF) squadron. (RAF Museum)

landing grounds and for this reason they did not appear on any aeronautical charts. The aircraft stored there were heavily camouflaged, and most of the sites were guarded by Army units or local Home Guard companies, although some SLGs were also protected by guard dogs. In fact they were the first Service sites to use RAF guard dogs. Perhaps the most famous SLG was at Woburn Abbey, the ancestral home of the Duke of Bedford.

All the SLGs were numbered 1 to 50, and the first one to be brought into service in December 1940 was at Slade Farm, Oxfordshire. Brinklow, as its number (No 46) indicates, was one of the last SLGs to be prepared and brought into use. Brinklow received its first aircraft, Handley-Page Hampdens, in October 1941 and was placed under the control of No 29 Maintenance Unit at High Ercall. Certainly from late 1943 until Brinklow closed in late 1945, various training aircraft from Ansty and Church Lawford used the landing ground, albeit intermittently.

Hockley Heath

There were four Relief Landing Grounds (RLGs) in Warwickshire, of which Hockley Heath was certainly the busiest and best utilised.

Shortly after the outbreak of war twenty-four RLGs in England were swiftly brought into use and by early 1940 this number had doubled, with many more sites being requisitioned and developed. RLGs were all grassed airfields of quite varying sizes and really required the minimum of preparation and construction work. All that was needed was a couple of reasonably level fields, the removal of hedges, perhaps the provision of drainage, the erection of about half-a-dozen prefabricated huts and the installation of a fuel storage tank. In many instances the odd Bellman hangar was provided, but more often than not a number of Blister hangars.

Hockley Heath, situated at an altitude of 450 feet above sea level, could lay claim to being the highest 'airfield' in the county. The grassed landing ground was sited slightly to the north-west of the village whence it gained its name and was bordered in the east by the A34 from Birmingham to Stratford-upon-Avon. Originally, the landing ground offered two grassed landing runs of 1,250 and 800 yards in length but these were later extended to 1,700 and 1,300 yards, respectively. It was perhaps better supplied with facilities than most RLGs, with seven Blister hangars, fuel storage tanks for 4,000 gallons of fuel and a sufficient number of Laing and Nissen huts to accommodate over seventy permanent personnel who were based there. Like virtually all RLGs, it came under the control of Flying Training Command but was directly administered by the nearby RAF station at

The ubiquitous Tiger Moth: they were much in evidence at RLGs.

Student glider pilots being shown the instruments.

Elmdon. From late 1941 Hockley Heath was used by Tiger Moths of No 14 EFTS, based at Elmdon, and in August of the following year Oxfords and Tutors from Church Lawford used the landing ground. Then, in February 1943 No 5 Glider Training School moved in, equipped with Master II glider-tugs and Hotspur gliders. At this stage of the war all glider pilots were recruited from army personnel, with the objective that they would be as highly trained and disciplined as infantry troops, well able to make a positive contribution to the land battle when they had landed their gliders. Nevertheless, all trainee glider pilots had been originally selected for flying training by a joint Army/RAF selection board. Before they arrived at the Glider Training School they had already undergone a basic flying course at an EFTS and would now receive instruction on glider techniques over a twelve week period. The school remained at Hockley Heath until late 1944, by which time most of the trainees were RAF pilots. Hockley Heath was then used by several other training aircraft, latterly North American Harvards of No 20 Flying Training School at Church Lawford. Towards the end of 1945 the Air Ministry relinquished its control of Hockley Heath and it was then used for a certain amount of private flying before closing three years later.

Leamington

Leamington was one of a coterie of three RLGs that were sited in an area around Warwick and Royal Leamington Spa. It was situated close to Harbury, just off the Fosse Way, and for the major part of the war Leamington was used for the repair and reconditioning of Hampden and Whitley bombers. However, it was also employed on occasions as an emergency landing ground for training aircraft from both Ansty and Church Lawford.

Southam

Southam was another small grassed RLG, which was situated at Southam Fields, to the east of the village and running alongside the A425 to Daventry. It had been laid out with two landing runs of 800 and 600 yards long, certainly more than adequate to accommodate the various training aircraft that used the landing ground from 1940 to 1944. Southam was placed in Flying Training Command and was directly controlled by No 9 EFTS at Ansty, and it was the school's Tiger Moths that began to use the landing ground from the summer of 1940.

In 1941 the RLG was provided with a number of Laing and Nissen huts for the seventy or so airmen stationed there. It was also supplied with six Blister hangars – two Extra Over and four Standard. These afforded ample storage and maintenance facilities, with the miniature technical site grouped in the south-west corner of the landing ground.

Extra Over Blister hangar, few of which have survived.

Besides the many inevitable Tiger Moths buzzing around Southam
with their trainee pilots making their endless practice landings and
circuits, Oxfords and more especially Tutors of No 2 Central Flying
School at Church Lawford were in greater evidence from 1942
onwards. When No 9 EFTS at Ansty closed down in mid-March 1944,
virtually all flying ceased at Southam and by the end of the year the
landing ground was handed over to the Ministry of Works for
storage.

Warwick

Not very far from Southam, at least by air, was another RLG. It was
sited about 1½ miles to the south-west of Warwick and slightly north
of the A429. Warwick opened for flying in December 1941 and the RLG
was mainly used by No 2 CFS and No 18 (P)AFU, based at Church
Lawford. Blister hangars were then de rigueur for RLGs because of
their ease of construction, and certainly Warwick was no exception; it
was supplied with two 'Over' types and another two that were erected
in the south-west corner of the landing ground. Also in this corner of
the RLG were eight Nissen and Laing huts, which were used for flight
offices, accommodation and mess rooms. Warwick remained in use

until the end of 1945, mainly by aircraft of No 18 (P)AFU, then based at Snitterfield. Like most wartime RLGs Warwick had closed down by the end of 1945.

Bombing Ranges

Besides all the wartime airfields and various landing grounds, there were, to my knowledge, three practice bombing ranges in the county, which were used by the various OTUs operating in the area. For quite understandable safety reasons, these bombing ranges were sited, where possible, in fairly secluded and isolated areas. The ranges required little more preparation work than the provision of a large white concrete circular target, although sometimes the target was in the shape of an arrow, and one or maybe two brick-built quadrant towers on high land overlooking the target area. From this vantage point an observer would take bearings on each flash bomb burst, fix the position and radio the result back to the parent airfield of the OTU concerned, who in turn would then pass the information back to the trainee crew. During night practices the target was illuminated by lamps and the trainee crews dropped parachute flares as target markers.

One of the county's bombing ranges was situated between Grand-borough and Sawbridge, about eleven miles east of Royal Leamington Spa, another at Prior Hardwick, some eight miles to the south, and the third at Shotteswell, four miles north of Banbury. Most of the land around these ranges was open to the public, but small red crosses were nailed to field gates to warn them of the dangers of wandering too close to the range, and of course the inevitable red flags signified the bombing range itself.

15
SIR FRANK WHITTLE
(1907–1996)
'the father of the jet engine'

Frank Whittle was born on 1st June 1907 at Earlsdon, Coventry and it might be argued that he was the most famous and influential figure the county produced in the twentieth century. When he was sixteen Whittle entered RAF Cranwell as an aircraft apprentice – No. 364365 – and during his three years there he so impressed his instructors that in 1926 he was one of five apprentices to be awarded a coveted flight cadet scholarship at the RAF College, thus joining the other 'elite' students – Peter Townsend (later Group Captain) was one of his contemporaries. By 1928 he had gained his pilot's wings, being rated 'Exceptional to Above Average'. He was posted to a famous fighter squadron, No 111, at Hornchurch, Essex and flew Armstrong Whitworth Siskins, which were produced in his home town. Whittle was later sent on a flying instructor's course at the Central Flying School at Wittering and on completion of the course he was appointed as a flying instructor at No 2 Flying Training School, Digby. It was here that his remarkable flying skills were recognised, when he and an instructor colleague, Flying Officer Campbell, demonstrated a crazy flying routine in two Avro 504Ns at the RAF Display at Hendon in June 1930. Later in the year he was posted to the Marine Aircraft Experimental Establishment at Felixstowe, Suffolk as a float plane test pilot.

Nevertheless, Whittle's major interest was aeronautical engineering, and more particularly the design of aero engines. In 1928 he had written a thesis entitled *Future Developments in Aircraft Design*, wherein he discussed the possibilities of rocket propulsion and of gas turbines

Group Captain Sir Frank Whittle. (RAF Museum)

driving propellers. In August 1932 he was selected to attend the RAF Officers' Engineering School at Henlow, Bedfordshire, which had gained a fine reputation for producing highly trained aeronautical engineers, each entitled to use the esteemed annotation (e) after his rank. After completion of the course Whittle spent six months in charge of the Aero Engine tests at Henlow. Thus far Whittle's service career could almost be described as meteoric; in just ten years he had progressed from a mere boy apprentice through the RAF College to become a commissioned officer, first as a fighter pilot, followed by flying instructor, then test pilot and now as a qualified aeronautical engineer. He was the epitome of a highly qualified and very professional RAF officer, exactly the type that Lord Trenchard had visualised in his concept of the peacetime Service.

In the summer of 1934 Whittle was seconded to Peterhouse College,

Frank Whittle's birthplace in Earsldon, Coventry. (Midland Air Museum)

Cambridge and spent much of the time working on his proposed turbojet engine rather than academic studies. Nevertheless, two years later he attained a First Class in the Mechanical Sciences tripos. Since his days at Cranwell he had been concentrating his mind on the theory and practicalities of substituting gas turbines for piston engines in the propulsion of aircraft. Indeed, he had taken out his first patent for a turbojet engine in 1930 but the patent lapsed in January 1935 because he lacked the necessary £5 to renew it.

Whittle was now fortunate that two ex-RAF officers, Rolf Dudley Williams (later knighted) and J. Collingwood Tinling, offered to raise sufficient capital for his further research. New patents were taken out and in April 1936 Power Jets Ltd was formed with £10,000 capital. Whittle managed to persuade the Air Ministry of the importance of his research and somewhat reluctantly they agreed to his working part-time on the project as 'consultant engineer' for 'not more than six hours a week'. He also managed to interest British Thomson-Houston (BTH) at Rugby in his concept, and some of the company's workers were contracted to Power Jets to build the first experimental jet engine at BTH's gas turbine factory at Rugby. It was known as the WU or Whittle Unit. The first test run took place on 12th April 1937. This prototype was not capable of powering an aircraft; so over the next eighteen months various modifications and reconstructions were made to produce a more reliable and powerful engine. Because it was felt that the experiments were becoming a trifle dangerous to conduct at the existing factory at Rugby, the experimental work was transferred to a disused BTH foundry – the Ladywood Works at Lutterworth, Leicestershire – and subsequently, because of a lack of space at Lutterworth, Power Jets' design staff moved to office accommodation at Brownsover Hall, some three miles outside Rugby.

Up until this stage the Air Ministry had shown little interest in his research and experiments although they had provided a contract worth a meagre £1,900. The redesigned engine made its first trial run at Lutterworth in October 1938 and the Air Ministry pledged a further £6,000 and placed Whittle on the Special Duties List, enabling him to devote himself full-time to his engine. In the following year, the Air Ministry, on the recommendation of Dr David Pye, the Director of Scientific Research, who had been most impressed with a test run at Lutterworth, now took a positive interest. In July, Power Jets Ltd received a contract for a flight engine – W1 – to be designed by Whittle and built by BTH. It was also clearly stated that this contract would

Gloster E.28/39 at Farnborough during 1942.

continue even if war broke out. Ten months later the Air Ministry authorised the manufacture of three more jet engines.

The Air Ministry selected Gloster Aircraft Company to produce an airframe for Whittle's engine. The company's Chief Designer, W. George Carter, had been present at Lutterworth for a test running of the engine, and clearly the two men were of like minds. The Ministry's precise specification – E.28/39 (Experimental Jet Test-bed) – was passed to Gloster Aircraft on 3rd February 1940 for the production of two prototypes, with a clear indication that the experimental aircraft should be based on fighter requirements: the design should allow for the provision of four .303 inch Browning machine guns. The design drawings did show a space for the guns but the two prototypes were unarmed.

By April 1941 the first E.28/39 (W4041), now named *Pioneer*, was ready for its taxiing trials at Gloster's own airfield at Brockworth. It was a neat small low-wing monoplane, really not much larger in length and height than a Tiger Moth and with a slightly smaller wing span. In the evening of 7th April Gloster's Chief Test pilot, R.E. 'Gerry' Sayer, watched by Whittle and Carter, took the aircraft on its first taxi trials. The following day the aircraft reached 50-60mph and actually left the ground to a height of about six feet and a varying distance from 100 to 200 yards. Whittle taxied the aircraft himself on a couple of occasions; it must have been a proud moment to see the culmination of his dreams of some thirteen years.

It was decided that the first test flight would take place from RAF Cranwell, where the long concrete runway and flat surrounding countryside would be a more suitable and secret location. Some days were spent at Cranwell reassembling the aircraft and replacing the W.I.X engine used only for taxiing with a W.I flight engine. At 19.35 hours on 15th May 1941, Gerry Sayer took off from the south airfield in the Gloster E.28/39 after a run of about 600 yards, the first British turbojet aircraft to fly. After a flight of about seventeen minutes the aircraft landed safely. Other than Whittle, Carter and a few Cranwell officers, there were few officials to witness the flight and no official film unit to record this most historic event. Whittle merely recorded in his notes the bare statement 'E28 flew for the first time.' Six days later Sir Archibald Sinclair, the Secretary for Air, and a party of officials visited Cranwell to view this 'propellerless aircraft'. Ten flying hours were completed over thirteen days before routine maintenance was needed on the engine. The aircraft achieved a top speed of 370mph at 25,000 feet, well above that of the fastest Spitfire. After the success of these flights, it was decided that the more powerful W.1A would be installed, so the aircraft was again dismantled for return by road to the Gloster works.

In October, a Whittle engine, working drawings and three engineers from Power Jets were sent to the USA (in the bomb-bay of a Liberator!) to assist General Electric Company in their development of a turbojet engine. Whittle was flown to Boston in June 1942 to help General Electric to overcome some problems, and on 1st October, some seventeen months after E.28/39, the Bell XP-59A Airacomet with two General Electric Whittle-type engines made its maiden flight – the first American jet aircraft. Largely unknown to the rest of the world, Germany's first jet engined aircraft, the Heinkel He 178 had first flown in August 1939.

The next stages of the development of the E.28/39 took place at Edgehill, an Oxfordshire airfield close to the Warwickshire boundary, which was a satellite airfield for No 21 OTU, based at Moreton-in-the-Marsh. This airfield was presumably chosen for its location; it was convenient for Gloster's works and also relatively well hidden away, about nine miles north-west-north of Banbury. The first flight trials began on 4th February 1942, under high security, with Gerry Sayers again at the controls. A blade failure in March brought a brief halt to the programme, but Sayers managed to achieve speeds of 330mph at 15,000 feet. The Ministry of Aircraft Production had placed the production contract for Whittle's engines with Rover Motor Company. Whittle had anticipated that Rover would only be sub-contractors to Power Jets. By March Rover had completed eight W.2B engines and Power Jets were rather reluctant to install one in *Pioneer* without a comprehensive test run in a Wellington Test Bed, which when approved was undertaken by Rolls-Royce in a Wellington at their airfield at Hucknall. This was the beginning of Rolls-Royce's involvement in turbojet engines.

During the summer of 1942 the test flights of E.28/39 continued at Edgehill, often in front of senior military officers, including a number of American VIPs. Sadly, the test programme received a serious setback when Gerry Sayers was killed in a flying accident in October, and it fell to Michael Daunt to replace him, but it would be a number of months before the test flights were continued.

In February 1943 the second prototype, W4046, powered by a Rover W.8 engine, arrived at Edgehill, and it was flown by John Grierson, another celebrated test pilot. During its trials the aircraft managed to exceed 400mph, and on 17th March Grierson flew the aircraft to Hatfield in order that it could be demonstrated to Winston Churchill. This was the first cross-country flight made by a turbojet aircraft. Hitherto test flights had been confined to a narrow corridor some two miles wide and about thirty miles in distance. The first prototype, *Pioneer*, now powered by a Power Jets W.2/500 engine, had been delivered to the Royal Aircraft Establishment at Farnborough, where it was flown for the first time by RAF pilots, who collected various aerodynamic information on the aircraft's performance and handling qualities. On 30th July, whilst on a test flight, the aircraft's ailerons jammed at 37,000 feet and it went into an inverted spin; Squadron Leader Davie managed to bale out but *Pioneer* was lost in the subsequent crash. Towards the autumn W4046 was also sent to Farnborough and at the conclusion of a test flight programme it was subsequently placed in the Science Museum, South Kensington for permanent exhibition.

In the meantime, Power Jets Ltd had grown considerably and employed a work force of almost 1,000. During 1942 the company had moved to a new factory at Whetstone near Leicester, which was probably the first purpose-built factory to manufacture jet engines. Design work on the RAF's first operational turbojet fighter was showing considerable progress. Back in August 1940 Gloster Aircraft Company had been given Air Ministry approval for George Carter's

Power Jets' W2/700 engine on display at the Sir Frank Whittle Jet Heritage Centre at the Midland Air Museum. (Midland Air Museum)

preliminary study for a twin-engined low wing monoplane. Carter had opted for two engines, largely because of the relatively low thrust produced by the then current Whittle engine. However, de Havilland opted for a single engine in the Vampire, their turbojet fighter which first flew in September 1943. The Air Ministry's specification F.9/40 was issued in November, and on 7th February 1941 an order was placed for twelve prototypes, although in fact only eight (DG202 to DG209) were ultimately produced by Gloster. The specification required six 20mm cannons, but because of lack of power Carter restricted the number to four. In June the Air Ministry notified the company that the initial requirement would be for two hundred and fifty aircraft.

The first prototype (DG2020), already named the Meteor, powered by a Rover W.2B engine underwent its taxiing trials at Newmarket Heath from 29th June 1942. However, delays in the production of flight-standard engines greatly extended the development and test programme. There were several aircraft and aero-engine companies developing their own versions of Whittle's turbojet engine besides Power Jets itself: Metropolitan-Vickers Ltd with its Metrovick F.2, de Havilland with the Halford H.1, Rover, of course, and towards the end of the year Rolls-Royce had taken over the development of Rover's W.8B engine. Each of these engines would be used to power one of the prototype Meteors, only further complicating and prolonging the test programme.

It was not until 5th March 1943 that a prototype Meteor (DG206) made its maiden flight under Michael Daunt's control and it was in fact powered by two de Havilland Halford H.1s. This was followed by the flights of two more prototypes (DG202 and DG205), both with modified Rover W.2B/23s, on 12th June and 24th July respectively. Later in November another two (DG203 and DG204) took to the air, one with Power Jets W.2/500 engines and the other with Metrovick F.2s. However, it was not until 12th January 1944 that the first of twenty production Gloster G.41A Meteor F.1s made its maiden flight and it was provided with Rolls-Royce W.2B/23C Welland engines. The Meteor F.1's maximum speed was 415mph.

1944 proved to be an auspicious year for Frank Whittle in many ways. With the first successful flight of the Gloster Meteor F.1, the Air Ministry decided to make public the whole turbojet achievement and overnight Group Captain Frank Whittle became a celebrity and a household name. He was made a Commander of the Order of the British Empire and other honours would follow. However, Whittle felt that all this publicity was a little premature, largely because it gave Germany the knowledge of the advanced state of British turbojet technology. Actually, Germany's first turbojet Messerschmitt Me 262 had first flown in mid-April 1941, and the first Me 262As would enter the *Luftwaffe* in July, almost at the same time that the first Meteor 1s arrived with No 616 (County of Yorkshire) squadron on 12th July.

Whittle was certainly more than a little disenchanted with the way the production of his engines had been contracted out to other companies without his prior knowledge and changes made to the engines without consultation. Matters were not improved when, in April, Power Jets Ltd was nationalised, the only gas turbine company to be taken out of private control. It was renamed Power Jets (Research and Development) Ltd and the directors were appointed by the Minister of Aircraft Production. In future the newly constituted company would not engage in production but rather it would foster the gas turbine industry as a whole, offering its technical expertise.

At least Whittle had the satisfaction of seeing his brainchild powering RAF operational aircraft when No 616 squadron made its first operational Meteor sorties on 27th July, and on 8th August two of the squadron's pilots claimed the destruction of their first V1 flying-bombs. On 5th November 1945 a Meteor IV piloted by Group Captain H. J. Wilson captured the first post-war speed record at 606.38mph, only to be surpassed the following September by Group Captain E. M. Donaldson at 615.78mph. 3,662 Meteors of various marks were built up until 1955, including 1,072 by Armstrong Whitworth at Baginton, not that far from Whittle's birthplace. Whittle had been banned by the Air Ministry from flying because his technical expertise was too valuable to the country to be put at risk. However, he did get the opportunity to fly a Meteor in October 1945, when he piloted a Meteor F.1 (EE221) from Bruntingthorpe, Leicestershire. It was fitted with a Power Jet engine. Few airmen could claim to have flown an aircraft powered by an engine of their own design. Since September 1944 Power Jets' unit, based at Blaby near Leicester, had maintained a small flight of aircraft at Bruntingthorpe for test flying purposes.

Frank Whittle was not in the best of health and in January 1946 he resigned from the board of Power Jets (Research & Development) Ltd; the jet age had lost its founder. Later in the year the company was taken over by the National Gas Turbine Establishment so even the name of Power Jets disappeared as well. Whittle accepted a post as Technical Adviser on Engine Production and Design to the Controller

The first jet fighter to enter the Service – Gloster Meteor FI. (RAF Museum)

(Air) at the Ministry of Supply. Sadly, in April 1948, after twenty-five years of service (man and boy), he retired from his beloved RAF on medical grounds, at the rank of Air Commodore. In May Whittle was awarded a tax-free sum of £100,000 on the recommendation of the Royal Commission on Awards to Inventors and in the following month he was knighted as a KBE. On retirement from the Service, Sir Frank became very involved in civil aviation, acting as a technical adviser to British Overseas Aircraft Corporation and helping to plan its first Comet jetliner operations. The inaugural scheduled turbojet liner service to South Africa by a de Havilland DH.106 Comet on 2nd May 1952 must have been a proud moment for Sir Frank; a mere fifteen years since the first bench test run of his original engine, WU, at Rugby.

In 1976 he emigrated to the USA and set up home in Columbia, Maryland. He was in great demand in the States as a consultant and lecturer, as well as being appointed Navair Research Professor at the nearby US Naval Academy in Annapolis. Ten years later HM Queen Elizabeth II invested him with the Order of Merit, which is limited to twenty-four of the most distinguished people in the country. He published *Jet* in 1953 and *Gas Turbine Thermodynamics* in 1981. Sir Frank

Whittle died at his Maryland home on 8th August 1996 at the age of eighty-nine years. He was survived by his second wife and two sons from his first marriage. A memorial service in Westminster Abbey was held in his honour the following November.

The Midland Air Museum at Baginton was responsible, in June 1982, for placing a plaque on the house in Earlsdon where he was born, and five years later the museum opened the Sir Frank Whittle Jet Heritage Centre, a splendid and comprehensive display which illustrates, with exhibits, photographs and text, the remarkable story of 'the father of the jet engine'. Recently two full-size fibreglass models of E.28/39 have been placed on view, one on a roundabout just outside Lutterworth and the other at Farnborough. They were built by the Sir Frank Whittle Commemorative Group at Lutterworth.

A passing thought: one cannot help but wonder what Sir Frank's views would have been on the sad demise of Concorde in 2003!

16
CIVILIANS AT WAR

Many years have passed since the start of the Second World War and yet certain names can immediately evoke vivid memories of this long and dreadful conflict, and perhaps none more so than Coventry. On a single night in November 1940 the medieval 'City of Three Spires' experienced a terrifying blitz that extensively damaged the city centre and its fine cathedral church of St Michael. Such was the ferocity and devastation caused that Coventry became synonymous with the wanton destruction of war, especially when inflicted on the civilian population. This dreadful night of bombing became the accepted paradigm to measure other British cities and towns forced to suffer a similar fate when they too were 'Coventrated'.

On a sunny Sunday morning in early September 1939, millions of anxious people gathered around their wireless sets to listen to what the BBC described as 'an announcement of national importance'. They heard Neville Chamberlain, the Prime Minister, mournfully inform them that 'the country is at war with Germany'. Most people genuinely felt that it would be all over by Christmas (shades of the Great War!); certainly, few, if any, realised that almost six years would pass before the war would be finally over. During this time they stoically endured and survived untold hardships and privations, countless wartime restrictions, food rationing, death and destruction from the skies and the loss of loved ones. The 'People's War', as it is now known, touched the lives of every person in the land, adult and child alike, whatever their social background or, indeed, wherever they lived, although the last obviously determined the severity of their sufferings. As Lord Woolton, the Minister of Food, presciently recorded in his diary during the dark days of 1940, 'It isn't the

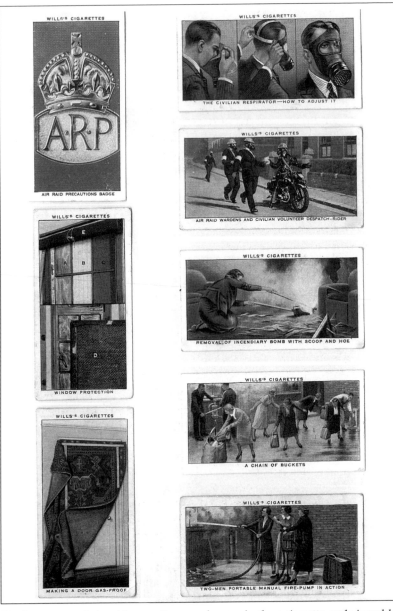

The importance of air raid precautions can be seen in these cigarette cards issued by W.D. & H.O. Wills in 1938.

Government of this country that's going to win the war – it's the people.'

The declaration of war did not really come as a great surprise; most people viewed it as a relief from all the suspense of the summer months. Earlier in the year every household had been issued with the *National Service Handbook*, which gave details of how they could contribute in a national emergency – demolition workers, telephone operators, ambulance drivers, fire watchers, canteen helpers, messengers and nursing support – these tasks were additional to the formal Civil Defence organisation that was already in place. The public was well aware that the country was inexorably being placed on a war footing. The various Air Raid Precautions had been established, public air-raid shelters appeared in streets and parks, trenches were dug, air-raid sirens erected and ARP posts and static water tanks were placed in surburban streets. The universally detested gas masks had been issued (thirty-eight million in September 1938) along with dire warnings that they should be carried at all times in the event of a war, and sandbags had suddenly appeared around public buildings.

In July four Public Information leaflets were sent to every house in the land – *Some Things you should know if War should come*; *Your Gas Mask*; *Your Food in War-Time*; and *Evacuation, Why and How* – although they clearly stated: 'This does not mean that war is expected now'! Only Birmingham and Smethwick were listed as 'evacuable areas' in the Midlands, and strangely not Coventry. In late August the Emergency Powers (Defence) Act gave the Government sweeping and almost draconian powers over the country and its people, and the mobilisation of the Armed Forces along with the call-up of Reservists and Territorials presaged the imminence of war.

The most ominous sign of the impending conflict was the mass evacuation of children and mothers from London and other major cities, which was set in motion on the morning of 1st September. The sight of tens of thousands of children with name tags, carrying their gas masks and a few treasured possessions, provided some of the most moving images of the war. It was estimated that some 90,000 children in Birmingham were eligible under the Government Scheme but in fact only about 50,000 left the city, bound mainly for towns and rural areas in the neighbouring counties. Coventry, after considerable pressure from the civic authority, had been belatedly included in the scheme – or at least those children living in the more populous parts of the city centre. In the event, some 8,000 Coventry children were registered by

The evacuation of children in September 1939 provided 'some of the most moving images of the war'. (Imperial War Museum)

their parents but only about a half presented themselves for evacuation to towns relatively close to Coventry. Some private schools in both cities moved en bloc to 'safer' country areas. Within months many evacuees had returned home, but during 1940 as the threat of air raids materialised the Government introduced additional schemes. In November/December, after the heavy air raids, over 22,000 children left Birmingham, and the whole of Coventry was declared an 'evacuation area'. However, by 1942, the number of Coventry children still evacuated was some 4,500 and this figure was almost halved by the end of the year. Indeed, it was not until April 1945 that the Government made official arrangements to bring the estimated 1.04 million evacuees home finally, although during the previous six months almost half had returned voluntarily.

The first month of the war saw the Government tightening its rigid control of the country. In addition to the War Cabinet a number of new ministries were formed, several of which greatly impinged on everyday life. Throughout the war the civilian population was bombarded with a plethora of information, advice, and instruction mainly from two ministries – Food and Information. Printed leaflets, radio broadcasts, newspaper adverts and street posters abounded; it was impossible to avoid constant demands to save, waste not want not, dig for victory, make do and mend, etc. Of the two ministries, the Ministry of Information was almost universally distrusted. The public (with justification) suspected it of withholding news – good or otherwise. Indeed, in 1940 over 50% of the population admitted to listening to William Joyce (Lord Haw-Haw) and his propaganda broadcasts from Hamburg in order 'to glean some news that the Ministry of Information keep from us'. The ministry's censorship of newspapers and broadcasting almost became farcical.

The National Services (Armed Forces) Act, which was passed within hours of the declaration of war, made all fit men aged between eighteen and forty-one liable for military call-up. A further Act in 1941 extended the call-up to women, and it was abundantly clear that the Government would call upon every able-bodied man and woman to do his or her duty, whether in the armed forces, industry or civil defence, and housewives were considered to be 'serving the country on the Kitchen Front'.

The blackout regulations were strictly enforced, often by over-zealous ARP wardens on their regular 'lights patrol'; 'Put that light out' was an early wartime catch phrase. Probably the blackout transformed conditions of life in wartime Britain more thoroughly than any other single factor. During September 1,130 persons (half of them pedestrians) were killed in road accidents, over double the number killed in the previous September. This was despite the fact that kerbs, lamp-posts, steps and trees had been painted white. In fact Birmingham Corporation reported that it had painted three hundred and fifty miles of kerbs! Even the imposition of petrol rationing on the 21st had little effect on the number of traffic casualties, but it must be admitted that only one household in fifteen owned a car. The basic petrol ration was completely withdrawn in March 1942, except for those classified as 'essential users', which resulted in virtually all private cars being taken off the road.

In late September the National Register was established, a comprehensive census of every household in the country. It enabled the Government to issue National Identity Cards to every person (including children). They were required to be carried at all times and produced on demand to anybody 'in authority'. Identity cards would

The two most important documents on the 'Home Front' – Ration book and Identity Card.

be closely followed by the provision of ration books. These two records were the most important and precious documents in wartime Britain. Soon ration books – stolen or forged – could be obtained for the price of £5 per book.

The first War Budget was also introduced in late September and brought 'an unprecedented level of income tax' – 7s 6d (37½p) in the £1 – with large increases in the duties on beer, spirits, wines, tobacco and sugar, and a special excess profits tax of 60%. This was merely the start of quite exorbitant levels of wartime taxation, which were accepted with a resigned forbearance because 'after all this war must be paid for'. Perhaps the almost total lack of consumer goods in the shops made the punitive rates of taxation a little easier to bear, as there was precious little for the public to buy with their hard-earned wages.

Nevertheless, despite the vastly changed world, the country relatively quickly 'slipped very easily into war habits', according to one wartime diarist. This patient and tolerant acceptance of a strange new lifestyle was helped by what had become known as the 'Phoney' or 'Bore' war. The anticipated and forecast heavy air attacks had not materialised, and there appeared to be a total lack of military action (except at sea by the infamous U-boats). Places of entertainment that had closed immediately on the outbreak of war had now re-opened, and cinemas especially were well-attended, as they would be throughout the war despite all the air-raids and the inconvenience of the blackout and poor public transport. The epic film *Gone With the Wind* became the first of many outstanding box-office successes.

On Christmas Day 1939 King George VI broadcast his Christmas message, continuing the tradition established by his father in 1932. His reserved and hesitant manner allied to his distressing stammer seemed to give his words greater moment and sincerity and further endeared him to his subjects. He said, 'We feel in our hearts that we are fighting against wickedness and this conviction will give us strength from day to day to persevere until victory is assured.' The sentiment was no doubt shared by most of his subjects. He and Queen Elizabeth became a powerful symbol to the British public throughout the war, with their regular visits to bombed cities and towns, factories and military bases. King George visited Coventry two days after the infamous blitz and he made visits to Birmingham in April and December 1940.

The winter of 1939/40 tested the resolve of the country to the utmost. It proved to be the most severe for over fifty years, with week upon week of hard frosts and heavy snowfalls, followed by flooding in

February, although this topic was forbidden to be reported in the newspapers because of official censorship – 'it might aid and abet German bombers'! Indeed, this also applied to weather forecasts. Coal was in short supply due to the severe conditions, and many households had to contend with the added misery of burst water pipes. From 8th January food rationing was introduced – first butter, bacon and sugar, shortly followed by cheese and meat. A wide range of everyday goods disappeared from the shops and queuing became a normal feature of daily life. It almost became a national obsession; cynics said, 'If you see a queue join it.' The uncertainty of what the future held in store only added to the strain and distress suffered during the long and harsh winter; the general mood of the country seemed to be for 'the war to begin properly and get it over with'. With the benefit of hindsight the majority of the people considered this first wartime winter to be the worst period of the war.

The weather, the blackout and restricted travel services ensured that the BBC became the country's chief solace during the dark winter evenings; three in four households owned a wireless set. The BBC's regular news bulletins became essential and compulsive listening, as they would throughout the war, with newsreaders, such as Alvar Lidell, Frank Phillips, John Snagge and Stuart Hibbard becoming familiar and well-loved voices. However, it was the comedy shows – *Hi Gang!*, *Band Waggon* and, of course, *It's That Man Again* (*ITMA*), that became the nation's favourites. They brought much humour into the drab and bleak war years. From 1940 *Workers' Playtime* and *Music While You Work* did much to alleviate the long drudgery of factory work. The radio was instrumental in creating the first wartime celebrity – Vera Lynn, the 'Forces' Sweetheart'. She was a vocalist with the Ambrose Orchestra and her haunting *We'll Meet Again*, first performed in the autumn of 1939, captured the mood of the country and became, perhaps, the most evocative of all wartime songs.

When Easter came at the end of March, it brought fine weather and blue skies. Many families escaped to the coast for at least a day, almost as if they had a premonition that this would be the last 'peaceful' holiday of the war. On 4th April Neville Chamberlain made a most ill-considered speech in the light of following events. 'After seven months of war I feel ten times as confident of victory as I did at the beginning ... one thing is certain Hitler has missed the bus.'! Four days later Denmark and Norway were invaded and the 'Phoney War' had come to a sharp and abrupt end. On the last day of the month the

Vera Lynn – the first wartime celebrity.

first civilian casualties as a result of enemy aircraft attacks occurred at Clacton-on-Sea, Essex. The 'People's War' was about to begin with a vengeance.

The invasion of the Low Countries and France in May, their swift defeat and the Dunkirk evacuation suddenly changed the whole nature of the war. The threat of invasion was now a very real and sombre probability. Largely as a result of the ill-fated Norwegian campaign, Chamberlain was forced to resign. He was a tired and broken man and terminally ill with cancer; he died in November. Chamberlain, with his close family links with Birmingham, was praised by the lord mayor as 'one of the city's most distinguished sons'. The formation of a National Government under Winston Churchill emphasised the perilous state of the country.

The elevation to Prime Minister of this inspiring and charismatic war leader proved to be a matter of 'cometh the hour, cometh the man'. Winston Churchill had an innate ability to inspire the British people whatever their poilitical persuasion. His stirring and unforgettable speeches during the country's darkest days seemed to express the indomitable spirit and deep feelings of the country. On 13th May he addressed the House of Commons for the first time as Prime Minister. He said: 'I have nothing to offer but blood, toil, tears and sweat. We have before us an ordeal of the most grievous kind ... You ask, what is our aim? I can answer in one word. It is victory. Victory at all costs – victory in spite of all terrors – victory, however long and hard the road may be, for without victory there is no survival.' 'Good Ol' Winnie', with his trademarks – the 'V for Victory' sign and inevitable cigar – was universally feted and cheered wherever he travelled. He made several journeys to Birmingham and Coventry to see at first hand the bomb damage, as well as visiting aircraft factories. Throughout the coming years it would be revealed that 85% of the country approved of his conduct of the war.

The deep concern felt in the country about a likely invasion was further fuelled by the issue of *Rules for Civilians in Case of Invasion* to every house in the country. It gave a mass of instructions – 'hide maps, food, petrol and bicycles ... but above all to stay indoors'. Signposts were taken down, as were the names on railway stations, and maps were removed from shops. From June church bells were silenced and would only ring again to signal an enemy invasion. The Treachery Act was passed in May, designed to deal with enemy agents and Fifth Columnists – a term originating from the Spanish Civil War – who

Winston Churchill – 'Good Ol' Winnie' with his famous 'V-for-Victory' sign.

were described as Fascists and aliens who might assist the enemy. Thousands of aliens were placed in 'protective custody' and all foreigners were treated with the utmost suspicion. Posters carrying slogans such as 'Careless Talk Costs Lives' and 'Be Like Dad, Keep Mum' appeared everywhere. It was a most tense and anxious time; even carrying a camera might lead to arrest. Newspapers published instructions on what to do 'If the Enemy reaches your Village'. But as usual *ITMA* managed to bring some humour to such grave and parlous times and captured the spirit of the nation with its character Funf the spy and his catch phrase: 'This is Funf speaking'.

The dire plight of the country was emphasised by the broadcast on 14th May by Anthony Eden, the new Secretary of State for War. He appealed for 'large numbers of men between the ages of seventeen and sixty-five to come forward and offer their services'. Their principal task would be to oppose the enemy's airborne troops as they landed. These volunteers would not be paid but they would be provided with a uniform and arms (eventually!) and were required to serve a minimum of ten hours a week. It was hoped to raise a force of 150,000, but within a fortnight 400,000 had enrolled and one month later the number had reached almost one million. The force was originally known as the Local Defence Volunteers, although Eden privately called it the 'Broomstick Army'. At first the LDVs received little more than their armbands – the initials were jokingly said to stand for 'Look, Duck and Vanish'! In late July they were given their more familiar name – the Home Guard – largely as a result of Churchill's insistence.

Almost every town and village had its own battalion or company along with countless works' platoons. At the peak there were 53,000 Home Guardsmen in Birmingham alone. They took their duties very seriously, manning road-blocks, patrolling their territory during the hours of darkness, guarding crashed enemy aircraft and later manning anti-aircraft batteries as well as replacing army units on certain defence duties. The Home Guard became a quite professional force, and over twelve hundred Home Guardsmen were killed and fifteen George Crosses awarded. It holds a rather special place in the folklore of the war and was, of course, immortalised by the BBC's fond and affectionate portrait of this unique citizens' force – *Dad's Army*.

By June 1940 there were 1.7 million men and women engaged in some form of Civil Defence duties – ARP, Fire & Rescue, Casualty and Police. It was reported that Birmingham was spending £5,000 a day on Air Raid Precautions, but nevertheless the threat of air raids was

Birmingham and Coventry were heavily protected by barrage balloons. A Junkers 88A was brought down by a barrage balloon at Witheybrook, Coventry on 16th September 1940.

still not taken too seriously by the majority of people; despite the fact that daily they saw the silver barrage balloons in the skies overhead. Birmingham and Coventry were especially heavily protected by the balloons, generally referred to as 'pigs'. Nevertheless, they were one of the abiding images of the war and those who lived close to a site bestowed a personal name on their balloon (the writer recalls one being called Horace!). Undoubtedly, the barrage balloon defences provided some measure of protection and their presence overhead gave at least a feeling of security, daily evidence that they were being protected from air attacks. The barrage balloon defence was especially successful during the V1 flying bomb onslaught. Balloons brought down over two hundred and seventy V1s. Unfortunately, they also accounted for more friendly aircraft than enemy. Collisions with the vicious steel cables was an ever present danger. The first known RAF aircraft to strike a balloon cable was a Hampden of No 106 squadron, which crashed onto the cricket ground in Coventry on 24th May 1940, killing the three airmen. The first enemy aircraft known to have been brought down by the balloon defences occurred on 13th September 1940 at Newport, Gwent and three days later the second enemy bomber to fall foul of a balloon – a Junkers 88A-1 – crashed at Witheybrook, Coventry. Two German airmen were killed, the other two baled out.

The whole question of air-raid shelters had caused endless debate in official circles. Despite the provision of thousands of communal surface brick shelters, it was recognised that they would accommodate only about 10% of the population. There were seventy-nine in Coventry able to shelter some 30,000, maybe about 13% of its citizens. Furthermore, these shelters were universally detested as forbidding places – dark, dank and damp, and prone to flooding – many viewed them as death traps, and there were certainly instances of them collapsing at the slightest blast because of, it was thought, an incorrect cement mix. Of course, the many factories and works in the county had made their own arrangements to provide shelter for their workers. The Government offered all households an outdoor shelter at the cost of £7 but free to those with an income less than £250 per annum. Known as Anderson shelters from their designer Dr David A. Anderson, they were of a curved corrugated sheet design, intended to be sunk several feet into the ground and then covered with earth or sandbags as a protection against bomb blast. The shelter was said to provide adequate protection except from a direct hit, which was officially considered 'a very remote chance', although there were several tragic instances of that happening in Birmingham, with fatal results. By mid-November 1939 the 100,000th Anderson shelter had been delivered to Birmingham. Nevertheless, many families in Birmingham and Coventry were convinced that such protection was quite unnecessary, as 'we are too far from Germany to be bombed'. Of course many homes in the city centres did not have gardens and when it was clear to the Government that many families (estimated at 60%) preferred to shelter in their homes either under the stairs or in cellars, they produced an indoor shelter – the Morrison, named after Herbert Morrison, then in charge of Civil Defence. However, it is the Anderson shelter that became the defiant image of the early war years and without doubt these shelters (some 2.25 million) saved countless thousands of lives.

Even before what was described at the time as the 'miracle of Dunkirk', the War Cabinet had been clearly informed by the Chiefs of Staff that 'Germany could not gain air superiority unless she could knock-out our Air Force and the aircraft industries, some vital portions of which are concentrated at Coventry and Birmingham'. Thus it could be said that the fate of the two cities was sealed, especially after the Battle of Britain, which denied the *Luftwaffe* its expected victory in the air.

Certainly, both cities were vital centres of aircraft, aero-engine, tank and military vehicle manufacture as well as of other essential military material. At Coventry there were Daimler, Armstrong Whitworth, Rootes, Standard, SS Cars, Alvis, Coventry Climax, GEC, Humber, and so on, all heavily engaged in war work. Birmingham had for instance Vickers Armstrong, Rover, Austin, Fisher & Ludlow, Dunlop, BSA, Wolseley, ICI, SU Carburretors, Joseph Lucas, and even Cadbury's had turned over to war work. Indeed, by 1944 over 400,000 Birmingham people were employed in such vital work – the highest percentage of any city or town in the country.

The work was physically hard and demanding, the normal hours were from seven in the morning until at least seven in the evening – seven days a week. Almost every worker, male and female, exceeded their hours in response to the continual demands for increased production. It should also be remembered that many workers after the completion of their normal shift of work were then engaged on some form of civil defence activity, even if it was 'only' fire-watching; from October 1940 it was made compulsory for those between sixteen and sixty years to complete at least forty-eight hours per month. Furthermore, they were clearly instructed that 'the protection of their workplaces takes preference over the protection of their homes', a most harsh order. When one also considers the frequency, length and ferocity of the air raids during late 1940 and early 1941, it is no small wonder that one worker recalled that 'sleep, or a lack of it, became elevated to a position of national importance'.

The handful of bombs that fell by mischance on Ansty aerodrome in mid-June 1940 really heralded the onslaught of bombing endured by the hapless citizens of Birmingham and Coventry from August 1940 to May 1941. It has been possible in this brief account merely to outline the major aerial attacks on Birmingham and Coventry but this does not belittle or diminish the immense destruction, untold misery and heavy loss of life as a result of these many air raids. According to official sources, only London and Liverpool suffered more air raids, a greater tonnage of bombs dropped and heavier casualties than Birmingham. Coventry, despite the infamous November blitz, was placed behind

Glasgow, Plymouth and Bristol, although it seems invidious, if not to say rather macabre, to prepare a 'league list' based on such a catalogue of wholesale suffering and destruction.

Birmingham, with a population of 1.04 million, was the third largest city in the country, whereas Coventry was considerably smaller (about 238,000) and more compact. The city centre still retained its old medieval narrow alleys and lanes where shops, houses and flats jostled with small factories and numerous workshops, one of the reasons to explain why Coventry's devastation was so complete. The first recorded bombs were dropped on Erdington, Birmingham on 9th August by a lone enemy bomber and they brought the city's first civilian fatality – an eighteen-year-old on leave from the Army. Four days later Castle Bromwich aircraft factory was the target and seven people were killed. However, on Sunday 25th/26th August Birmingham's city centre was bombed by about fifty aircraft and the 19th century market hall was destroyed; twenty-five people lost their lives in this first major raid. This was followed the next night by an air raid that lasted six hours, with the BSA factory being damaged. Coventry had experienced its first air raid a week earlier but remarkably with no injuries. The city was also targeted on 25th/ 26th, with six people admitted to hospital. Three nights later sixteen people in the Hillfields area of Coventry were killed. A German news bulletin which was issued on 30th August grimly promised: 'The attacks of our *Luftwaffe* so far are only a prelude. The decisive blow is about to fall.' A dire and distressing warning of the harrowing and frightening ordeal to be faced by the civilian population over the months ahead.

Both cities experienced increasingly heavy air raids during September and October, with barely a night's respite from the alerts. On 6th September the *Birmingham Mail* proudly proclaimed: 'Not daunted. Birmingham's Fine Morale. Standing Up to the Raids. Work Goes On As Usual.' Unfortunately, October proved to be a particularly harsh month, especially for Birmingham. On the night of the 15th fifty-nine were killed in the city and on three consecutive nights – 24th to 26th – heavy damage was sustained with a high loss of life. The raid on the 26th was described as 'a night of hell', when over two hundred and seventy major fires blazed in the city.

The dreaded and woeful air-raid sirens sounded in Coventry when neighbouring Birmingham was being bombed and should the early evening have arrived without their wailing and mournful sound,

The dreaded air-raid siren.

people commented that 'Old Jerry's late tonight' or 'Jerry's having a night off', such was their frequency and regularity. On 14th/15th October some one hundred and forty bombs rained down on Coventry's city centre for the first time, inflicting heavy damage, and the *Luftwaffe* returned the following night. It was after these two air raids that many Coventry families left the city nightly to gain 'a good night's sleep' in the nearby countryside, either with relatives or friends, or in church halls or farm buildings, with some content to sleep under bridges or in their cars. The letters SO marked on house doors informed rescue workers that the occupants had left for the country. This 'trekking', as it was officially described, became a feature of everyday life in other British towns and cities that sustained similar heavy bombings. It was steadfastly ignored by the Government for many months, as it was thought that these mass nightly 'evacuations' demonstrated a serious breakdown of public morale and it was anxious that nothing should be done to encourage such movements. In fact, 'trekking' was a natural and understandable response to heavy bombing and was the only action that people could take, especially as there was not any clear and official alternative. By the end of October Coventry had suffered the loss of 176 killed and 650 seriously injured in seventeen air-raids, but, sadly, Birmingham had endured heavier attacks with more extensive damage and a greater loss of life.

The month of November brought Coventry its night of destiny as the German High Command planned a major operation code-named *Moonlight Sonata*, a massive bombing assault on the industrial Midlands, timed for a period of full moon in the middle of the month. The *Luftwaffe* had pioneered the method of guiding their bombing formations by radio beams and also it had introduced the concept of a pathfinder force (KG100), which would first light the targets with flares and incendiaries, the resultant fierce fires providing a blazing beacon for the successive waves of bombers. On the evening of 14th November the *X-Gerät* radio waves intersected over Target 53 – *Koln* (codename for Coventry) – the die was cast.

The sirens wailed out a few minutes after seven o'clock in the evening and the all-clear was sounded at six o'clock the following morning – almost eleven hours of continuous and relentless bombing by some four hundred and fifty Heinkel IIIs and Junkers 88s. Thirty thousand incendiaries, five hundred tons of high explosive and many parachute mines rained down on a few square miles. The destruction wrought by this intense and ferocious bombardment was catastrophic.

266

The centre of Coventry after the horrendous bombing of 14th November 1940. (Imperial War Museum)

A third of the factories were put out of commission for several months and another third heavily damaged. Hundreds of shops and almost three thousand houses were utterly demolished with another 70% sustaining various degrees of damage. The cathedral was gutted, with only the shell and remarkably the 300 foot spire left standing. All the essential services – gas, electricity, water, telephones and transport – were put out of action, and the fire and rescue teams were overwhelmed by the scale of the devastation and the number of fires; one rescue worker was convinced that 'This is the end – we'll be dead lucky if we see the sun again'. Rest centres, many of them damaged, could not cope with the number of homeless families. Roads were impassable for a mile from the city centre. The final death toll was 568 killed and 863 seriously injured.

For the first time ever air power had been directed at a relatively small city with the express object of its annihilation. On 15th November the German High Command issued a news communique, along with a reconnaissance photograph entitled Coventry – *covientriert*. The caption read: 'The non-stop attack of strong formations under the command of Field Marshal Kesselring was particularly successful. Numerous factories making aircraft and other factories important to the war effort were bombed with bombs of every calibre. The utmost devastation was caused. After this large-scale attack, which was an answer to the British bombing of Munich [on the night of 8th November], the English invented a new word 'to coventrate'. With this word, which could be translated as ''complete destruction'', the success of the German attack was admitted.'

The outrage of the wholesale bombing was condemned throughout the free world, and messages of sympathy and support along with financial aid poured in and the name of Coventry entered into the history books. As the *Birmingham Gazette* proclaimed two days later, 'Coventry – Our Guernica'. In the aftermath of the raid when the true and awesome extent of devastation was revealed, the people of Coventry were in a state of trauma; most were convinced that 'Coventry is finished'. The large number of unexploded bombs, the restoration of essential services, the lack of drinking water and hot food and the homeless were the first major problems to be tackled. There was also the terrifying thought that the *Luftwaffe* might return again that night, which did not happen. King George VI, after his visit to the city on the 16th, recorded in a letter, 'Poor Coventry is in a very sorry state. The people were all dazed from the shock of it.' On 20th and 23rd November two mass civic funerals were conducted when a total of 422 people were buried. However, by the end of the month life slowly began to return to the city, and the people felt that, having survived this terrible ordeal, they could now 'face anything'.

On 19th/20th November it was the turn of Birmingham – Target 52 *Regenschirm* (Umbrella) – to endure nine hours of bombing by 350 aircraft, when, according to one eye-witness 'the whole city seemed ablaze'. Two nights later a force of two hundred bombers attacked the city; the onslaught lasted almost eleven hours. Over six hundred fires were blazing and by the end of the night it was reported that only one-fifth of the city's water supply was available. The two nights of terror and mayhem had left over six hundred and eighty dead and one thousand or so seriously injured. Whole areas of the city had been flattened; nearly two thousand houses were destroyed and thousands more damaged.

Early in December, on the evening of the 3rd, a relatively small force (fifty) bombed the city centre, which resulted in thirty-six fatalities. On the following night the raiders returned and some high explosives fell on St Andrew's, the ground of Birmingham City Football Club at Small Heath, wrecking one of the stands. A week later the long-suffering 'Brummies' endured their longest raid of the war. Some two hundred aircraft bombed for over thirteen hours, 263 people were killed and almost the same number seriously injured. On the following day (12th December) King George VI made an unscheduled visit and he was shown the devastated areas of the city and talked to many of the homeless; he was cheered wherever he went. At the end of the year Birmingham had suffered thirty-six air

Auxiliary firemen fighting a blaze in Birmingham – April 1941. (Imperial War Museum)

One that did not get away! Heinkel III H-8 crashed at Earlswood, Warwickshire on 11th May 1941. (RAF Museum)

raids and Coventry twenty-one.

Other than some minor incursions during the first three months of 1941, the *Luftwaffe* did not return in force until the week before Easter. On 8th/9th April Coventry was bombed by over two hundred and thirty aircraft. They dropped some 315 tons of high explosives and 25,000 incendiaries across an already devastated city centre. The Coventry and Warwickshire Hospital sustained heavy damage. There was a minor raid two nights later, and the total casualty figures amounted to 451 killed and 780 seriously hurt. Birmingham suffered a particularly heavy raid on 9th/10th April, followed by another severe attack the next night. It was estimated that over the two nights 525 tons of high explosives and 83,000 incendiaries had rained down on the city. Huge fires raged in the Bull Ring but amazingly the steeple of St Martin's church survived; the Swan Hotel, the oldest in the city, was destroyed, as was the Prince of Wales Theatre. Over eleven thousand ARP wardens were on duty that night. In the two raids about 350 people were killed and hundreds more injured. Rugby was also targetted on this night, with a loss of life. One of the enemy bombers – Heinkel III H-8 – was shot down by anti-aircraft fire; it crashed at Earlswood, Birmingham. It was over a month before the *Luftwaffe* struck again, on 16th/17th May about one hundred bombers raided Birmingham, striking both Wolseley Motors and ICI Chemicals, but fortunately casualties were relatively light – however, more than thirty were killed. This was not the case in Nuneaton, which was bombed largely as a result of navigational errors. There eighty-three people lost their lives.

In retrospect, 1941 can be viewed as the nadir of the country's fortunes, although it was no longer fighting a lone battle after Germany invaded Russia on 22nd June and the country was exhorted to support 'our gallant ally'. Even Joseph Stalin was fondly referred to as Uncle Joe! Otherwise, there was very little on the military fronts to bring cheer to the beleaguered nation, with serious military reverses in North Africa and Greece, although the BBC's celebrated 'V for Victory' campaign, really designed to foster resistance to Germany in occupied Europe, captured the public's imagination, and defiant Vs, chalked or painted on walls, appeared around the country. The Home Front, as the Government insisted on describing wartime Britain, was bearing the full force of the war so far. By the end of 1941 over 43,600 civilians had been killed, which was three-quarters of the total of the whole of the war. This figure was more than the number of soldiers and airmen killed in action. Food rationing had become even more stringent; fresh eggs had all but disappeared to be replaced by a powdered egg substitute (imported in huge quantities from America); milk was placed on ration, to be followed by soap in 1942. Although bread was never rationed, the white loaf became a memory of long-past happier times and was replaced by the 'national wheatmeal loaf', a dark and coarse bread, never the family's favourite. Clothes and footwear rationing by means of coupons began in July, and later a points system was introduced for tinned goods. The paucity of goods of all descriptions fuelled the black market, where any item could be obtained but at a price. However, in early December there was a faint ray of hope that the war situation might change for the better, when, on the 6th, the United States of America entered the war, but this was countered just weeks later with the news that Hong Kong had fallen to the Japanese.

December also brought an unprecedented measure not equalled in either Germany or Russia – the conscription of unmarried women between the ages of twenty and thirty years, later extended to nineteen-year-olds with the upper age limit raised to fifty-one, largely to release younger women for work in aircraft factories. The conscripts were given the choice of any of the three women's auxiliary services, Civil Defence or industry. However, thousands of women, both married and single, were already filling jobs vacated by men serving in the armed forces, and by mid-1943 there were over three million women engaged in some form of war work, the greatest number in the aircraft and munitions factories; others on trains and buses; and many delivering milk and post. Many were also working in previously male-dominated industries such as ship-building. The independence of women can be seen as one of the major and most significant social changes brought about by the war.

At the outset of the war many women had taken up voluntary work,

WVS – the 'Women in Green' busy at work with one of their Queen's Messengers Convoys.

Cadbury's cocoa caravan was a welcome sight in all bombed areas. (Cadbury Ltd)

perhaps most notably in the Women's Voluntary Service. The WVS had been formed in 1938 with the intention of encouraging women into Civil Defence and was dubbed by the newspapers as the 'Housewives' Service'. These 'women in green', as they were more generally known from their grey-green tweed suits, made a large and vital contribution to the Home Front throughout the war, often working in most trying and difficult circumstances. They assisted with the evacuation of children and families during 1939 and were in the forefront in providing assistance and support to the victims of the air-raids. Perhaps their most public role was the provision of Queen's Messenger mobile canteens in bombed cities and towns, from which they served hot drinks and meals to the homeless people and rescue workers. The day after the Coventry raid the WVS was in the city centre providing hot drinks, and in three days they served 50,000 hot meals. In Birmingham it was a similar story; they also operated more permanent canteens in ARP depots. The WVS organised the distribution of clothes and other items to bombed families, operated reception and rest centres for servicemen and were engaged in the collection of salvage. No task, however onerous or distressing, seemed to be beyond their capacity.

The other conspicious female war workers were the girls of the Women's Land Army with their distinctive uniform. The WLA had been revived by Lady Denham in June 1939, and by the outbreak of the war some 17,000 had volunteered. The girls were drawn from all walks of life but mainly from the industrial cities and towns, no doubt attracted by poster images of a 'Healthy and Happy Life' in some rural Arcadia. The reality was somewhat different: their work was long, hard, exhausting, and undertaken in all weathers. The wages were extremely low, especially compared with munitions work, and the accommodation in the WLA hostels was often inadequate and regulated under a strict regime. Furthermore, they had to earn the respect of a mainly sceptical farming community. At its peak, during 1943, the WLA numbered over 87,000 and had become an essential part of the wartime rural scene, making a valuable contribution to the war effort. By 1944 Warwickshire's farms were providing all the flour, potatoes and milk for Birmingham, Coventry and other towns in the county. The WLA survived well after the war and was not disbanded until October 1950.

The summer of 1942 brought to a close the *Luftwaffe*'s heavy attacks on the Midlands. On 13th June the Lockheed hydraulic brake factory at Royal Leamington Spa was bombed, one of the last precision raids of the year, and there was an early morning attack on the same factory on 16th July, when four people were killed and production was seriously affected. Nuneaton was bombed on 24th/25th June by about thirty-five aircraft. The raid lasted for about an hour and caused considerable damage and twenty-eight casualties.

During July both Coventry and Birmingham came under heavy attack on two successive nights – 27th/28th and 29th/30th; these air raids where thought to be the *Luftwaffe*'s response to Bomber Command's heavy raid (400+ bombers) on Hamburg on the 26th/27th. These two nights of bombing proved to be the last major raids suffered by Birmingham and over the two nights when 'incendiaries came down in showers', over 170 people were killed. On 3rd August Coventry had its 380th air-raid alert when a small bomber force attacked Stoke Heath. This raid heralded the end of the city's bombardment; in total 1,253 people had been killed and over 1,850 seriously injured. However, it was not until 23rd April 1943 that

Birmingham's prolonged and costly aerial onslaught finally ceased. In seventy-seven air-raids about two thousand tons of bombs had fallen on the city resulting in untold devastation, and killing 2,241 people (including 211 children under sixteen) and seriously injuring another 3,010. Both Coventry and Birmingham had been forced to pay a very high price for their industrial and engineering heritages and their large contribution to the war effort.

Those who lived through the grim austerity of the wartime years cannot forget the continual Government demands to save any and every item for salvage – books, bottles, rags, bones, jam jars, old aluminium pots and pans, glass, newspapers, scrap metal and even kitchen waste – indeed this saving culture, born out of the harsh wartime conditions, coloured their peacetime years. There were non-stop salvage drives, with schoolchildren being actively engaged on the collections. Perhaps the most famous collection was the compulsory removal of iron railings from parks, public buildings and private houses to be melted down for the production of aircraft, tanks and munitions. But without doubt the greatest success story of the war was the National Savings Movement, which had started back in November 1939 as the War Savings Scheme, with the aim to raise £475 million in a year, although it just fell short of the target by £8 million. Nevertheless the National Savings Movement proceeded to go from strength to strength, with savings groups established in every street, office, factory and school. Despite the penal rates of taxation, it was estimated that at least 25% of the average weekly income was given up to savings, compared with a mere 5% pre-war. The most dramatic and successful aspects of the Movement were the national drives organised through-out the war, from the Spitfire Fund in the summer of 1940 through War Weapons Week (1941), Warship Week (1941/2), Wings for Victory (1943), Salute the Soldier (1944) and Thanksgiving Week (1945). Every city, town and village took part in these drives, with an agreed target based on their populations. The target for Birmingham during Warship Week in October 1941 was £10 million and what was then believed to be the largest poster, portraying Admiral Nelson and 'England expects' was displayed on the city hall. The special weeks were accompanied by sports events, carnivals, concerts and military parades, which did much to brighten life in wartime Britain, if only briefly. It was later reckoned that in one year alone (1944-5), the war had cost the country £4.8 billion, an illustration of how important the National Savings Movement was to the Government.

The civilian population were constantly exhorted that 'food was a munition of war'. The early success of the 'Dig for Victory' campaign, which persuaded people to turn their gardens over to the production of vegetables and use all available land for allotments (by 1943 there were 1½ million), was followed by a welter of advice and information from the Ministry of Food. Under the leadership of the ebulliant and enthusiastic Lord Woolton (the second most popular politician after Churchill), housewives and mothers were bombarded with 'food facts' and 'food hints'. In the Government's concern that all families had the opportunity of at least one cooked and nourishing main meal a day, it encouraged the establishment of community feeding centres or 'British restaurants', as they were renamed by Winston Churchill. They were non-profit-making and run by the local authorities. Breakfast cost 4d and a three-course midday meal 1s with a cup of tea an extra 1d. By 1943 there were British restaurants in most cities and towns – some 2,000 in number – serving over 600,000 daily midday meals. Lord Woolton proudly boasted that the country's diet was now better than it had ever been, despite food rationing. Some sixty years later nutritionists are now claiming that the wartime diet was far healthier than today's eating habits!

By the end of 1942 many people felt that at long last 'we have turned the corner'. According to the BBC news bulletins, Bomber Command was nightly inflicting heavy damage on German targets, and in the late summer the United States Army Air Force had entered the European air war and the 'Yanks' in their smarter uniforms, flush with money and a seemingly endless bounty of goods and foodstuffs were beginning to make an impact on the wartime scene. The first real victory by land forces – El Alamein – was celebrated on 15th November with church bells sounding once again. Churchill was cautious in his praise: 'This is not the end. It is not even the beginning of the end. But it is perhaps, the end of the beginning.' This Sunday was also declared Civil Defence Day, as 'a witness and reminder of the great defensive effort of two years ago'.

The country now entered its fourth year of the war and it seemed to most people to have lasted for an eternity. All the annoying and frustrating wartime restrictions were still in force; food and clothes rationing was as exacting as ever, and over 70% of the population was engaged in some aspect of war work. Nevertheless, there now appeared to be some light at the end of the very long tunnel and most people were confident that it was merely a matter of time before

The stand-down parade of the Home Guard: Victoria Square, Birmingham, 3rd December 1944. (via R. Mortimer)

victory would come. From April church bells were heard again each Sunday, the terrifying night raids had largely ceased and the bombed cities and towns were slowly returning to some semblance of normality. Towards the end of 1943 there was a great feeling of expectancy in the land patiently awaiting the news of the 'Second Front'. However, this seemed to be merely wishful thinking when, in January 1944, the *Luftwaffe* launched its heaviest bombing offensive (the 'Little Blitz') since 1941, mainly directed at London and the south-east.

It was the familiar voice of John Snagge that delivered the historic news at 9.30am on 6th June 1944: 'D-Day' has come. Early this morning the Allies began the assault on the north-western face of Hitler's European fortress.' According to reports, there was 'an almost tangible release of tension in the country'. The progress, and setbacks, of the Allied land forces in France was closely followed and most of the population genuinely believed that the war would be over by Christmas, despite the arrival of Hitler's secret weapons – the VI flying bombs and later the V2 rockets. During the autumn, matters were slowly improving on the Home Front. Much to everybody's relief the universally detested blackout restrictions were partially lifted from 17th September and certain goods slowly began to reappear in the shops. Cigarettes were at long last more plentiful but now matches were almost unobtainable! However, food rationing was still ever present and would remain so well into the post-war years. In November Civil Defence duties had been relaxed and on the first of the month the Home Guard, which now numbered 1.7 million, was stood down. On Sunday 3rd December stand-down parades were organised throughout the country and HM King George VI paid fulsome tribute to this remarkable force in a radio broadcast: 'You have given your service without thought of reward. You have earned in full measure your country's gratitude.'

Despite the continuing attacks of flying bombs and V2 rockets, Christmas 1944 was still a time for modest celebration. Extra food and sweet rations were allowed and poultry was in greater supply but nevertheless family circles were still far from complete, with loved ones away fighting either in Europe or the Far East. The final victory in Europe seemed to take a long time in coming but when it did on Tuesday 8th May every street, hamlet, village, town and city in the country celebrated VE day. Precious stocks of food had been carefully and secretly squirrelled away (hoarding food was a criminal offence) for the great and momentous day and hundreds upon thousands of street parties were held throughout the country. Once again the people crowded around their wireless sets to hear 'Good Ol' Winnie' broadcast to the nation. Later in the evening HM The King addressed the country, as he had done on the first day of the war, which seemed such a long, long time ago, 'Let us remember those who have not come back . . . Then let us salute in proud gratitude the great host of the living who have brought us to victory. Armed or unarmed, men and women, you have fought, striven and endured to your utmost. Today we give thanks for our great deliverance.'

Thus the 'People's War' had ended but the country was not completely at peace until Victory against Japan Day was proclaimed on 14th August. The long, bitter and harrowing conflict on the Home Front had taken a heavy toll: over 60,500 civilians killed another 86,100 seriously injured with more than two million people made homeless, with the loss of treasured possessions and memories. The scars of this protracted battle were plain to see in the gaunt ruined buildings and flattened bomb sites in Birmingham and Coventry and

The ruins of Coventry Cathedral, as they are today, a poignant memorial to the sufferings and huge sacrifices made during 'The People's War'.

other battered cities and towns. Since those grim days the visible scars have long disappeared under the wholesale redevelopment of those city centres. The shell of the old Coventry Cathedral with its splendid and spectacular new cathedral close by, and the Peace Gardens in Bath Row, Birmingham with the surviving Bell Tower of St Thomas's church destroyed on 11th December 1940, are poignant memorials to the sufferings and huge sacrifices made, not only by the citizens of those two cities but by people of Warwickshire, over sixty years ago.

BIBLIOGRAPHY

During my research I consulted various books. I list them below with my grateful thanks to the authors.

Armitage, Michael, *The Royal Air Force: An Illustrated History*, Cassell, 1993

Bannerman, Kenneth P., *A Towering Control: The Story of British Airfields*, ISE, 1958

Bishop, Edward, *Mosquito: The Wooden Wonder*, Airlife, 1980, Second Edition

Bolitho, Paul, *Whittle 1907–1996: Warwickshire's Genius of the Jet*, Warwickshire County Council, 1998

Bowyer, Chaz, *Wellington at War*, Ian Allan, 1982

Bowyer, Michael J. F., *Action Stations: 6. Military Airfields of the Costwolds & the Central Midlands*, Patrick Stephens, 1983

Calder, Angus, *The People's War: Britain 1939–1945*, Jonathan Cape, 1969

Chinn, Carl, *Brum Undaunted: Birmingham during the Blitz*, Birmingham Library Services, 1996

Chorley, W. R., *Bomber Command Losses: Volume 7 Operational Training Units 1940–47*, Midland Publishing, 2002

Chorlton, Martyn, *Leicestershire & Rutland Airfields in the Second World War*, Countryside Books, 2003

Collier, Richard, *1940: The World in Flames*, Penguin Books, 1980

Coombs, L.F.E., *The Lion Has Wings: The Race to Prepare the RAF for World War II: 1935–1940*, Airlife, 1997

Cruddas, Colin, *In Cobhams' Company*, Cobham plc, 1994

Douglas, Alton and Jo, *Birmingham: The War Years*, Brewin Books, 1995

Douglas, Alton, Gordon Stretch and Clive Hardy, *Coventry at War: A Pictorial Account 1939-45*, Brewin Books

Falconer, Jonathan, *Bomber Command Handbook: 1939–1945*, Sutton Publishing, 1998

Golley, John, *Aircrew Unlimited: The Commonwealth Air Training Plan during WWII*, Patrick Stephens, 1993

Hickman, Tom, *What did you do in the War, Auntie?: The BBC at War 1939–45*, BBC Books, 1995

HMSO, *Front Line, 1940–1941: the Official Story of the Civil Defence of Britain*, HMSO, 1942

Hylton, Stuart, *Their Darkest Hour: The Hidden History of the Home Front 1939–1945*, Sutton Publishing, 2001

Jackson, A. J., *Avro Aircraft since 1908*, Putnam Aeronautical Books, 2000, Third Edition

Longmate, Norman, *Air Raid: The Bombing of Coventry, 1940*, Hutchinson, 1976

Longmate, Norman, *How We Lived Then: A History of Everyday Life during WWII*, Hutchinson, 1971

Millgate, Helen D. (Editor), *Mr Brown's War: A Diary of the Second World War*, Alan Sutton, 1998

Negus, Geoffrey and Tommy Staddon, *Aviation in Birmingham*, Midland Counties Publications, 1984

Piper, Ian, *605: No 605 (County of Warwick) Squadron R.A.A.F.*, Ian Piper, 2003

Price, Alfred, *The Spitfire Story*, Arms & Armour, 1995

Rawlings, John, *Fighter Squadrons of the RAF & their Aircraft*, Crecy Books, 1993

Richards, Denis, *The Royal Air Force, 1939–45*, HMSO, 1953

Smith, David J., *Britain's Military Airfields, 1939–45*, PSL, 1989

Smith, Graham, *Taking to the Skies*, Countryside Books, 2003

Taylor, H. A., *Airspeed Aircraft since 1931*, Putnam, 1971

Thetford, Owen, *Aircraft of the Royal Air Force Since 1918*, Putnam, 1995, Ninth Edition

Webb, Edwin and John Duncan, *Blitz Over Britain*, Spellmount Ltd, 1990

Whiting, Charles, *Britain under Fire: The Bombing of British Cities*, Pen & Sword Books, 1999

Williams, David E., *A View of Ansty: 1935–1982*, Rolls-Royce Heritage Trust, 1998, Historical Series No. 25

Williams, Ray, *Armstrong Whitworth Aircraft*, Chalford Publishing, 1998

Wixey, Ken, *Armstrong Whitworth Whitley*, Hall Park Books

Zamoyski, Adam, *The Forgotten Few: The Polish Air Force in the Second World War*, John Murray, 1995

INDEX

SQUADRONS